STARTING YOUR OWN BUSINESS

THE GOOD, THE BAD, AND THE UNEXPECTED

STARTING YOUR OWN BUSINESS

THE **GOOD,** THE **BAD,** AND THE **UNEXPECTED**

David Lester, Founder of startups.co.uk

This edition first published in Great Britain in 2008 by
Crimson Publishing
Westminster House
Kew Road
Richmond
Surrey
TW9 2ND

A catalogue record for this book is available from the British Library.

ISBN 978-1-85458-401-4

Printed and bound in Great Britain by MPG Books Group

Acknowledgements

I now realise more than ever just what goes into creating a book, and as a result have even more respect than before for those who do this regularly. I am really grateful to the team at Crimson who have helped turn my manuscript into this finished product you hold in your hands, especially Beth, Holly, Lianne, Sally, Lucy and Andy. This book would have been very different and considerably less good without you.

I would like to thank the many other people who have contributed encouragement, ideas and constructive criticism to early drafts, especially Matt Thomas, Peter Shaw and Allison Harper.

Lastly, I would like to dedicate this book to my wife, Sue, who has not only supported me brilliantly throughout this longer-than-expected process, but also has contributed significantly to the ideas, the approach and the writing itself. Thank you.

CONTENTS

Foreword
Introduction

Foreword

I learned so much about business on *The Apprentice* and working for Sir Alan that I thought I would be well prepared to set up my own business. That experience was amazing, and working for Sir Alan Sugar is probably some of the best training you can get as an entrepreneur, but starting your own business is completely different to working for someone else. No matter what obstacles are thrown at you or opportunities come your way, you have to make it happen; there's nobody telling you what to do next or giving you advice.

That's why I have set up the Bright Ideas Trust, which aims to help people starting their own businesses by finding them a mentor to guide and advise them. It's proven that new businesses where the founder has a mentor are much more likely to succeed than those without. The Bright Ideas Trust will also invest small amounts of money in new businesses to help get them started properly. It's a charity, so all profits it makes from these investments will go back in to investing in more businesses.

I learned the importance of this the hard way, by setting up my own business–and male grooming business. I'm thoroughly enjoying it, but I could never have imagined just how many things there are to do, and how hard it would be to get the information I needed.

I was delighted to see this book, which offers a lot of the answers you'll need to start your own business. It's really easy to read, but best of all it is full of real business examples from someone who has been through the pain and joy of starting his own business and succeeded. It's the first book I've seen which is as honest about mistakes as about things that have gone well–and you can often learn more from those mistakes than from the successes.

If you, like me, are starting out on a new business journey, this book could really help you. I wish you well with your new venture.

Tim Campbell
Winner, *The Apprentice* 2005
Founder, Bright Ideas Trust

Introduction

Starting your own business will change your life. Literally. Running a business can be a fabulous way to earn your living and live your life. It can be enormously satisfying and let you take greater control over your own destiny. It might even make you lots of money.

Are you sick of your job? Or just frustrated that others around you are not doing what you know they should do? Good. That's a great starting point to set up on your own. I think now is a fabulous time to start a new business. There are loads of opportunities and the rise in capabilities and use of the internet is making it cheaper and easier to start a business anywhere. But be sure you understand that it won't be easy: it's very risky. Most new businesses which get started don't make it, and if you are to succeed then your new venture will dominate your life, especially while you get it going. You're probably worried about giving up a regular salary too. Good. That concern will help drive you on to succeed, so long as you are confident in your new business.

I love small businesses. The best things about small firms are that it's possible to stay really close to your customers, that everyone who works in them knows how much they matter, and that as the person in charge, you can do what you know makes sense for your business – being your own boss is enormously satisfying. All too often large companies can't, because what's right for one part of the corporation doesn't make sense for another. It's a big advantage for small businesses, especially when you first start up.

Who am I to tell you all this and why should you read this book?

There are lots of books around about starting a business – why is this one worth the time and money? In short, because this is different. Not only is it written by someone who has been there and done it themselves, successfully, with a variety of businesses, but it's also full of what matters: what it is really like to run a business – the emotions as well as the practicalities; the highs, the lows, and the bald realities. It's not theory, it's practice. And I'm not some weird uni dropout; I'm a normal, real person.

I run my own business today. So every day I still face many of the issues you will encounter when setting up your own business, which means I still understand the issues, and feel the emotions you'll be going through as you set up your own business. (It also means that much of this book has been written at night!) As part of my work, I have spoken to hundreds of people starting and running their own business; in fact, it's what we do – my company specialises in providing information to small business owners. So I've heard what most people find challenging about starting out, and I hope to give you some direct answers you'll really want; answers which are practical enough for you to use straight away.

More than that, this book is different to most others about starting up because many of the other books out there explain the mechanics, rules and regulations about starting up, but don't say much about building a business that will actually survive. This book is entirely focused on starting something which can survive and thrive.

I've crammed this book with real examples from my own business experience – there's good, bad and totally unexpected. I've included details of some of my mistakes. We all do make mistakes, even the most successful entrepreneurs out there. Mistakes are great ways to learn – even more so if you can learn from other people's! Most of these mistakes come from businesses I've been involved with, since it's harder to get other people to talk about their mistakes rather than their successes; it's not because my businesses make more than most!

So, who am I and what have I done? I got bored while training to become an accountant, so I set up a computer games business as a hobby, when I was 22. I started the business with £12,600; some was money from friends and relatives and some was my own investment from money I had earned through summer jobs as a student. The business, called Impressions, did well enough early on that I left accountancy to run it full-time. It grew until it was making profit of over £1m per year before I sold it almost seven years later.

After that, in 1999, I set up Crimson Publishing, to publish information for people starting and running small businesses. I had spent five years in the USA and saw just how much better the information was there than in the UK, so when I came back I decided to change that. The website we launched (www.startups.co.uk) has become by far the most popular independent small business website in the UK. We also publish the UK's most popular magazine for established entrepreneurs, put on dozens of events for small businesses every year, and publish business books like this one. It has worked so well that we are now the UK's leading information provider for small businesses. If you're interested, you can read more about how I started and built this business in My Story at the end of this book.

I've also invested in a dozen small companies, two of which I am very involved in. A few have done extremely well, two have gone bust, and the rest are still growing. I have also been a director of one which floated on AIM. I've read literally hundreds of real business plans from companies trying to raise money.

If you haven't guessed already, small businesses are my passion. That's why I've written this book. Do let me know how you get on with your own businesses, as well as any comments on this book. You can email me at: david@smallbusinessexpert.co.uk.

Often an introduction like this might end with a 'good luck' wish. Not this one. I believe that while luck can play a part in the short term, you need to make your own luck with a small business. It's up to you – after all, that's why you're doing it; to control your own destiny. If you are sufficiently determined, you can overcome the challenges you'll undoubtedly encounter, and make it work. So hang on, and enjoy the ride!

01

SECTION ONE
Before You Start

CHAPTER 01

Do you really want to start your own business?

What's this all about?
- Find out what it's like to start a business
- See what it takes
- Is it right for you?

(?)

The media have made running your own business seem glamorous these days. There are lots of stories about people who've started a business from scratch and gone on to make millions, and even hugely successful prime-time TV shows about entrepreneurs. Sir Richard Branson is one of the best-known celebrities in the UK, with Sir Alan Sugar, Sir James Dyson and others also enormously famous – and rightly so. These people have all succeeded every bit as much in their own world as David Beckham has in his, or Madonna in hers. They've earned fortunes, and they inspire us all.

Running your own business definitely has elements of glamour. It feels great to see your own business card with 'managing director' or 'proprietor' on it; great to see your shop open for the first time, or your van delivered with your business logo on it. It is also a huge high to make your first sale, your first profit, and more.

THE HIGHS AND LOWS

I used to say that running a business yielded higher highs than anything else. I now have two young children, and for me their births certainly matched those highs. But either way, business highs are up there with some of the best feelings we can have. I will never know what it feels like to score a winning goal in a cup final, but I'm sure the best moments running your own business come pretty close.

You should expect your own business to also deliver possibly the lowest lows you can imagine, too. Children and professional football can surely match those also; but the real point here is that most people's normal jobs can't. They will cause people to stay within a narrower range; not reaching the same highs or the lows. To start your own business and seek those highs, you need to be willing to face those lows and come out the other side.

The title of this chapter probably sounds like a strange question for a chapter in a book all about starting a business. However it's arguable that anyone who hasn't done it before doesn't really understand what it is like to set up and run a business. My father told me before I set up my first business that it is far easier to start a business than to get out of it. I was a bit put out at the time, thinking what a negative comment from someone who I had hoped to get more support from, though of course, my father was right; he had run his own business for most of his life.

There were times when I really wanted to get out of running that first business, but I couldn't. It didn't all go according to plan, and after growing to four employees I had to cut it back to just myself and one part-time person; we were losing money, and having started it with only about £12,500, we soon owed more money than we had. I had personally guaranteed more than £500,000 worth of debts, despite the fact that I had no savings at all, and so if the business had failed I would have been bankrupted. I spent many, many sleepless nights trying to work out how to juggle the payments to the suppliers yet still keep the business going.

Those were the times when I would have leapt at the chance to walk away from the business – but you can't just do that. I managed to turn the business around, with the support of a few other people, and the business grew to be highly successful.

You should expect immense pressure, responsibility, and lack of freedom – in fact, all the things you want to escape from when you set out to become your own boss. I have met literally hundreds of other entrepreneurs. They've all had challenges along the way, and most really struggled to get through to viability.

WHAT DOES IT TAKE?

I am often asked what I think it takes to set up a successful business: of course it takes a variety of qualities and skills. But there is one thing that it takes above all else: the desire to win. Some people are happy to try hard, some even to try their best. To succeed at running your own business, though, you need to be absolutely determined to make it work. There will undoubtedly be hurdles and problems, some you can predict and more that you can't. Many people who start simply won't want to do what it takes to overcome some of these issues. They will have reached their limit. So it will ultimately come down to how badly you want to succeed. If you want to badly enough, you will find a way through.

There are definitely some people who are well suited to setting up on their own, and others who aren't, though opinions vary as to whether entrepreneurs are born or made. I believe that people who start businesses need to be a little bit arrogant. I also think that they need to be a bit naïve. (I admit I'm definitely both!) You clearly need to believe that your idea is better than whatever is out there already; and if you knew everything that is likely to happen after setting up your business, you might well decide not to start it. One of the major factors in deciding whether a young business succeeds or fails is whether its founder can cope with the bad times, and come up with ways to get round the obstacles every business faces as it develops. It needs determination, courage, and often some creative thinking to find ways around problems.

Lots of research has been done to try to isolate these characteristics, with mixed results. Whatever the sources, there are some clear characteristics you will need to have if you are to succeed. You need to be:

✓ PASSIONATE

You need to really love the product or service your business is selling, and to learn as much as you possibly can about it. You need to spend vast amounts of time thinking about it and really caring about getting it right for customers. This will be all but impossible without passion.

✓ SMART

I mean market-stall-trader smart, not rocket-scientist smart. This is very different from 'well educated', too. You need to be comfortable with simple numbers (basic arithmetic and percentages), and able to pick up on trends, gaps in a market and people's reactions to your early products. You then need to be able to work out the right way to move forward in light of any suggestions for improvement, after working out which of these matter and which don't.

✓ A RISK TAKER

You need to be willing to take risks: starting a business is risking your own livelihood and probably money, and you need to be able to handle that risk without cracking up. It will be stressful at times, and it's critical that you can keep a clear head and make sensible decisions.

✓ RESILIENT

Otherwise known as bounce-back-ability, you'll need this in spades to cope with the setbacks, rejection and criticism that you'll surely encounter at times. It's important to remain positive though it can be tough at times.

✓ ENERGETIC

You'll have more to do than you can imagine, and frequently it will all need doing now; you'll need, therefore, not only to work hard, but to work fast. Forget any ideas about taking extra holidays or time off during the day – your life will be more 9am–9pm (if you're lucky) than 9am–5pm.

✓ A SELF-STARTER

If you're used to being told what to do and are quite happy with that, setting up your own business is probably not for you. But if that's you, I'm surprised you've read this far! Once you have decided to start, nobody is going to tell you what to do and when – it's down to you. You need to be comfortable that you can start with an empty diary, desk and contacts list and create something from nothing. Are you going to talk about it in the pub, or actually get on and do it?

✓ A MULTI-TASKER

In most established businesses people have fairly specific, narrow roles. When you set up your own business, initially you, and any partners, will have to do everything. You will need to keep lots of different issues in your mind, and work out your priorities to ensure that everything gets done on time to make the business happen. It's one of the biggest surprises for founders who have worked for a while for other companies before starting.

Age

I haven't included age in this list – I've met successful entrepreneurs of just about all ages. You need to be over 18 to be able to sign legal documents, but both the Darling brothers, who started hugely successful games business CodeMasters, and Dominic McVey, who made a fortune selling scooters, started before they were 18. I'm not sure there's any upper limit: if you've got the energy and passion, age won't stop you. We have both a Young Entrepreneur and a Silver Fox award at our annual Startups Awards, and every year I'm amazed at how many great businesses come forward for both.

Experience

Do you need experience to succeed? Strictly speaking, you don't need to have worked in the same sector before in order to make your new business take off. But you do need to know something about it. I had never worked in computer games before I set up my games business, but I had spent loads of time playing and reading about games. There's an enormous difference between experience as a customer, and work experience within a sector; I think everyone should have at least some decent experience as a customer. While people do start businesses straight from school or uni, I think it's easier if you've worked somewhere else first; you'll have seen how other people run things, and learned from it, whether your experience was good or bad. Not essential, then, but a good idea.

Education

I have not included 'well educated' in the list of characteristics or qualities you will need to succeed. I spoke recently at a conference for 13-year-olds, teaching them about business. It was a great event, and one I wish I had been to when I was that age. Not surprisingly, one of the questions I was asked concerned what education or qualifications you need to set up or run your own business. The answer is none really, but that can be misleading.

Of course, you'll need expertise at whatever it is you want to do – whether that's being a plumber for a plumbing business, or having a science degree for a scientific business. The real question is what general education you need.

It is well known that a lot of prominent businessmen have dropped out of university. Bill Gates is perhaps the most famous, dropping out of Harvard University to go and form Microsoft. Charles Dunstone, the founder of the hugely successful Carphone Warehouse also dropped out of university. Theo Paphitis, on the other hand, who made a fortune from changing and growing Ryman, La Senza and several other retail chains, left school at 16 without any qualifications at all.

So it is quite clear that to run a small business you don't need a degree, or probably even any formal examining qualifications at all. But let me talk of a friend of mine who runs his own business and is dyslexic. This wasn't spotted at school, so he ended up without any formal education qualifications, and without much education. Despite all this, he is running a business, and making it work, but it is far harder for him because he struggles to read long documents – inevitable in almost every business.

The other thing you really need, above all, is a grasp of numbers. You certainly don't need to be a mathematician, but you really do need to be very comfortable with multiplication and addition, and with percentages. You'll need this to be able to know how much to spend and to charge people.

You should also be honest with yourself about what your strengths really are and aren't. Think about all those excruciating auditions for potential music contracts on reality TV shows – loads of people really think they can sing when they clearly can't. Ask people around you to be cruel to be kind and check that you really are good at what you think you are, and then find ways to fill the gaps. Nobody is good at everything – it's just a case of knowing what help you'll need, and getting on with finding that help.

Hard work

However smart and passionate you are, you will also need to work hard to get a new business started. It sounds obvious I know, but I mean harder work than you probably realise (I know just how patronising that sounds, but bear with me). For my first business I worked about 70 hours a week for over five years as the norm; busy weeks were often over 100 hours. Research continues to show that people who run their own businesses work harder than people who are employed, with the average being over 45 hours a week. You will soon realise that it will take longer to get a business up and running than it will to keep it ticking over once it's been set up.

You should think hard before you start about what this means for your non-work life, especially your family and close friends. There's no way I could have got married and had a family when I was building my first business – I couldn't have taken the extra stress of needing to support them, and they wouldn't have put up with my working the hours that I did.

It is possible to create a more relaxed business if you're not trying to grow a major corporation. Just how hard you will need to work depends on what you want to achieve. Increasingly, many people are choosing to make quality of life a higher priority than a traditional career, and sometimes starting a business can be a way to achieve this. There are plenty of people who run part-time businesses, for example. The next chapter looks closely at the different types of business you could start.

REDUCING THE RISKS

You will probably have heard lots about how hard it is to start a business, and that most new businesses fail within a year or two. The statistics are pretty consistent, and you should believe them. It really is very hard indeed to get a business to succeed from nothing. But luckily, plenty of people do so.

You do need to be willing to take risks if you are to start a new business. It's one of the essential qualities I listed above. But you also need to be able to judge when to take a risk and when not to – to assess a situation and weigh up the pros and cons. It's madness to take some risks, while others might well be worthwhile.

You can take action to reduce your own risks in various ways. Make sure you're truly committed to seeing your idea through, for starters. It's easy to have a flash of inspiration, start something, and then give up when you first hit some major obstacles; sadly, plenty of new businesses do just that. Other businesses fail because they run out of money; most businesses take more money and more time to succeed than the founders expect. Plan properly before you start to make sure you can get the finance your business needs.

—▷ STARTUP TIP

Find someone you trust who knows about business to go through your plan before you have spent much time or money on it. Make sure they think it is sensible before you proceed – or at least understand and overcome their concern, and are still confident that you are right.

Many people start businesses which haven't been thought through sufficiently, and therefore never had a chance of succeeding. Unfortunately, the most blatant example of this I have come across was a magazine I started. We saw a gap in the market for a magazine giving personal financial information to younger people, many of whom were in a financial mess. There were a number of established magazines which were covering the investment area, but were tailored to older people. We would make money from advertising and selling the magazine in newsagents. We researched our competitors to give reasons why advertisers should use us rather than them, and employed a team to write and design the magazine.

We showed potential advertisers a 'dummy issue' in order to persuade them to advertise in the first issue. Here we found our fatal flaw. We had compared the other magazines' newsagent sales well, but had somehow ignored their yearly subscribers. All the competitors had a lot of subscribers – this was in fact the majority of their circulation. So without any subscribers at all, our proposed circulation was very much smaller than the other magazines'. There was no reason for the advertisers to switch to us – so our advertising revenue didn't come in.

How could we be so stupid? The fact is that we were very busy (launching three magazines) and we somehow overlooked it. It's also fair to say that we were all rather pleased with ourselves for discovering what we thought was such a good idea. We were proud. And pride, as is so often the case, came before a fall.

I still smart when I think back to this. I put several people out of work when we shut the magazine down. I wasted a lot of time, close to £50,000, and tarnished our reputation with the trade. I can't change the past, but I want to make sure I don't do something this stupid again.

ALONE OR WITH PARTNERS?

Starting a business on your own is hard and can be lonely. Not so much in a saddo, Billy-no-mates sense, but in the sense that you will have nobody who you can really trust to discuss things with. You'll probably have plenty of friends, a partner, or maybe some business colleagues who you can talk to about your business, but there's a world of difference between saying something is a good idea, and getting off your rear end, and risking hard cash to pursue it. It's amazing just how strange it feels to be literally on your own with serious problems – especially if, like me, you're used to having colleagues or a boss to talk things through with.

When I started my first business it was with friends. We were trying to get some computer games published, and the publishers who were interested were all asking us to make changes that we didn't really think were sensible. So one day I said 'why don't we do it ourselves?' Everyone agreed this was a good idea, and so the next time we met we considered it some more. Again they all agreed, so I went off to research what it might cost us to publish our own game. I put some numbers together, and we all thought that we could make a go of it. But when it came time to say 'right, how much were we all willing to risk?' I ended up putting in 90% of the money, even though some of the others had as much money as I did. They were only willing to take a small risk. From then on, although I used some of them for advice (and received some great advice) I knew that ultimately we had different positions: I was taking the biggest risk, and effectively it was 'my' business – certainly I was the only one personally guaranteeing the debts! I would have preferred to have more equal partners.

However, I know other people who have started a business in equal partnership, and it has gone badly wrong. If two business partners fall out, even a good business can fall apart. I've known couples in a relationship who have split up after setting up a business together. You need to face up to the realities that things can change, sometimes with drastic consequences.

The highs and lows of starting a business will test most business partnership relations at times. Think of most music bands – these are effectively business partnerships. Even the good ones which succeed tend to suffer major disagreements, which eventually lead to the band breaking up at some point.

Money is usually at the root of many of the musician disagreements – and most business disputes. This seems as true when things have gone really well (as there's plenty of money to share, greed can kick in and one or more partners thinks he or she deserves a larger cut than the others) as when the business has gone wrong.

Only you can decide whether you are the sort of person to cope with these pressures, either alone or with partners. But you should think about it long and hard before you get too committed to your new venture. Make sure to put down in writing the basis of your agreement – ideally get it reviewed by a lawyer. You probably think it's a waste of time and money, but you're better off getting it done properly when you're all good friends than ending up arguing about what the deal was if you end up falling out.

SO IS IT RIGHT FOR YOU?

At the end of the day, when a group of people are sitting in a pub chatting about whether or not to do something like setting up a business, some people will say 'OK then, let's do it,' while others won't.

If you forget about the pub conversation by the next day, it's probably not right for you. If you wake up thinking about it, and can't stop thinking about it, like I did, you've got a chance.

There are always plenty of reasons not to start a business. Most of us would lose a significant sum of money if we start something and it doesn't work. Worse still, we'd be giving up a salary at our current job. And perhaps we'd feel a failure if it doesn't work out. If you've got a family that you're supporting financially, or a mortgage, it's more of a risk. If it's your own business, what's going to happen when you're sick, or need to look after family members? If you're lucky enough to be able to start a business with no financial commitments, it's easier to take the chance.

I remember that when I was doing my A-Levels it struck me, looking round a large room full of students, that a few of the people in that room would probably be successful, the others less so. I decided that I wanted to be one of the ones that would succeed. Is it as simple as that? Sometimes, it is. It's about confidence. Have you got it?

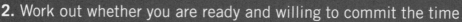

ACTIONPOINTS

1. Ask yourself honestly; have you got what it takes?
2. Work out whether you are ready and willing to commit the time
3. Consider whether you have got the right partners, if any
4. Decide if your family or personal life will allow you to put in enough hours

CHAPTER 02

What sort of business do you want to start?

What's this all about?
- What do you want from a business?
- What types of business are there?
- Franchises
- Which is best for you?
- What can you afford?

You probably already know what product or service you want your business to make or sell if you're reading this book. If so, there are still a number of important decisions to make about what type of business you set up. These will determine whether you get what you want from your business. Equally, however, I come across plenty of people who love the idea of running their own business but don't know quite what. This chapter, therefore, also has some ideas about what types of business you might want to consider setting up.

Do you want to run a business part- or full-time? Would a virtual business work for you? Is there a way to fund it all yourself or will you need other people's money to get it up and running? The answers to these revolve around what you want to get from your business, and when, which is often dominated by what you want to put into it.

WHAT DO YOU WANT FROM YOUR BUSINESS?

I've known a few people who set out to start a business in order to sell it as soon as possible for a large amount of money. I've known others who have started mail order businesses part-time to earn a little extra money on the side. If I ask you whether you want to make a fortune from your business, I'm sure you would say yes. Who wouldn't want that, right? But I am pretty sure that that isn't the main reason you want to start a business.

You don't need to want to be the next Richard Branson in order to start your own business. But you do need to have an idea of what you want to do. When I left my full-time job as an accountant to run my computer games business, my father asked me whether I thought I would be able to earn a living from it. I hadn't really thought about what I wanted to achieve with the business before that. By then I was already targeting £1m revenue and £100,000 in profit, which felt like really good numbers to get to. When we first set the business up, though, our objective was to earn a small amount of money on the side by doing something we wanted to do. The loftier ambition came later.

On the other hand, One Small Step One Giant Leap, now the UK's leading children's shoe shop chain run by my good friend Nick Schwefel, was set up to grow fast; knowing it wouldn't make money until it had at least 10 shops. This is important because from the start this meant Nick knew he had to raise far more cash to get the business to sustainability than many businesses need.

In my experience, the best businesses are born not from desire to make enormous sums of money, but from a real passion for a particular business. James Dyson did not set out to become a multimillionaire; he was convinced he had found a way to improve the vacuum cleaner, and was utterly committed to getting that made and into people's hands.

I've also seen some fabulous businesses started by people who were either made redundant or had become unhappy with their employer, and who thought they could set up in business doing similar work themselves. At that stage the primary objective is simply to earn a living.

Increasing numbers of people want to get off the rat race, wanting instead to set up their own business as a way of improving their quality of life through flexible work patterns or living on the coast or in the country. Almost all these people have visions of a wonderful way of life, earning a relatively modest income but enabling more time spent with family or enjoying particular hobbies. Most of the businesses started in these sorts of situations are businesses many people think they can run; such as a bed and breakfast, pub, café or similar.

TYPES OF BUSINESS

Part-time businesses

There are over three million registered businesses in the UK, yet nearly 90% of those have no staff – these are mainly 'self-employed' people, who effectively run their own business, though many won't think of themselves like that.

I started my first business part-time, really as a hobby, and I think it's a fantastic way to start if you can. It enables you to learn what it's really like to run a business without needing to give up your current job, and therefore rely financially on it. If the business works, you can grow it and go full-time when appropriate. Of course, you might be happy leaving it as a permanent part-time affair, and if that achieves what you want, fantastic. Sadly it isn't possible to do this with all sorts of businesses – for example it is hard to imagine setting up a shop, bar or café part-time.

Businesses that can work well part-time include: mail order, internet, eBay, consultants, party planers (such as Ann Summers or Usborne children's books) and even trades like plumbing.

⬆PROS
A great way to test a business idea
Lets you see if you really do enjoy running a business
No need to give up the day job

⬇CONS
Won't work for all business types
Can be difficult to limit the time it takes

Lifestyle business

A 'lifestyle' business is simply any business which is run primarily to deliver a good lifestyle for its owners. Typically these businesses aren't at all ambitious, but are very content to tick over at a nice level, without causing much stress to its owners.

⤒PROS
Low stress

The satisfaction of being your own boss

Plenty of time for life outside work

⤓CONS
Unlikely to make you rich

Hard to raise much money to set it up

Ambitious business

Some people are ambitious, and want to grow something significant. To set up a more ambitious business takes more of everything: energy, money and planning. Of course there are different levels of ambition, but if you want to grow a business it will affect everything you do from the start – from the sort of people you work with to the suppliers you select and how you fund it. Because you'll be placing a bigger bet, these businesses tend to be more risky – but could make you rich.

⤒PROS
Immense satisfaction and industry sector recognition

Potential to get rich

Easier to raise money

⤓CONS
Much higher risk

Will dominate your life

Virtual business

You might want to run a 'virtual' business. This is a business which has no staff or premises to speak of, and gets everything done by sub-contracting work. The real advantage of this is that you can set up quickly with a relatively small investment, and be highly flexible, growing simply by ordering more from your suppliers. It is increasingly possible to run virtual businesses using the internet, which enables your website to look as professional and serious as any other company's. Most of these businesses will be online. For example you could set up a website to sell books; you could find a consultant to set up your website and a book supplier to warehouse, pick, pack and dispatch the books, all automatically. So once you have instructed suppliers, all you would need to do is literally sit back and watch as money rolls in.

PROS

No need to take on staff

Very low cost to start

Easy to grow or shrink over time, within reason

CONS

Not suitable for all types of business

Limits the ultimate size you are likely to reach

Can be easy for other competitors to launch similar businesses

eBay business

eBay, the internet auction site, is a very big deal these days, with millions and millions of customers globally. Thousands of people have set up businesses just to trade on it, and some are selling well over £1m of goods every year. The big advantage of starting a business on eBay is that the website has already gathered a vast audience to its site, so setting up a business there is a little like setting up a shop in a shopping centre which reaches most of the country. This can work really well for niche businesses, specialising in narrow product areas. Of course the other thing to remember is that this 'national shopping mall' is vast, with many, many other shops there, so it's also a highly competitive place to do business.

PROS

Easy access to an enormous global market

Customers find you – all you need to do is make yourself available there

No human selling skills needed

CONS

There are already loads of people doing it

Very price sensitive, so it's hard to get rich

Franchising

If you aren't at all sure what sort of business to start, and really just want a bit more freedom and the ability to earn more from your own hard work, you should consider franchising. Franchises are business models which you can buy, usually for a particular geographic region. Fast food and print shops are some of the better-known franchises, though there are literally thousands to choose from. When you buy a franchise you pay a lump sum initially for the right to set up a new unit of a chain, using their brand. The franchisor (the business selling the franchise) trains you and helps you set up, and you then pay a percentage of your revenue as an ongoing fee. Chapter Four talks more about franchising.

⊞PROS
Gentler way to run your own business
Low risk due to proven business concept
Dedicated training and support
Comparatively easy to fund by bank loans

⊟CONS
Can be expensive to start
Unlikely to make you millions

FUNDING CONSIDERATIONS

Some businesses need far less money to set up than others. Do you need to spend money up front, for example on premises refurbishment, equipment, or creating a new product? Do you need to buy lots of stock in advance, or can you get what you need quickly, easily and often?

You should think carefully about whether you want to start a business self-funded, or with the help of other people's money. It can be hard to raise money from other people, and doing so could get in the way of you feeling like you're in control. If the main reason for starting your own business is to be your own boss, you might want to try to find a business which won't need outside funding. On the other hand, if you are trying to start something specific which will definitely need more money than you have, then you have no choice but to try to raise the money.

If you're sure you want to start a business but haven't finally decided what business to start, I'd really recommend starting one with a smaller funding requirement – it will make life simpler and more pleasant.

CONSIDER BUYING A BUSINESS

You don't have to start from scratch. Whatever size of business you want to *run*, you have several choices about how you *start*. Instead of starting from scratch, you could buy a successful existing business doing what you want to do, or buy a somewhat similar business and adapt it. Buying businesses is far more common than you might think, and please don't rule it out without thinking about it. It needn't cost more than setting up from scratch, either; Chapter Three looks at this in detail.

HOW IMPORTANT IS IT TO KNOW THE SECTOR BEFORE YOU START?

It will be much easier for you if you are setting up a business you know about already. When I set up the computer games publisher business, I already had quite a bit of knowledge about how the industry worked, from my own and friends' experience. When I set up my second business, publishing magazines, I had very little experience of that sector, and despite my much stronger knowledge of business in general, my lack of knowledge of the media sector meant that I ended up making some very expensive mistakes.

Another advantage to setting up a business in a field you already have experience in is that you are likely to have contacts in that sector. This might help you find the right staff, where you can trust the people you know – they know what they're doing, might work harder for someone they know, and you won't need to spend money finding them; plus, you will have a good idea of what they are capable of.

Knowing suppliers, too, can be really useful. One friend of mine was able to set up a business with much better terms than most startups would get just because several suppliers knew and liked him, and wanted to help him out; in his case, this meant that they gave him quite a bit more credit than they would usually, so he was able to start his business for less money than it would normally need.

Yet knowing potential customers already is probably the most significant benefit. This is true whether your customers will be consumers or businesses. Imagine a hair stylist who has worked at a place for years, and then decides to open her own salon; there's a good chance that many of the clients whose hair she has done before will go with her to her new salon, providing the new business with crucial early custom. For business customers, it can be very hard for a new business to get seen by the right level of potential buyer. This can be especially true if you are trying to sell products to large retailers. But a business started by someone who the retailers already know is more likely to be seen and treated seriously than a business they know nothing about.

Despite these advantages, many successful businesses are set up by people who haven't worked in the sector before – innocent drinks is a good example here. Its founders had good business experience, but not within soft drinks. And they have succeeded spectacularly. So don't rule out running a business just because you haven't worked in it before.

A little knowledge can be dangerous. If you've got plenty of experience as a customer, but no work experience, you might well think you can improve on what's already on offer, but not realise that there are some serious obstacles making it hard to achieve your ideas. Restaurants and pubs often look easy to run to people who haven't done it before – but there's an enormous difference between being a good cook at home, and running a busy, professional kitchen. Be cautious, and learn as much as you can before you start.

—▷ STARTUP TIP

If you don't have experience in your sector, get it while you plan your new business. This is especially useful in catering, where there is a huge difference between knowing how to make a cocktail, and being able to run a busy professional bar. Getting a job even just for a month or two in a similar business could teach you about systems and ways of doing things (as well as possibly ways not to do some things), which could end up making a big difference to your business when you do start it. Before starting Wagamama, founder Alan You worked at McDonalds to learn about how an efficient fast food restaurant works.

ACTIONPOINTS

1. Think through what you really want out of your business
2. Decide what sort of business will deliver that
3. Research whether you can raise the money that it will take (see Chapter Six for how to do this)
4. Consider working in the industry to learn how it really works

CHAPTER 03

Buying a business

What's this all about?

- Why consider buying?

(?)

- It can be cheaper than you think
- How to go about it
- Dangers to avoid

I wish I had bought a business as a starting point for Crimson (my company today – see Introduction or My Story). Buying a business sounds expensive, and feels like something that might be more appropriate for a book aimed at established businesses. But actually, buying a business instead of starting one is often a really smart way to start.

For example, it is relatively straightforward to buy an existing shop, café, bar, bed and breakfast, post office or restaurant, and then either continue running it as it is, or adapt it to your own plan. What a great way for you to learn about running a business, especially if it comes with some staff who already know what they're doing.

When I set up Crimson I had almost no experience of the publishing world. I did consider buying an existing publisher and launching some of my product ideas within it, but I mistakenly thought that it would be an expensive way to go about things. I thought I knew better and that I could create something successful for far less money than it would take to buy it. I was wrong. Today, I regret not doing that. It ended up taking a lot longer and a lot more money to build up the business to a sensible level than I had expected – and more money, in fact, than it would have taken to buy a business and build on it.

THE RISKS OF STARTING FROM SCRATCH

This word 'risk' is significant. Most entrepreneurs I have met don't think that their ideas are risky. You can see the same confidence in most of the people seeking money on *Dragons' Den*; none of the entrepreneurs think that their business is very risky – yet all the investors do. In reality, most new businesses don't last three years. Sometimes that is because the new businesses weren't run well, or thought out properly, or didn't have enough cash to get to profitability. There can be all kinds of reasons. But the facts speak for themselves – starting up a new business is risky.

There are very real reasons for that. It is much harder to start momentum for a new business than for an existing business to keep things ticking over. Although most of us complain about various aspects of our lives, we're often quite slow to switch to an alternative when it presents itself. Yet most entrepreneurs think that they have come up with a better option, and are then surprised by how slow it is to get customers.

No potential customer really knows how good your new business is, so they would need to take a risk by buying from you the first time. Banks say that most of the time about 20% of their customers would admit to considering moving to another bank, for example. Banks call these customers potential switchers. Yet despite being at least a little bit dissatisfied, only 4% actually end up switching. That means that most of these somewhat unhappy customers are not actually unhappy enough to move. That inertia applies to most aspects of our live. 'Better the devil you know' is a common response from people. A brand new business needs to overcome this if it is to succeed.

All this helps explain why I am such an admirer of people who have started a business entirely from scratch: it is incredibly hard to build up a good business from scratch.

WHY BUYING CAN BE BETTER THAN STARTING

There are several reasons to consider buying a business rather than starting from scratch:

1. It's already making sales
2. It can provide a ready-made team of trained staff
3. It provides an existing, proven setup
4. It's one less competitor for your new business

These reasons should make it quicker for you to achieve your goals, and with less risk.

Even without making any changes, you would have an existing group of customers. If you start to improve on the business you have bought, potential customers might trust it more easily (since it has been around for ages) than they would a brand new business.

If you want to start a food or drink business, such as a restaurant, café or bar, then buying an existing business might be a very smart way forward. For a start, the premises might already have a license to serve alcohol and is highly likely to have the appropriate planning permission for your type of business. You will need to transfer license, but the fact that one has been issued for the premises already will be helpful. Better still, you might find that the cost of taking over the existing operation is cheaper than buying the equipment you need, especially for a kitchen. Remember that cafés or restaurants need lots of equipment to set up, and while they may not have worked as businesses, this was probably not down to shoddy equipment. So taking over premises from a failed restaurant might be a great way of buying some good quality gear for less money.

CAN BUYING TURN OUT CHEAPER THAN STARTING?

Buying a business sounds like an expensive thing to do. But when you take into account the losses a startup business will probably incur early on, buying a business might actually not be very much more expensive; it might even prove cheaper in the long run. Of course, you simply won't be able to buy a business if you want to create something brand new and very different. But buying something with a view to changing it into what you want might work for you. Even if you hadn't considered buying a business before, try making some simple comparisons of, for example, how the first two years of your business might look if you started it yourself and how it might look if you bought an existing business and adapted that. You might be surprised at how small the difference is.

This can be really applicable to retail and leisure establishments; businesses like cafés or restaurants also then have the added advantage that by buying an existing business they are at a stroke removing a competitor as well as getting some sales momentum from day one.

How much do businesses cost? You can literally buy a business for £1. You have probably heard of people who have done this; Theo Paphitis bought businesses like Ryman and La Senza for negligible sums like this; Ken Bates famously bought Chelsea Football Club for £1. This sounds odd until you realise that the businesses you can buy for £1 have some real problems in them; typically they will have substantial debts that you need to repay. Unless you know an industry very well, I would advise not buying a business in trouble (it still might be worth taking over the premises of a failed business, though, so long as you don't take on any staff or debts you don't want). It's a mistake that people, especially entrepreneurs who ooze self-belief, make. They think they can buy something that's failing, spot the problems, sprinkle on their own brand of magic dust and turn it round or sell for a fast, fat profit. It's almost never that easy – attempting a turnaround is a bad idea for the first-time entrepreneur.

All businesses are worth whatever someone will pay for them. There are standard formulae for valuing a business, and ranges of values for different types of business. If a property is an integral part of the business, as with a pub or a farm, then land values will play a major part in setting the value of the business. Some businesses might be able to make more money from a site than others; so for example, a shop site could easily be worth more money to a fashion retailer or coffee bar than to a hardware shop or builders' merchant. What it is 'worth' will therefore depend on who wants to buy it.

Where property is not involved, the value of a business is normally several times the normal profit the business makes. For small private businesses, somewhere between three and six times normal profit is probably about right. If a business can prove it has much stronger growth prospects than most businesses, the number could go higher. Dotcoms, for example, can sell for substantially higher multiples of their profit.

Some commonly used terms explained:

NORMAL PROFIT
I have used the phrase 'normal profit' here; what I mean by this is the profit a new owner would expect the business to make, which might well be different to the actual profit a business made in any one year. Small business owners often pay themselves very large salaries, for example, which might reduce the apparent business profits, but a new owner wouldn't necessarily want to do that – what matters to the new owner is what level of profits to expect in a normal year. Be careful the other way round, too – sometimes a small business owner might not pay themselves anything at all, or might do the jobs two normal people would do but just take out one salary. The key is for you to understand how much profit you would make from the same business.

GOODWILL

The word 'goodwill' often gets banded about when you're buying a business. 'Goodwill' is basically the extra amount a buyer pays for the business on top of the value of its assets. The idea is that the momentum and quality of the business you're buying will make it quicker and easier to make a profit than if you just went out and bought all the assets on their own. The better the business, the more the seller will want you to pay for its goodwill. You should talk to your accountant about what it might be worth to you.

MORE AFFORDABLE THAN YOU THINK

Another advantage of buying a business rather than starting from scratch is that you might well find banks more willing to lend you money. If they can see that a business has consistently made a profit over a number of years, it is easier for them to predict that this will carry on, and they can then lend against that future profit. Obviously when someone starts a business from scratch, there is no history of profits for a bank to lend against. This means that in practice, while it might cost a little bit more to buy a business, it might also be more affordable for you, taking into account a bigger bank loan. Banks always love lending with the security of property in the picture, so if you decide to buy a business with a property, it should be easier to get substantial bank funding.

If you are serious about buying a business, you should get some professional advice. Typically an accountant will be a good place to start; they can look at the books of any business you consider, and give you advice as to what this might be worth to you. You should also consider a consultant with experience in your industry sector, to give you tips on what to look for, and what to avoid. While this advice will cost you, unless you know the sector really well it is likely to be well worth the cost. Remember that, just as with buying a house, the agent promoting businesses for sale work for the seller, not the buyer.

DANGERS TO AVOID

Of course, buying a business isn't always the right thing to do. If the business is not doing very well (a common reason for its owners wanting to sell it) and you don't know much about running a business like that, it could be a very quick way to lose money. Research suggests that most people who buy a business don't achieve all that they wanted to when they bought them. This sounds negative and you should remember it as a note of caution – a buyer doesn't know everything about a business at the time of purchase and it is easy to assume that things will be easier or better than they end up being. There are of course acquisitions which deliver far more than expected, too – but they are rare.

Things to watch out for when buying a business include:

- Declining sales
  - You should expect sales to be a little bit higher than last year for most businesses, just to keep up with inflation. If they are lower, why? Make sure that you understand any drop in sales, and think about how much further sales might drop in the future.
  - Are sales about to decline? It could be that there are substantial industry changes which haven't yet reached the business you are contemplating buying, but which will imminently. The internet and growth of the supermarkets into new product types are hurting many small retailers, for example.
- Potential new competitors
  - Has a new business recently opened in competition to the business you're considering buying? Is one about to? If so, it could seriously reduce the value of the business you want.
- Key staff
  - Some businesses are really dependent on one or two key members of staff. This might be the head chef in a restaurant, for example. If they leave, you could lose sales or have to spend a considerable sum replacing them and training new staff, when maybe their expertise is one of the things you wanted to buy. If this is important to the business you're considering, check carefully with the seller, and ensure you will get some money back if they do leave after the deal.
- New investment needed
  - The business you're investigating might need serious sums spent on premises, or IT equipment, which could come as a real shock if you don't think about it in advance. If premises come with the business, get a survey done, and have someone check any equipment over before you sign.

The best way to ensure that there is nothing major to worry about is to get formal promises in writing from the seller. These are called 'warranties' and it is normal to get them when you buy a business. I always want a seller to warrant to me that they know of no reason why the business will be worse in future than it has been under their ownership. I also try to keep some of the money I pay them back for at least a year; that way, if they have deceived you (whether intentionally or unintentionally) and it turns out the business is in worse shape than you had been led to believe, it will be easier for you to get some compensation from the seller. How reliable the warranties are though, will depend on how trustworthy your seller is; and it is important to consider how easily you could get your money back if you sued. A warranty that is subsequently proved to be clearly false won't help you if the seller has moved abroad with the cash. Be careful.

HOW TO BUY A BUSINESS

There are several stages to buying a business: finding a business you want to buy; talking to the owners and finding out more about the business; negotiating a price and agreeing a contract.

If you're interested in finding businesses currently for sale, startups.co.uk is a good place to start. Its section on buying a business will let you search for the type of business you are interested in, and give you examples of what is on offer, for free, within a couple of minutes. The businesses will often quote asking prices; consider these as far less rigid than asking prices on a house – frequently the businesses are not worth anything like the asking price. The website lets you request more information if you want to. This can be a good idea even if you have no real interest in buying a business – at least you can get to see some details of how similar businesses really work.

You should also look at the trade papers for your sector, where there are often small adverts at the back detailing businesses for sale. But it may well be that the business you want to buy isn't openly 'for sale'. Don't let that put you off. Just as with houses, if you approach someone and ask if they might be interested in selling, the answer will be yes more often than you might think. I have found the best thing to do is to phone the owner, and have a very relaxed, tentative chat about what their future plans for the business might be, and explain that you are interested in starting something in the same sector, and that you might be interested in buying a business if the right one was available at the right price.

You should look carefully at the figures of any business you are considering. This should include:

- The latest two sets of annual accounts
- Sales by month for the current year, split by type of product
- Expectations for the next two years (this might be a few sentences of explanation rather than a formal forecast)
- Details of all staff, with salaries
- Length and value of any leases, eg premises

It's a must to get an accountant who understands the sector to look at these figures with you if this process is new to you; this will save you money in the long run.

If you decide you would like to buy the business, you need to work out both what it is worth to you and how much you think you can get it for. Hopefully you will be able to pay less than the value you place on it; certainly if you need to pay more than it is worth to you, don't! It is very easy to get caught up in the process and end up paying more than you really should, so try to stay cool, and always be willing to walk away if the owners ask for more than you feel it is worth to you. The business planning techniques in Chapter Seven should help you work out what that is.

If you do decide to buy a business, it's important to use a lawyer who has done lots of similar deals, ideally in the same industry type. That way, they will already know what to look out for, and can save you time and hassle.

Once you have bought a business, it's really important to let all the staff know where they stand from day one. They will all be worried about their own future, so you need to meet them all to explain at least a little about your plans for the business, and where they might fit in. It's also important that they understand you are the boss; you won't really know what the team dynamics are until you've been running it for a while, but there may well be some things you'll need to change; some of the staff may remain loyal to the old boss and regime, especially if you want to change things a bit. I am amazed by just how threatened people can be by change, especially if they have been there for a long time. It's usually well worth showing that you understand that, and making a point of helping the staff get used to your changes.

IS IT RIGHT FOR YOU?

So, should you buy a business instead of starting one from scratch? Only you can really answer that. It will depend on your experience with the business sector you have in mind, and on your objectives.

If there is another business available which is very similar to what you want to do, then it's a good idea to at least talk to the owners. In the retail or catering sectors, it is often a good idea to buy something. If you want to start a dotcom, you might find it hard to pay (or justify) the price someone will be willing to sell a business for – you'll probably find it much cheaper to build it from scratch.

CASE STUDY
IN MY EXPERIENCE

When Crimson began publishing books in March 2006 I decided to try to buy a small book publisher to gain their expertise and a network of established suppliers.

I drew up a list of target businesses that were interested in selling through asking contacts in the book business and subscribing to the trade magazine (*The Bookseller*).

I spoke to a number of the owners of these businesses and mentioned I had heard that they might be interested in a conversation about the business's future. I asked for some financial information if I felt there might be a possibility of buying a business.

From this information I tried to work out what the business might be worth to Crimson. Then I would go back with a draft offer, or politely say that I did not want to take it further.

I ended up making an offer for a business where the owner was retiring; he had run the business for over 30 years, so his reason for selling was genuine. We negotiated the price and the structure of the deal, and then agreed terms.

The owner was especially keen for me to look after his staff. This is very normal for small businesses. We also agreed that he would work for the business for a few months after the deal, to give me a chance to learn the ropes. Solidifying the deal then took some months. I went to their office several times, with my accountant, to look over the figures and contracts. The deal was done in September 2006, when we became the proud owners of Vacation Work, the leading publisher of gap year and living and working abroad books.

We have integrated Vacation Work into Crimson now. The business is working very well, and I am delighted to have bought it. It has certainly helped us learn about some of the differences between book and magazine publishing faster than we would have done otherwise.

ACTIONPOINTS

1. Think about whether buying a business could help you
2. Draw up a list of what buying would achieve that would make it better than starting
3. Read trade magazines and talk to people in the trade to learn how much buying a business might cost
4. Draw up list of possible businesses to buy
5. Approach those businesses; negotiate with any which are suitable and interested
6. With your accountant, check the business out really thoroughly
7. Use a lawyer to draw up a sensible contract
8. Make sure the deal still delivers your objectives, and at a sensible cost
9. Do the deal

CHAPTER 04
Franchising

What's this all about?

- What is a franchise?
- What are the pros and cons?
- How to find the right franchise for you

(?)

D ull word, good concept. Franchising is almost a halfway house between starting a business from scratch and buying one. It involves you opening up a branch of an existing business, which helps you set up and run it, and in return, you paying them an initial fee and a small percentage of your takings from the business.

An established company (called a 'franchisor') creates a business package, which it sells as a 'franchise' to someone like you, who then becomes 'a franchisee'. This gives the franchisee the right to operate a business under the franchisor's name, in return for a one-off initial fee, and then an ongoing fee which is a percentage of turnover.

Franchising is very large already, and growing fast: in the UK, franchised businesses turn over more than £10bn, and employ nearly half a million staff. There are all sorts of franchises, from fast food outlets and cleaning businesses, to print shops, estate agencies and even dating agencies. Franchising is huge in America, which is why some of the biggest names in franchising are American businesses. McDonalds and Burger King both have some franchised restaurants, as do household names like Domino's Pizza, Kall-Kwik, Prontaprint, Dyno-Rod and more.

Companies like these often use franchising as a way to grow faster than they could on their own. It's a good idea to understand why a company might rather sell you a franchise to run rather than open the branch themselves. There can be very good reasons why they do – usually it is a great way for them to find highly motivated branch managers, or to grow their own business without needing to find all the money themselves.

WHAT'S THE UPSIDE FOR YOU?

The advantages to someone looking to start a business are that you get a proven business concept, a known brand, good training and support. If you were to open the same type of business from scratch rather than as a franchise, you'd probably pay almost the same in startup costs, but wouldn't get any of the help. Think about the Domino's Pizza or McDonalds cases; it is likely that their brand name and national marketing campaigns alone would be enough to more than double the revenue a branded restaurant might make over a similar restaurant you could open yourself – if you think about all the pizza leaflets you get shoved through your door, are you more likely to use one with a name you know, or a name you don't?

This also means that it is far less risky to open a franchised outlet than to start the same type of business yourself. You get all the benefit of knowledge that the franchisor has learned in its life, as well as being able to buy in supplies from quality, tested suppliers at prices which are sensible. The franchisor should train you and provide you with an operating manual which will help you learn how to run the business well. They can also tell you what sort of revenue and profits to expect and when, based on their past experiences. They will probably also give you good advice on what sort of premises to find (if they are retail) or tips on marketing. Some will even give you some early customers to get you started, or have a strong enough brand name that you get some early customers very easily.

Banks like franchising precisely because it is so much lower risk than starting a new business. This often means that they are comfortable lending people quite a bit of the money needed to start a franchise. Many franchisors have agreements with some banks to lend franchisees a set percentage of the money they will need, too, which will make it considerably easier for you to borrow the money.

And if you don't know what sort of business you want to run, but you know that you want to work for yourself, franchising could be perfect. There are enough franchises available that you should be able to find one suitable for your skills and lifestyle goals, and you'll get plenty of help setting it up. It's far less lonely being a franchisee than setting up on your own – as well as the support you'll get from the franchisor, you'll be able to talk to other franchisees, too. Better still, because the franchisor will get a percentage of your future turnover, it has a strong incentive to help you increase it.

... AND THE DOWNSIDES

There are two main disadvantages to starting a franchise. Firstly, it can significantly limit the amount of income you can earn, because the franchisor takes a percentage of the turnover as a fee. This should all be entirely clear before you commit to buying a franchise, though, so there shouldn't be any nasty surprises.

The second downside is that you are dependent on the franchisor doing a good job, both now and into the future. There have been some instances where franchisees have become unhappy with the way the franchisor was run – Benjy's sandwich shops is one recent example. You will benefit from any great initiatives the franchisor introduces, but if their marketing backfires, it could affect your sales. If you think you have a great idea to develop your business, for example by introducing a new type of burger or pizza, you probably wouldn't be allowed to do it by the franchisor. So while you would be running your own business, you would not be fully in control.

Sometimes franchisors can change their strategy and want to buy your franchise back from you. While they'll need to pay for the privilege, it might well not suit you to sell when they want you to, which could get awkward. PizzaExpress bought their franchises back years ago, and while this is still unusual, it does happen from time to time. Check your contract to see what rights you have if the franchisor does want to do this in future.

Most franchisors also check up on their franchisees, to ensure that their quality standards are maintained. This is perfectly reasonable, but does mean that if you let standards slip when you're going through a rough patch at some stage, your franchisor could get tough with you – and ultimately, might be able to kick you out of the franchise altogether.

If you do decide to go ahead with a franchise, you should certainly use a lawyer who has seen franchise agreements before and therefore knows what is reasonable and normal and what is not. You can find lawyers like this by asking the owners of franchises in your area (I'd try Mail Boxes Etc or a Kall-Kwik store near you – the owners I have spoken to there have always been really helpful).

Most franchises are pretty good, but some are badly run. This can mean that the franchisor doesn't do some of what it is supposed to, or that it does it badly. Marketing is often the area that franchisees feel isn't done well enough. There have been a few cases where franchisees have been very unhappy with their franchisor. If there are enough franchisees, they can often be powerful enough, together, to force the company to improve its service. It's important that you talk to a few current franchisees first, before you sign up for a new franchise, just to see how they feel.

You should be especially suspicious of franchisors making promises that sound too good to be true. There are some unscrupulous franchisors out to make a quick buck; the danger is that they could take your money and deliver very little back. Be wary, and make sure you talk to several other franchisees, and a lawyer, before you sign up.

HOW TO FIND A FRANCHISE FOR YOU

There are a number of franchising magazines that you might find, but you should be wary of them: most of the profiles you will see there are written by the franchisor, or at least paid for by them. Startups.co.uk has a dedicated section all about franchising, called Start a Franchise, found on the startups.co.uk homepage. There you will be able to browse through lists of all the franchises available in the UK by type, and see if any appeal. You'll also find the latest news about franchising, including any current known problems.

If you want to investigate it further, there are a number of franchising exhibitions around the UK. At each of these you can speak to lots of different franchisors about their offers, and very quickly get a sense of what it is all about. If franchising is a real option for you, I strongly recommend that you attend one.

Above all, try to talk to as many franchisees as you can before you commit to one yourself. I would literally go into some franchised outlets, and try to chat to the boss – just try to find a time when they aren't really busy! See if you can buy them a coffee, and pick their brains. They'll probably be flattered you've asked their opinion, and be really helpful. Try to ask what has happened which they hadn't expected, whether it has gone according to plan, whether they would recommend their franchisor, and if they have any tips or other advice.

Franchising is often sneered at by some entrepreneurs but if you'd like to run your own business but don't have a killer idea, are reasonably risk-averse and have good management skills, franchising can make a lot of sense and earn you a very comfortable living.

ACTIONPOINTS

1. Find out if there are any franchises in your sector, or which interest you
2. Consider if the pros of those franchises outweigh the cons for you
3. If so, learn as much as you can about the parent company and the business
4. Contact them and register interest in becoming a franchisee
5. Test a few different franchise branches out, as a customer
6. Talk to other franchisees about how satisfied they are
7. If you're happy, get a lawyer and negotiate a deal

CHAPTER 05
Will your business work?

What's this all about?
- What does 'success' mean to you?
- Is there a market for your business?
- Ways to test your idea
- Ways to make it work

C onsidering if your idea will actually work is crucial: if the business isn't viable, then no matter how hard you work, or how much money you invest in it, it simply won't ever work. You'd be surprised just how many people launch businesses that are highly unlikely ever to work. For a business to be viable, I mean that it has to make money – at least enough to survive comfortably after paying all its normal costs.

I was looking at a company recently that I was interested in buying. They had great products, but weren't making a profit. I could see that some of their costs could be trimmed, but the business fundamentally wasn't viable, because it was making far too little profit per product. The managing director told me that the solution was to produce far more products – but that would have meant investing a lot of money, potentially for nothing. She had failed to spot the real issue: they weren't making a proper profit on their core products, which meant the business was not viable. However many products they made, they wouldn't make the overall business work.

HOW DO YOU DEFINE SUCCESS?

Of course, before you can start to think about whether something will 'succeed' or 'work', you need to know what that means for you. Initially, try to work this out in terms of lifestyle or other objectives: what do you want to get from the business? This might be a little income on the side to help fund great holidays, a house deposit, or a better car. Or it could be a decent standard of living, or being able to sell in a number of years time for millions. It doesn't matter at all what the objectives are – what matters is that you define them for yourself, and put them into numbers: how much will the business need to make in order to give you success, and when will it need it by for it to be worth your while setting it up.

WHY WILL ANYONE BUY FROM YOU?

Whatever you want to achieve, your business will need to get customers buying from it. Every potential new business needs to work out why prospective customers will buy their product or services. This could be as simple as thinking 'there's no fish and chip shop in this town, and lots of people like fish and chips' but even here you need to understand how people really behave. Of course many people like fish and chips, and most places in Britain already have a shop selling them so finding a place without is a potentially good start. But people in that area will have lived without a fish and chip shop for some time which may mean that they've got used to using a Chinese takeaway instead, or that convenience food outlets aren't popular in that community. So, either way, getting customers to use a new fish and chip shop would mean your business has to change the way they behave and the choices they make.

To do that, you need to have good reasons why people will buy from you, and make sure that potential customers can clearly see those reasons. (Some people call these reasons unique selling points, or USPs for short.)

If we continue the fish and chip shop example, being the only shop in an area is a great start – if people want fish and chips, you're the only choice, which is a wonderful reason why they'd buy from you. It's always easier to be different (to whatever else is on the market) than to be better.

If there were another fish and chip shop in the same town, though, you'd have to persuade people who use the other shop to try yours. You'd basically have to persuade them that you're better. That might be cheaper, having better quality food, friendlier service, a cleaner shop, longer opening hours or a wider choice of food and drink, for example. Premium fish and chip shops seem to be more popular now, offering organic or line-caught fish, served on tables with white linen tablecloths. This means they are able to charge far more.

About 10 years ago a friend of mine wanted me to invest in a new restaurant he wanted to open. I didn't. The problem was that he hadn't thought enough about why people might want to come to his restaurant other than the fact that it would be a nice place. He didn't know what food he would cook – that would be up to the chef. No one else invested either, and the restaurant never opened.

Other common unique selling points include speed, service, convenience, nutritional value etc. You'll need to work out what will set your business apart.

GAP IN THE MARKET

Lots of people I meet tell me that they'd love to start their own business one day, but they're still waiting to spot a gap in the market. Most entrepreneurs I meet are forever seeing other opportunities for businesses, or gaps in the market. If you're really well suited to running your own business, you'll probably see plenty of gaps in all sorts of markets, and be talking about them with your friends and family long before you actually start your first business.

So what is a gap in the market, and how do you know it exists? You probably never know for sure it exists before you start, you just think it does. Gaps in the market are really ideas for businesses that are like existing businesses, but slightly different. The gap might be geographical, such as there not being a fish and chip shop in a particular place, or national, such as Harry Ramsden's, where someone thought there was room for a national chain of fish and chip shops, where previously there had only been individual shops or chains selling burgers or pizzas.

Looking at today's high street, it seems hard to remember what it was like without any coffee bars. Yet when Coffee Republic launched, there were none on most high streets. Its founders, Bobby and Sahar Hashemi, had seen these new coffee shops in New York, and felt sure they would work in Britain. It looks obvious now. Yet other people have felt the same about bagel shops, which are also very common in America, but which haven't worked as well over here. What works in one country may well work in another, though this shouldn't be assumed.

CASE STUDY
IN MY EXPERIENCE

The first magazine Crimson launched was called *What Laptop*. It was 1999, and there were even more computer magazines around then than there are now. Plenty of people thought I was mad to have this idea; 'surely there can't be room for yet another computer magazine', they said. 'If there was room, one of the other IT publishers would have done it'. But I thought there was a gap in the market. I had seen magazines like this in America, and the laptop share of the PC market was growing rapidly.

I did a little research and discovered that already laptops accounted for nearly 25% of the UK PC market. That suggested that a quarter of the people buying general computer magazines wanted to buy a laptop, yet laptop buyers were not very well catered for by the general magazines.

So I launched our magazine in August 1999, and it was profitable within three issues. It didn't sell quite as many copies as I expected, but it sold more advertisements, and ended up being more profitable than we had predicted. The gap in the market was there.

WHY HASN'T THE GAP BEEN FILLED?

It is really important to ask yourself why a gap hasn't already been filled, since it may well be that there are some good reasons which you haven't yet spotted that would mean your otherwise great idea won't work.

At the inception of *What Laptop*, (as described in 'In My Experience') I gave this some thought and concluded that the main computer magazine publishers wouldn't want to publish such a magazine since they would be getting more money from laptop advertisers by forcing them to advertise in their existing, larger magazine, because there was no alternative. It wouldn't be in their interest to take on extra staff and other costs to produce a magazine which would reduce the revenue of their existing magazines.

The only exception to my theory was Future Publishing, a large IT magazine publisher; I couldn't work out why they hadn't launched it, since they launched lots of new titles and could have done this very easily. (Eventually they launched a magazine to compete with *What Laptop*, then closed it down, and ended up buying our magazine from us.)

At the same time, as I was trying to work out whether there might be a good reason not to do this, I went into a newsagent and had one of those moments. There in front of me was a brand new magazine called *Mobile Computing*, focused on reviewing laptops. Although I was cross and worried that someone had spotted this gap first (an entrepreneur's constant worry) I was also pleased since it suggested more people agreed that there might indeed be such a gap.

I bought it and took it back to the office. Luckily, my team and I thought it missed its target audience; for a start it featured a scantily clad woman on the front cover, rather than a large picture of a laptop, which would not only alienate an important segment of the audience (laptops were often bought by women) but also potentially detract from the magazine being taken seriously by businesses, who were major purchasers of laptops. So we continued with our launch plans, and within a few months *Mobile Computing* shut, and we thrived.

IS THE GAP LARGE ENOUGH?

The tragedy behind the business I nearly bought which I mentioned at the start of this chapter is that the products themselves are extremely good quality. They have very good reviews in the press, and are generally liked. They are sufficiently different from their competition, and do genuinely fill a gap in the market. But the problem with the business is that they don't sell enough to make a profit. While there is a gap in the market, it's not large enough.

Years ago, I invested in a business called Soup Works. It had great branding, and a new concept for workplace lunches – all based around soup. The soup was significantly better than the fresh soup you can get in supermarkets, and the theory was that people would welcome a fresh alternative to the sandwich for lunch. The concept was interesting, the product fabulous, but the business failed. It just couldn't get enough customers to come regularly enough to pay the high rents and staff costs. Nearly, but not quite there. And nearly is not good enough in business, as you lose money and ultimately fail.

The key point to note here is that you need to not only be sure that there is indeed a gap in the market but also that there are enough customers out there who might buy your product or service. Also, that you can reach enough of them, within your marketing budget, to make a profit.

This is why the US bagel shops being set up here in the UK have not been as successful as the coffee shops. There are some people who love bagels, but not enough to make the bagel stores work well in many locations.

PREDICTING THE SIZE OF A MARKET

The hard part is that it's almost impossible to know in advance whether a market really is there. When we launched magazines, the major retailers wanted lots of market research from us to tell them there was a large gap before they agreed to stock them. We had remarkably little. I don't believe in research that asks people 'if this product existed would you buy it?' since it's such an artificial question. Ultimately, I believe that the only way to predict success is to look closely at the sales of similar products, and to try to compare. Try to work out what quantity they are selling, and what proportion of that you might achieve.

Most industries have some sort of research information you will be able to use – try the relevant trade organisation for your proposed business type. It's very easy to do loads of research from good sources, and end up with the wrong answer. How? By believing all that you read.

To explain this further, most of the estimates you come up with will be a combination of what quantity of something you might sell, and at what price. I've made two mistakes here, and have seen other entrepreneurs make them, too.

The first is to believe the prices you see quoted in catalogues or price lists: very frequently, larger customers will pay much less than a quoted price. This is very fair and sensible, but unless you know what sort of prices different customers actually pay, you can't get an accurate estimate of your revenue potential.

I should know; I made this mistake when I started Crimson. I assumed advertisers in some competitive magazines paid more per page than they actually do, which made it look as though the other magazines were far more profitable than they actually were. I had even asked certain people, too, and had been told that the high prices I was assuming were about right. (Beware of bragging – lots of people want you to think that their business is more successful than it really is). You should ask enough people the same question so that you can compare their answers. If you're not sure who to believe, think about who would really know. For example, to find out advertising prices, you could ask an advertising agency what prices they typically pay.

The second mistake is to assume that all quantities sold are the same. Take books, for example. Publishers give discounts to retailers and wholesalers; bigger customers can get bigger discounts. Then there are unusual customers like book clubs, who will often buy very large quantities of a book, but pay much less per copy. So when you hear about a book which has sold a million copies, for example, it is quite easy to assume that they were all sold at normal trade prices, when in fact many of them might have been sold at very low prices to a book club. The difference this makes to the estimated sales revenue of your new business could be enormous.

Again, the way to solve this is to ask people who might know. For example, to find out typical discount rates which you might need to give away if you are selling to other businesses, try asking likely trade customers. I often used to phone people and explain that I was in the process of setting up a new business, and just wanted a few minutes of someone's time to help me learn more about how it worked. Often people were very helpful, despite being busy. Indeed, if you ask the right people, then they might feel better disposed towards your business when you do launch, especially if you have taken their advice.

The founders of innocent drinks were pretty sure their idea for a new business was good, but weren't sure if it would take off. So they took a stall at a music festival, and sold some early versions of their smoothies there. They asked people to tell them if they should give up the day jobs to set up a business making smoothies – customers could put their empty cups in a bin marked 'Yes' or one marked 'No'. At the end, the 'Yes' bin was full, and they decided to set up. The rest is history. It wasn't a formal survey, or conventional, but it was enough to persuade them that plenty of people would pay for their product. Often, that's as much certainty as you'll get.

WILL IT WORK TOMORROW AS WELL AS TODAY?

To judge how future-proof your business will be you need to consider trends within your own proposed business sector. For example, as supermarkets have been growing over the last few decades, the number of independent butchers and bakers has fallen significantly. Had you opened an extremely good bakers' shop 15 years ago, it might be struggling now because more and more people are buying their bread from supermarkets, however well you are running your shop. It is possible to succeed in a declining market, but it's far harder than succeeding in a growing market. Greggs, for example, has grown its chain of high street bakers' shops to a major national chain even as supermarkets' expansion have put other bakers out of business.

⇾ STARTUP TIP

You should be able to learn these industry trends by reading the sector's trade magazine for a few months, and by talking to people – especially at the trade organisation. Literally pick up the phone to them, say that you're in the process of setting up a business and ask if you could you speak to someone there to answer a few questions. Most people are surprisingly helpful when you make the first step and, politely, ask them business questions.

Most of us are pretty focused on the world the way it is today. When I say 'the world' I actually mean 'our bit of the world, as seen through our eyes'. But we live in a world which is changing fast. Faster, in fact, than ever before.

What do I mean? The internet has changed many aspects of our lives, from how we buy books and music and increasingly financial products like insurance, to what airlines are successful – Ryanair and easyJet have been made far more successful by internet booking which keeps their costs so low. Six years ago, it's very likely you had never heard of Google. Now, I doubt there's anyone reading this book that hasn't used Google; you have probably used it multiple times today. Tens of millions of people are already using sites like Facebook and Bebo to catch up with friends and meet new people.

India and China are growing fast. You probably know that already. But do you know just how fast, and what it means? There's a whole book's worth of information on this very subject, so I'll be brief. China and India have already grown and will continue to grow faster than almost all of us in Britain realise. In just 10 years time there will be more people in China earning an average European income than the populations of England, Germany, France and Italy put together. If nothing else, that's an enormous market of new people with plenty of money to spend. But their income and education levels also mean that, for far less money, they will continue to be able to do far more of what we do in the UK today, undercutting UK and other western economies.

At the same time we probably have global climate change, and last but by no means least, we have an aging population, brought about by better diet and medical care, and a declining birth rate. This means that a smaller workforce will need to fund a larger retired population in the future. Somehow.

SO WHAT?

Well, in short, you need to think about how these trends might affect your future business. It probably wouldn't have been a smart move to have opened a high street travel agent 10 years ago, for example, given how the cheap airlines and the internet have opened up independent travel. And more bookshops close every year now than open.

On the other hand, a website business might be a very smart idea now, and even better if it uses or supplies China. If you're planning to open a shop, for example, consider how it will be affected by growth of the internet; this might be an opportunity, or a threat to your plans. Hairdressing and similar service businesses are less likely to be affected by cheaper Chinese imports or the internet.

Quite what global warming means is hard to predict – but an expansion of tourism and open-air dining in Britain seem like good bets to me, as does growth in demand for related products like air conditioning.

I genuinely believe that there are lots of great opportunities around right now for starting new businesses. I just think it's always better to go in with your eyes open, fully aware of how things seem likely to change. Andy Grove, ex CEO of Intel, the huge microchip company, named his autobiography *Only the Paranoid Survive,* which is a phrase I refer back to often.

SO WILL YOUR BUSINESS WORK?

Businesses don't work by themselves – someone, almost always the founder, has to make them work. Even a great business idea will struggle to work if run by someone who doesn't care or doesn't work hard enough. On the other hand, if you're really motivated, work hard and are sensible, you could make even a weak business idea a success. People matter more than the idea, in other words. Imagine a normal town or area, full of restaurants – then a new one opens up, offering what appears to be nothing very different. This happens frequently in Richmond, where I work, for example. If the food is decent, but nothing special, the décor decent, the prices average, but the service special, the restaurant will probably survive, and might even do well, on the back of its owner's hard work.

I've put my own tips to help you make your business work together later in this book, in Chapter Twenty-Three.

ACTIONPOINTS

- You need reasons for people to buy from your business
- *Different* is often easier than *better*
- Are there enough potential customers willing to pay for your product?
- Can you get to them cost effectively?
- What are the trends in your industry?
- How will your business deal with the changing world?
- You will need to *make* your business work

CHAPTER 06

How much money will you need?

What's this all about?
- How to work out the break-even point ⟨?⟩
- How to predict profits
- Work out how much funding you will need

Your business will fail unless you master this chapter.

Sorry to be so dramatic, but I really think it's true. Unless you know what is in this chapter you won't be able to make good decisions for your business.

There are really two questions which are crucial to the future of your business: how much will it take to set the business up in the first place, and after that, how much profit, if any, will it make and when? By the end of this chapter, you should know how to answer both these questions.

A few words about numbers. Most people think that accounts are complicated and boring, and that they can leave them for other people. They are partly right – business accounts can sometimes get very complicated, and, for some, very dull. But for most businesses, the accounts information you will need is surprisingly simple, and far from dull. In business, numbers and accounts are a way of measuring progress, and will help you make better decisions. The numbers don't dominate or drive decisions, but rather give you information so that you can make the right business decisions.

I think it's crucial to understand the numbers behind a business properly if you are to stand a chance of running a successful business. It really isn't that difficult to learn, but it really is important to grasp. It will all be far easier if you think of it in relation to the business sector you are passionate about, so try to think about your business as you read through the next section.

The danger of not making financial predictions in advance is that you might start something which is never likely to make money, or something which could make a profit one day, but will take longer to get to profitability than you can afford. Either could be disastrous and spell the end of your business.

First, I'm going to explain how to estimate your business's likely costs and income. After that I'll go through calculating how much it will cost you to set up your business. Then, I'm going to show you how to work out whether business should be profitable or not. After that, I'm going to explain how to work out how much money you will need to set up and maintain your business. Right at the end, I'll discuss how to use all these numbers to work out whether this is a business you still want to start. There will be some repetition, and some of the terms are different but sound similar, so if you find you get confused it may be worth going back and re-reading parts, or using the glossary at the end of the book to understand some of the terms.

HOW TO ESTIMATE COSTS AND INCOME

Of course, you won't know what all the costs are going to be precisely, let alone precisely how much customers might spend with you, and when. So what you need to do is make some estimates. The better these are, the more accurate your forecasts will be. If you assume too much income, which almost every founder does, your new business will seem destined for amazing success, while if you assume too little, or too high costs, then you will predict failure. Usually I start out with rough guesses in my very early versions of numbers for a possible new business, then do some work to try to find out what real numbers might be, and build up a more and more accurate picture over time.

Costs are the easiest thing to estimate: you ought to be able to get quotes for everything you need before you commit to starting up. You have to do this research at some stage anyway, to find the suppliers your business needs, so do it early to make sure your forecasts are accurate. If you explain to prospective suppliers that you are in the process of starting up a new business, they will probably be willing to help in the hope of getting your business when you do start.

Whenever you estimate things, you can round up or round down. I always start out by trying to round my income forecasts down, and my cost forecasts up (which is the most conservative approach). That way, I feel comfortable that if I have missed something out or underestimated somewhere, there is a little bit of slack already built in.

The hard part is to know how cautious to be. If you are too cautious and assume higher costs and lower income, you could well end up predicting failure. There's no point in starting a business which won't work. Of course one of the points of this planning exercise is to tell whether the business looks like it will be viable. If there are any other similar businesses to yours, try to base your numbers on what you think they might be doing. It's unwise to base your numbers on the most successful business in the sector, though, unless you're completely clear that that is what you are aiming at.

Lots of businesses start from the total market size and say 'I am sure we can at least achieve 10% of that' (sometimes the 10% is 1%, if the market is huge). This is a very dangerous way to try to forecast sales, since it is starting with something really large and then making a wild guess, thinking that 10%, 1% or whatever, sounds small enough that you feel that surely you can do at least that much. A much better approach is to take a similar business and then try to work out whether you'll do a bit better, a bit worse, and so on. Best of all is to get a selection of similar businesses, then compare all their figures and work out where you ought to aim for. By far the best way to find out these figures is to talk to other business owners; a good bank manager might also be able to let you know figures from businesses he or she knows, anonymously.

Your income will be your selling price times the quantity you expect to sell. If you charge VAT (see Chapter Eleven to find out) then don't include VAT in your income here, since it doesn't belong to your business. You should forecast your revenue on the same time periods that you used to forecast your costs. Some examples of early income experiences from now successful businesses are:

Coffee Republic: after a great first day at their very first coffee bar (when they sold £500 against a target of £300) their daily sales stayed at a little over £200 for months and months, which was considerably less than they had forecast and they needed.

A Well-Known Travel Book: when a now well-known travel book launched, its publishers expected to sell 50,000 copies in the UK. That is a huge amount for a travel book in the UK, and its distributors suggested printing more like 5,000 initially. The publishers generated a lot of publicity for the book, which initially sold about 3,000 copies but went on to sell over 100,000 copies over the next two years, exceeding those expectations.

HOW MUCH WILL IT COST TO SET UP YOUR NEW BUSINESS?

When you set up a business you have a number of costs which you will only pay once. Once you've paid them, you shouldn't need to pay them again. They're therefore very different from ongoing running costs, which you will continue to incur as you operate the business. For some businesses these are tiny, for others they can be enormous.

Every business is different, but the following are some helpful guidelines as to typical costs. Please check with suppliers you would like to use as to how much they might charge you for working with your business. You probably won't need all these items initially, so just select those you think you will need and put down the amount you think you'll need to spend on that item. It may be that your business has some other items not listed that you'll need to spend money on as well – be sure to think about every aspect of the business and try to imagine all the costs there could conceivably be.

- Registering the name and creating a logo
- Buying business stationery
- Creating a simple website
- Setting up a limited company
- Registering for VAT and PAYE
- Accountancy advice on starting up
- Paying a premium to take over a lease on business premises
- Legal costs for your new business premises
- Fitting out your business premises:
  - Signage
  - Equipment
  - Furniture
  - Air conditioning
  - Security
  - Electrician
  - Architect or other design fees

- Hiring staff
- Buying initial stock of materials
- Creating early sample products
- Launch marketing spend

Please note that most suppliers will charge VAT on top of the amounts they quote you. Although you will get this back if you register for VAT, you won't get it back straight away, which means you will need to pay it first and then get it back later on (I talk more about VAT in Chapter 11).

ONCE IT'S SET UP, WILL IT MAKE A PROFIT?

Once a business is set up and open for business, it has two sorts of on-going costs: fixed costs that you pay regardless of whether anyone buys anything from the business or not, and variable costs which you incur only when someone buys something.

Usually these fixed costs consist of things like:

- Rent, rates, service charge for your business premises
- Staff costs for any staff who you pay on a monthly salary basis, rather than by the hours they work
- Utilities (while these vary depending on how much you use them, for most business types they tend to be pretty stable regardless of how many sales the business makes)
- Insurance

The good news is that these are fairly easy costs to estimate – that's about the only good news about fixed costs (I always try very hard to keep these to an absolute minimum). Businesses often refer to these costs as 'overheads'.

Although I have said that these costs are fixed, you will find that as your business grows beyond a certain level, you might need to raise the level of overheads. It might be, for example, that you need to move to larger premises in order to fit more people in. In general terms, though, these costs are called fixed because they tend to be fixed for at least a few years.

Variable costs, which go up and down with sales, usually consist of whatever you are selling. If your business is a shop, these will be the costs of whatever goods you sell and any extra staff you take on to cope with the sales; if your business is a manufacturer, it will be the costs of your raw materials and any non-fixed staff costs. Businesses often call these costs 'the cost of goods sold'.

Gross profit

If you subtract these variable costs from whatever sales income you get from your customers, the amount you have left is called 'gross profit'. Your gross profit margin is really useful for planning. By 'gross profit margin' I mean the percentage that is left of the sales income.

So if you have sales of £100, and spent £50 on the goods you sold to your customers, you have £50 left. That is a 50% gross profit margin. If you had spent £40 on the goods that you sold, your gross profit would have been £60, which is a 60% gross margin; had you spent £60 on the goods, your gross profit would have been £40, or a 40% gross margin.

If you take your fixed costs away from your gross profit, whatever is left is the profit or loss your business has made. When your gross profit is the same as your fixed costs, your business is breaking even. If the fixed costs are higher, your business is making a loss. If the gross profit is higher, then the business is making a profit.

Breakeven level

You can work out what level of sales you need to make to break even by dividing your fixed costs by your gross margin:

Fixed costs / GM% = Breakeven sales value

So if you have fixed costs of say £8,000 a month, and a gross profit margin of 40% (which will be typical for many small shops, for example) then you need to sell £20,000 every month in order to break even.

If you know the average price you sell things for, then you can work out how many items you need to sell in order to break even by dividing that breakeven level of sales by your average selling price.

Think about what the numbers would be for your new business. I would put your numbers onto a spreadsheet; that way you can save it, then come back to it over time as you get more information, and get more and more certain about how the business should work. You can download a free sample spreadsheet template from my website (www.smallbusinessexpert.co.uk) if you would like to.

Most businesses, though, sell a variety of different products, and might well make different profit margins on each of them. The way around this is to take an average. You can certainly try to work out how much of each type of product you think you'll sell, but it's also a good idea if you can to find out what 'industry norms' are. So restaurants are often said to spend one third of their income on supplies of food and drink.

It doesn't really matter whether you calculate the gross margin and fixed costs for a month or a year; it doesn't affect the calculation at all. The only thing to be careful about is to be consistent, so everything is put down on the same basis. Things like rates for a year are typically charged in 10 equal payments, so I normally take 10 times one month's payment, then divide by 12 to get a 'normal' month's cost.

If this is all new to you, don't worry; just read it a few times, then try to do the sums yourself, with your own business in mind. Try playing with a few different options: try charging a lower price and see how many more units you would need to sell. Or raising the price, and seeing how many fewer you need to sell to still break even.

Making a profit

Of course, there's no point in starting a business just to break even. You can use the same approach to work out what level of sales you need to achieve in order to make a pre-tax profit. Think about how much profit you would like to make from the business in order for it to be worth your while. Just add this profit figure onto your fixed costs, and divide the total by the gross margin as with the breakeven analysis. You'll get the level of sales you would need to achieve to make that profit.

This is really useful for working out whether you think a business might be viable – have a long think about the sales level you would need to hit to achieve your target profitability. Does it look OK, or a bit scary? Are there other businesses like yours doing that level of sales? Or would yours need to sell more than most in order to hit that level? You need to end up being comfortable that you can at least hit a level of sales which will make enough profit for you to want to carry on running the business.

CASH FLOW

Profit and having money in the bank are different. I know it seems odd, but it is entirely possible to have a profitable business which doesn't have enough funds to pay its bills. Equally, having money in the bank does not mean that your business is successful. This is a fundamental business concept it's important to grasp.

As this book is going to press, a very large British bank has suffered very publicly from precisely this: Northern Rock. It has been a profitable bank for many years, but suddenly found itself unable to pay its bills, and had to borrow money from the Bank of England, which led to vast numbers of its savings customers losing confidence in it, and pulling their savings out. This in turn has led to an 80% fall in the company's share price, and it looks as though the bank will not be able to continue as an independent company. All because of cash flow issues. So take note, to avoid something remotely like it happening to your business!

All businesses need 'stuff' in order to operate. For most businesses, that stuff will consist of premises, kitted out with equipment; stocks of raw materials or finished goods; marketing materials such as catalogues; a website and people. That has all cost money to buy. The day your business opens ready to make its first sale, you will have spent some money getting it to that point.

If your business grows, it will need more stuff to be ready to make more sales in the future. Some businesses are able to fund that new stuff using money from profits they have already made; others can't. It will depend on all sorts of factors such as how fast your business receives the money it earns from sales, how long suppliers give you to pay them, how large your profit margins are, and many other factors.

The amount of money you need to fund this difference between when you have to pay people and when you get paid is known as 'working capital'. It is usual for the amount of working capital a business needs to grow as the business grows. There are a number of ways to fund this, which I talk about under Raising Finance later in the book.

(If you're setting up a business as a consultant, or freelance provider of a service such as journalism or beauty therapy, then your main 'product' will be your time, and so you won't have quite the same issue – you can't exactly buy more hours of your own time! So if you are profitable, so long as your clients are paying you sensibly, you shouldn't face cash flow problems.)

So what? The big issue here is that it is very hard indeed to predict how much funding a business will need. It feels counterintuitive, but a business which is performing less well might need less than one performing better. All businesses need to make sure they have enough money to survive – not to do so is both madness and against the law (this law is there to protect suppliers from businesses which won't be able to pay their bills from ordering supplies).

FOUR STEPS TO PREDICTING HOW MUCH MONEY YOU NEED

The way to predict how much money your business might need is called a cash flow forecast. It is a really crucial part of the planning process. This is not a one-off exercise. When you have done it once, you need to think about it, adjust some assumptions, and see what difference it makes. Ultimately, you need to be comfortable that you can make your business survive in all the circumstances you think are possible, since you can't be sure exactly what will happen.

Once you have been through the cost and income estimation process we've already talked about, forecasting cash flows is a simple extension of that. Again, this is best done with a spreadsheet; the template you can download from my website (www. smallbusinessexpert.co.uk) shows a typical cash flow model.

Step one

The first step is to work out what money you will receive, and when. Normally, cash flows are done by month. The normal types of money any business might receive are:

- Cash sales
- Payments from customers who bought on credit
- Payments in advance from customers
- VAT refunds
- Bank loan
- New share capital
- Cash from sale of other business assets

Note that many businesses don't receive the payment from their sales in the same month as the sales are made. It is normal for businesses which supply other businesses to send an invoice to a customer when some work has been done, or goods supplied; this invoice is simply a document setting out how much is owed, why, how it should be paid, and by when. Just like people paying their personal bills, businesses tend not to pay their bills on time. Typically you should expect to get paid about 60 days after your invoice was issued, though 90 is more common in some industries – this makes a big difference to your cash flows, so check what is normal in your industry.

The total from all those items will be the total cash the business expects to have enter its bank account during a month.

Step two

The next step is to work out how much money the business needs to pay out in the month. The most usual categories for payments are:

- Payments to suppliers
- Wages
- Payments to HM Revenue & Customs (for VAT, PAYE)
- Rent, rates and service charge
- Payments for other 'stuff' – new assets such as vehicles, equipment, and so on
- Loan repayments

Step three

The difference between the total your business needs to pay out each month and the amount it gets in each month is called its net cash flow for that month. For young and fast growing businesses, this net cash flow can often be negative, which means that the business is paying out more money than it is getting in.

You should show the balance at the start of each month, then add the net cash flow for the month to get to the closing balance for that month. This closing balance is the opening balance for the next month.

Step four

When you're planning your new business you should project this cash flow for at least two years. Some people say they want to see three to five years' cash flow forecasts, but for a startup business I think it's likely to be a waste of your time doing it for more than two: so much can happen to a startup in the first couple of years that differs from expectations – the chances that your initial calculations are correct or applicable in year three are minimal. Of course, if your business needs it, perhaps because you know it won't make a profit until after the first two years, you might need to forecast for longer than that.

Now what?

You need to become really familiar with these numbers and calculations. As you learn more about the credit terms you will need to give your customers, and what terms you get from suppliers, you should keep updating this forecast. When I started Impressions, my games company, I would literally redo this several times a week, as I got new information.

The thing to look for early on is how much money in total the business will need before it starts to make positive net cash flows every month. This will be a combination of the amount it takes to set up in the first place, the amount it takes to run the business before it becomes profitable, and the cost of funding the business as it grows, even after it is profitable.

OVER TRADING

Profitable, growing businesses often need even more funding than less successful enterprises. It's surprising when you first learn this, but a business which does better than it is expected to is also in danger of running out of money; this is called 'over-trading' and can even lead to the business going bust if it isn't handled well.

How can this be? Well, let's say your business won't get paid immediately upon performing its service. While you are waiting to get paid, you still need to pay your own bills to keep the business running. And of course, these bills will be larger because the business is producing more to keep up with the growing demand. You need to pay your staff, too, and your overheads.

I know one entrepreneur in particular who tells me that his business is really fine because at the end of the year the forecast shows it has money in the bank. Sadly, the business needs more funding, because before it gets to the end of the year, its forecast shows it needs to pay out £150,000 or so more than it has. If the business can't get its hands on that £150,000, it probably won't reach the end of the year at all…

Once you know how much you are predicting the business will take to set up, you can think about whether it is viable for you or not. It may be that the total you think it needs is less than you are willing to put in yourself. That's ideal, and you're very lucky. If not, you will need to try to find an investor or bank to lend you the extra money. That may not be for over a year, but you still need to think about it before you start to make sure it is something which you can fund; otherwise your new business would go bust, unable to pay its bills.

Some businesses that are expected to be profitable may nonetheless not be viable. If a business will make just £100 profit, but takes £5m to launch, there isn't enough potential reward for a bank or investor, and you will find it extremely difficult to raise the money.

It is difficult, but for a viable business not impossible, to raise money to help fill a predicted funding gap – see Chapter Twelve for more on how to go about that.

WHAT IT ALL MEANS

Once you have got all these numbers in a spreadsheet, as accurately as you can, you should take some time to read the numbers, and think about it. Does it work at all? Have you got enough funding to begin with to reach the stage where you are generating enough that the business can carry on independently? If not, do you think you will be able to raise enough money to get there? Can you change some of the assumptions to reduce the amount of money you need?

When you have reached a point where you really think you've got your best guess in the figures, do two different versions, one with 10% more sales, and the other with 10% fewer sales. Look at the implications: what would happen if your sales levels do happen, but it takes far longer to get to that profitable level than you had assumed? Could the business survive?

Ultimately you need to get to a decision about whether to start or not. You should only start if you can see a realistic path to profitability, and think you have a good chance of getting there. I know from bitter experience, it is always, always easier to get to a good place with profits and a large bank balance on a spreadsheet than in real life running a business!

→ STARTUP TIP

It's very tempting to nudge your sales forecasts up a little more than you know you probably should, and to convince yourself you can probably cope with slightly lower costs than you really think you need. I've done it too many times. One good friend of mine did just that recently, and ended up starting a business he probably should never have started; it cost him all his savings and very nearly his house. Be really honest with yourself – if it doesn't look profitable with the numbers you think are accurate, don't start it. Instead, see if there is a way to change the concept so that the numbers become more positive naturally.

You need to think about your objectives: do you need to earn an income from this business, and if so does that need to be straight away? How confident are you that the business will be able to afford to pay you that income? In most startup businesses, the first thing that stops getting paid when times get tough is the founder's income. (If you're interested, another book called *How They Started*, which I edited, has stories of 30 founders' experiences of setting up, many of whom talk about this.)

Remember that I distinguished between initial setup costs and ongoing costs. That is important to assess how sustainable your business will be. But you still need to consider those setup costs. If they are very high, is the profit you think you will earn when the business is established, enough to justify the risk of putting your money into those setup costs?

Only you can come up with these answers. Please be cautious, and remember that almost all entrepreneurs are so keen on their own business that they assume the rest of the world will be too, and therefore their income assumptions are usually far too optimistic.

You've probably read about entrepreneurs that succeeded but who never talk about spending ages learning all about breakeven levels and gross profit. Some people make it sound as though they have ignored all this stuff and gone straight from rags to riches. I've met many of the well-known entrepreneurs in Britain, and can tell you that they're almost all very hot on this. They don't mention it because it's not the sexiest of things to talk about – accounts don't make for great headlines or engrossing TV programmes. Trust me, though: if you want to build a successful business, you need to know what everything in this chapter means.

ACTIONPOINTS

1. Find out what your core supplies will cost
2. Research what sort of income businesses like yours get
3. Learn how to do breakeven calculations
4. Work out what your overheads will be
5. Calculate how many sales you will need to make your target profit
6. Play with these numbers until you understand the effects of costs going up or sales going up or down
7. Put together your forecast sales, costs and profits for the first two years
8. Build a cash flow forecast linked to this profit forecast
9. Work out how much money it will take to get your business started

CHAPTER 07

Business plans

What's this all about?

- Why bother with a business plan?
- Does this need to be in a formal document?
- Plans to raise money
- Business plan software

(?)

his could be the dullest chapter in this book. Almost nobody gets excited by the prospect of writing a business plan. But you should if you're passionate about your business.

You already know that you need to work out how to set up your business – who will do what, by when – to get it up and running. That's obvious, right? And once it is set up, what needs to happen from then on to operate it? How much will it cost to set up and run it, and how much income do you think you will generate? Answering these questions is crucial if your business is to stand a chance of getting off the ground.

A 'business plan' is simply a document which answers these questions.

The first thing to say is that you should read the rest of this book before you write the plan. This chapter is in this section of the book because it is important to write the plan before you start your business – but in the plan you need to put down quite a bit of information which is covered in the next section. So it may be helpful to read this briefly now, just to get a sense of what you might need to include when you get to it, then return to this chapter when you know more about your business and are ready to produce your plan.

WHAT'S THE POINT IN WRITING A BUSINESS PLAN?

I think it's a really good idea to write your business idea down in a document, just to help clarify your thoughts. Especially at the start of a project, I often have several ideas I am very excited about, but haven't thought through. Putting them down on paper, and then discussing that document with someone else who knows a bit about it, is a great way to make sure that all the ideas are practical and can be made to fit together in a way which works.

Most of the successful entrepreneurs I have met say that they didn't do a business plan before they started. I think they're actually wrong; they did the plan, they just didn't set it out in writing. A new business is about as likely to succeed without planning, as the proverbial monkey is to write a Shakespeare play using a typewriter… not very. But this response from some business owners illustrates that lots of people groan at the thought of writing a business plan.

All you need is to put down your ideas for your business on paper. I think it's really important to do this, since the process of doing it forces you to think about things in a logical way, so the document reads sensibly. If you can't sum up in words what your business is going to be about, you will really struggle to persuade customers to buy whatever you're selling. But don't worry – it really doesn't need to be a big exercise.

I actually love reading business plans; they tell me a lot about the entrepreneur as well as about the business. As a business angel and a serial entrepreneur, I have written a dozen, and read literally hundreds of business plans. Big ones, small ones, good ones and terrible ones. I also went on a formal course on how to write them when I was working for what is now Ernst & Young. Some plans I have read have been so bad I stopped reading before the end of the first page; others made me want to invest almost straight away (just three of those!). And every business plan I have produced to help raise money has procured all the funding we wanted. The next section covers everything I think matters for business plans for startups.

Who is this plan for?

The main person is you, and any business partners you have. Your bank manager will probably want to see it at some stage, especially if you want a loan, and if you ever want other investors then they, too, will want a copy. But the real point is for you to set down in a document exactly what you want to do, why, and how. It's also something you can show to people you trust and respect so they can give you honest opinions about your idea before you start; I have always learned and improved from doing this – several minds are almost always better than one. It's so easy to get caught up in your own idea that you see it from one perspective; someone else will often see it from a different perspective, and will probably see some things you can improve.

Once you've started, you should go back and read the plan again, to remind yourself of what you set out to do. Sometimes you might have learned enough that the goals have changed; other times, you might find that you'd forgotten something which could get you back on track and really help the business. So it's well worth putting your goals, reasons, and passion down on paper in this document.

How big should this business plan be?

Probably between five and 10 A4 pages. More than that is probably silly unless you are going for significant outside investment money, less than that and you won't be going into enough detail to be useful. (See later on for plans to help you raise money.) When I started my first business, I wrote a letter to my bank manager with a few pages detailing what I planned to do. I didn't call it a business plan at the time, but that is what it was. Five to 10 pages is enough to get you a bank loan; if the bank says no, it won't be because your business plan was too short.

HOW TO WRITE THE PLAN

From the outset, you need to set out what your idea is, who it is for and why they are likely to buy from this new business. You should then talk about how you will let those potential customers know that your product exists, and write a bit about the competition. It's also a good idea to put down what staff resources you think you'll need. If you expect to give the plan to someone outside the business, it is probably worth putting down a paragraph or so about your own experience and background, too.

1. You should start by setting out your idea: quite simply, what is it? This very simple description of your proposed business should ideally be just one or two sentences, which provide a good sense of what your business will be about. Although brief, this intro is really important as it will either get the reader excited enough to sit up and pay real attention to your plan, or to relax and not give it much focus. No, that probably shouldn't happen, but we're all human, and in practice it really does happen.

You need readers to get the best possible sense of your new business. The description needs to show that you understand clearly what your business will do that's different, and why that should attract customers given the existing competition. You would probably be amazed by how few plans actually achieve this. Here are a few examples of descriptions which say enough to whet a reader's appetite:

Polish Nannies is a new agency specialising in helping parents in London find good quality, English-speaking nannies from Poland. Polish Nannies will source nannies from Poland, train them in first aid and English childcare needs, and advise them on moving to the UK.

Catch of the Day will be the first fish and chip shop in Brighton specialising in fresh fish and healthier meals. We will use light sunflower oil and offer grilled fish as well as fried, and a selection of salads and other side dishes to let Brighton's increasingly health-conscious customers continue to enjoy the fish and chips they love.

Pen Warehouse is a new online retailer offering customers in the UK a wide selection of pens, ranging from modestly priced to luxury brands. The website will let people buy the pen of their choice or refill cartridges or ink without needing to visit a large department store.

2. It's a good idea, though not essential, to go on to talk briefly about your targets for the business. Do you want to grow it into a large business, float on AIM, or simply stay as the best at what you do in your market? Whatever your goals, set them down simply to give the reader a sense of where you're hoping to go with the business.

3. I like to include turnover and profit expectations at this stage, too, saying what you expect the first year, second year (and third if you're doing a three year forecast) sales and profit to be. If you do want to raise money from a bank, it is worth saying so at this stage, setting out the amount you want to borrow, how long you want it for, or when you expect to repay it.

4. Next, explain a bit about you, the founder, and how the idea came about.

5. Then explain more about the market now: how or what people are buying or using now, and why your new business will offer something sufficiently attractive to make them switch.

6. It is important to acknowledge competition; at least half the business plans I have seen claim that the new business has no competition. The truth is that every business has competition, even if it is indirect: even if no other business does what yours does, you will still need to persuade people to start using your business, which will mean they have to stop using something else, even if it is unrelated.

All that should fit comfortably onto the first page. Then:

7. Try to include as much market information as you can which will be helpful. The global sales of fast food outlets might be an interesting fact but is too remote from your new fish and chip shop to be especially helpful. National or (even better) regional trends showing how people eat out more or eat convenience foods or fish more would be much more useful. One page on this should plenty. Half a page would be fine, but don't put in five pages of detailed market statistics that you've found on the internet; that would be too much detail. Your readers will expect you to have read the details and to just present them with the really important facts. Do put down the source of your information.

8. Then move on to describe how the business will operate. What premises will you use, what staff will you need, how will you let potential customers know about your new business, and how will you sell (online direct, mail order, a shop, to distributors or wholesalers etc). It's a good idea to give some sense of timing in this part of your plan.

9. It is also a good idea to have one or two pages with more detail about your product. For a restaurant you might want to include highlights from the menu, or a small map of your proposed location showing other restaurants; if you're a web business, include some sort of mock-up of your site (if you don't have any pictures to show yet, don't worry – just describe what you want to do in words). The point here is to give a full description of the business, making clear what will make it stand out from the crowd.

10. Then include your financial forecasts. I suggest including one page showing summary profit and loss forecasts for the first two or three years, and another showing the cash flow forecasts for the same period.

And that's it!

I've always found that I end up writing three or four versions of the plan. It is really worth getting the wording right, so it accurately describes your idea, and makes clear what your key objectives are, as well as what the drivers of your success will be. This is most important for you to refer back to months after you've started the business.

If you are using your plan to try to raise money, it can help to make small changes to it to take into account any feedback you get.

MORE SUBSTANTIAL BUSINESS PLANS

If you're planning to start a much larger business from scratch, or want to raise money from business angels or venture capitalists, you will probably need something more substantial and more formal than the document I have described above.

It is possible to go into immense detail about how these plans should look and feel; there are plenty of dedicated books just about writing business plans. Amazon has 2,500 results if you search for 'business plan'. Wow; that staggered me. Do you really need to read one of those? Probably not, though there are some good ones. If you need to raise serious money to get your business going, then you probably do need a more substantial business plan, and the better books about it might be worthwhile. Business angels or venture capitalists will expect you to have a pretty substantial, robust business plan and will also expect that that plan will cover a number of specific subjects. Most businesses aren't looking for this type of investment, and simply don't need the type of plan the books talk about.

Speaking (or writing!) as an investor myself, and as someone who has spoken to many other investors about this, there is a danger in following someone else's guidelines for a big business plan too rigidly. It is important to have a core structure and include certain elements that investors often want, but beyond that it is better to let your style and image come across, rather than trying to copy someone else's.

The structure of a typical substantial business plan is normally like this:

1. Contents
2. Executive Summary
3. The Market
4. The Product or Service, including Unique Selling Points
5. Competition
6. Barriers to Entry

7. Management Team
8. SWOT Analysis
9. Financial Projections
10. Funding Requirements
11. Exit Strategy
12. Appendices

1. CONTENTS

As a more substantial document (20–50 pages is typical) it can be useful to have a page of contents to help readers find their way to the bits they want easily and quickly.

2. EXECUTIVE SUMMARY

This is the most important part of the plan. It basically summarises each chapter of the plan in a paragraph, explaining what the business is, what stage it is at, what the purpose of the plan is (usually to raise money), the expected profits of the business, market overview, key unique selling points for the business, and details of key members of the management team. Opinions vary about how important it is to keep this to one page – I think two pages is OK, but it certainly shouldn't go beyond that. Investors need to know that you can summarise information concisely and well, and producing a good executive summary in no more than two pages is a simple test.

3. THE MARKET

Here you should describe the market you want to operate in. So for the fish and chip shop example you would talk about trends in eating habits in general, fast food industry figures, and the local market close to the site of the proposed shop. For the Polish nanny agency example you should discuss how many parents have children each year, how many nannies there are, whether that is growing or shrinking, why Polish nannies are a good idea for British families. It's important to use statistics from reputable organisations rather than putting your own thoughts down as though they were established facts. Searching on the web should provide quite a bit of information and trade organisations and magazines are usually good sources of this sort of information.

4. THE PRODUCT OR SERVICE

Once you have explained the market sector, it is easier to talk about your proposed product or service, showing what is different or better about it. You should go into enough detail to show that you have thought it through properly, so a reader can get a decent grasp of what is special about your idea – but not so much detail that you bore them! Remember, the plan will be read by investors rather than customers; you want them to invest in your business, not to buy the product. Most of the plans I see spend too much time describing technical details about the product which aren't needed in the business plan. Save yourself the time and effort, and keep it brief.

Make sure you state clearly what the unique selling points (USPs) of your business are within your description.

5. COMPETITION

It is a good idea to give a brief overview of the sorts of competition you will face – direct competition if there is any, and indirect competition otherwise. Briefly cover what the competitors tend to do as a group, and then talk about each major competitor individually, noting what sort of market share it has, how successful it is, how important this business is to it (sometimes it might be a peripheral activity for a much larger business, for example) and what sort of market position it has relative to you.

6. BARRIERS TO ENTRY

A 'barrier to entry' is something which makes it hard for another business to do what your business is doing. Investors want to invest in businesses which have a good chance of staying successful once they are up and running; if you watched *Dragons' Den* on TV, you will have heard the Dragons asking the entrepreneurs about this. For product businesses there may be some legal barriers to entry such as patents. Other common barriers to entry include hard-to-find expertise, high cost of entry, regulations or restricted licences, strong customer loyalty to competitors, hard-to-find suppliers. You should think about what might discourage someone else from setting up in competition with you if you are successful, and put this down.

7. MANAGEMENT TEAM

The management team is the single most important factor in whether an investor will put its money into your business or not. The general view is that great management will make an OK idea work better than an OK team and a great idea. In this section you should summarise the experience of your key managers. Be honest about any gaps that you have, explaining how and when you propose to fill those gaps. You probably don't need a financial director initially, for example, but if you have ambitious growth plans you probably will need one in due course. Talk briefly about the previous roles each team member has had in the past, naming any well-known employers, and describe what role each person will play in your new business.

You can include in an Appendix to the plan full CVs for each key team member if you think it would be useful. That's probably not necessary unless you want to raise more than £1m.

8. SWOT ANALYSIS

Nothing to do with flies, 'SWOT' stands for Strengths, Weaknesses, Opportunities and Threats. This 'analysis' is simply a list of all your business's strengths, weaknesses, opportunities and threats. A 'strength' is something you've got now which is really useful; this might be a new invention, or a great sales force, or the fact that nobody else is doing what you want to do yet. 'Weaknesses' are things you know about now which you would like to improve on. You should acknowledge these honestly, but also think about how serious they are, and how you can either fix them or work around them; they might include a lack of funding, or a particular management team vacancy. 'Opportunities' are things that your business can take advantage of, such as seizing a significant market share and building a brand name before any competitor has started. 'Threats' are things which might arise and make it harder for you to achieve your objectives; examples might include new competitors entering the market or a key member of staff leaving.

Use bullet points for each item. If there is anything that hasn't been addressed or doesn't belong elsewhere in the plan, include an explanation of it in this section. Try to keep this section as brief as possible – ideally the core SWOT summary should fit on one page.

9. FINANCIAL PROJECTIONS

The word 'projection' is simply another word for forecast in this context. For a more substantial plan you really ought to include a three-year forecast. I do see five-year projections, and occasionally this is necessary, but normally years four and five are so remote that the forecasts for them are not worth looking at. Stick to three years unless you expect your business's profitability to grow substantially more in years four and five. You should include profit and loss and cash flow projections. Depending on your business you might think it helpful to provide an extra page of analysis; perhaps the breakeven analysis of one key aspect of your business, or a breakdown of some key costs which you have summarised in the other forecasts.

If you are writing a new plan after your business has started, you should also include details of the financial performance you have actually achieved, as well as projections of what you expect to do in future.

10. FUNDING REQUIREMENTS

This is where you take the figures from your cash flow projections and talk about how much your business expects to need, and when. Then you should propose how you would like to raise this money. This is likely to be a combination of your own money, friends and family money, bank debt, and possibly other investors' money. You should put down the amount you would like to come from each source. Make sure you raise a little bit more than your forecasts predict you will need, to allow room for things to go a little bit more slowly than you would like.

It is perfectly normal to try to raise an amount of money now, but state that you expect to need to raise more money in the future; you don't need to raise all the money now.

I have seen plenty of plans which put down a proposed share price that the founder would like investors to pay. My advice is not to: if the number is too high, investors might be irritated or put off, thinking you either greedy or not very smart. I think the point of this plan is to interest potential investors enough to get you a meeting with them. Once you've got that meeting, they will decide then whether or not they want to invest; once they want to, you should be able to negotiate the terms. Having the price conversation earlier is a waste of time and risky.

11. EXIT STRATEGY

This is your description of how you expect investors to get their money back. People normally put down 'flotation or trade sale' here, meaning that they expect to sell the company or float its shares on a stock exchange. For bank loans, this is not relevant, since the loans will have a repayment schedule which will be fixed after discussions between you and your bank.

It is important to have this clause, mainly to show that you are aware of the need for investors to get their money back, and to give some indication of when you expect that to be. This time should be based on when you think the value of the investment will have risen enough to give the investors the handsome profit they will want.

WANT MORE HELP?

If you would like more help in producing a substantial business plan, you can buy a software package to help you. Startups.co.uk has more details of the latest versions. Or you could try some of the dedicated books; I'm sure there are some good ones, though I don't recommend any of the dozen or so that I have seen – they're typically too complicated, using long words where short ones would be better, and are very rigid.

Otherwise you could use a consultant to help. Medium-sized firms of accountants often get involved in this, though they will charge quite a bit of money to do so – probably between £5,000 and £10,000. There is also a dedicated consultancy associated with

London Business School called Business Plan Services which is totally focused on helping you with your business plan; their website is www.bizplans.co.uk.

ACTIONPOINTS

1. Decide whether you need a short or long plan
2. Write an initial version of the core sections
3. Incorporate your financial projections
4. Get feedback from someone who knows about business, and ideally your sector
5. Revise your plan until you're happy with it

CHAPTER 08
The decision

It's time to decide. Are you in, or aren't you?

It's a big moment, I remember mine well. It was June 1988. I was on holiday in the Lake District with some friends, still working for an accountancy firm. I was unhappy in my job (the first year of accountancy training is not very exciting, it must be said…) and had just been offered a more interesting, much better paid job. At the same time, I was working on some computer game ideas with some friends, as a hobby. I had to decide what to do. I took myself off to the lake to think. I considered the pros and cons of staying or leaving. In the end, I decided to stick with my accountancy training but to move to the 'entrepreneurial services' department so I'd be working with some exciting young business clients. I also decided to push the game development side to keep the creative side of my brain alive.

When I'd taken the decision, I felt a huge pressure lift, and felt strangely calm. Strange, because the decision I'd just made would lead to far more hours than if I'd taken the other job. But I knew, somehow, that it was the right thing for me.

There's so much about setting up a business on TV these days that if you haven't already, I would make a point of watching some programmes about other people who've set up on their own. Some good ones include *No Going Back*, or *Risking It All*. Both tend to get repeated frequently on digital TV channels, and both show people setting up their own business. It's great to watch other people – you can see, and cringe, at the mistakes they're making, most of which are pointed out by the programme presenter. But imagine you were that entrepreneur – could you do what they're doing? Are you excited at the prospect of facing their problems, doing their hours? Sure, the sectors are probably different; but the types of issue they face will be very comparable to yours.

For your new business startup to succeed, several things all have to be right. You have to have what it takes. The idea has to be viable. And you need to put in whatever it takes to drive the business from an idea to a sustainable enterprise.

It's easy to rush this phase. You've done your homework and are sure the idea stacks up; you think you can do it and you're excited by the idea. So was Iqbal Wahab, in the late 1990s, when he set up The Cinnamon Club, which he wanted to be the first Indian restaurant ever to get a Michelin Star. There's an excellent *Trouble At The Top* programme which covers what happened next. The chef Iqbal had found did get the first Michelin Star for Indian food; but it wasn't at The Cinnamon Club, which hadn't opened by then. I invested in the business on the back of Iqbal's business plan and his then chef, Vineet Bhatia's outstanding canapés. A year later I wanted to sue Iqbal for my money back, and it was all going horribly wrong. All credit to Iqbal, he worked and worked at it, and eventually got it off the ground, but with a different chef, a different location, and having spent nearly three times what he had first expected.

If you have a family, get their support. Then find some space; whatever works for you. Think long and hard about what you really want from your life. Will starting your own business deliver that? It's a journey, not an event. Are you prepared? Even if your family is fully supportive, it's you that will need to put in the hard graft; you that will face the problems, make the decisions, and hopefully lead the business to success. Do you really want that? Take note of this. Deciding to start your own business is a brave decision.

Before you've done it, it's easy to turn back, stay in your current job, or get a new job. It's safer. Once you embark on starting your own thing, you'll find it harder to get other people to take you on as an employee, and even harder to be one. It's hard to take instructions from a boss when you know what it's like to be one. So what would you do if your business fails? It's important to think about that. How would you feel? What shape would your finances be in?

You need to weigh all the issues up. And then decide: are you really up for it?

02

CHAPTER 09

Naming your business

What's this all about?
- How much does a name matter?
- How to choose a good name
- Check nobody else is already using it

C hoosing a name for your new business is one of the most enjoyable tasks. But business names matter: the right one can make it easier for you to succeed and gain business, while the wrong name could harm your chances of success. As the media love to report, large companies often spend millions of pounds choosing a name and logo. Indeed, there are businesses which specialise in creating names for new products and businesses. These are called branding consultants or agencies. We will come on to the concept of a brand a bit late in this chapter.

If you go back a hundred years or more, almost all businesses were named after their founder—Cadbury, Mars, Goldman Sachs, WH Smith, Marks & Spencer, and so on. Yet these days it is unusual for any major new business to be named after its founder. Dyson, the vacuum cleaner and household appliance manufacturer, is one of just a few I can think of in the last 20 years.

These days, many businesses often have names that instantly imply the values the business wishes to project, such as innocent drinks, the smoothie company, or Cobra, the beer. Other businesses are named after their very specific function, such as Friends Reunited or moneysupermarket.com.

Still others use invented words for their name, such as Ocado, the food delivery service. Though this word is apparently meaningless, presumably this was chosen as something that is evocative of high quality and healthy or indulgent, like avocado. Ocado was launched at almost the same time as a similar sounding but very different business, Opodo. I remember being a little confused and amused when these two were launched, since they both used radio advertising heavily. Both these businesses are web-based, and so they need their advertising to drive people to their website – yet as an invented word, people won't necessarily know how to spell their names even though they are phonetic. Ocado tackled this head-on, using a song which spelt out their name as a major part of their advertising. It's proved very effective, but at a significant cost in advertising. By contrast, I can't remember the last time I came across Opodo, and indeed it took me several goes to find their website while researching it for this book.

I'm sure that both these names came from a branding consultancy. These consultants follow similar sorts of procedures to try to generate the right name, and so it's not a surprise that they could both come up with something so similar. They were both trying to find something short, unique, memorable, positive, and easy to spell.

HOW TO CHOOSE A NAME FOR YOUR BUSINESS

I have spent countless hours generating lots of names at my various businesses; for products and for the companies themselves, and have really enjoyed this process.

A business name has various roles, one of which is to act a little like an army's flag – to inspire and unite a team of staff behind it. As your business becomes established, the literal interpretation of its name will matter less and less; but at the beginning the name is part of the 'first impressions' of your business and the right name will help establish it. It's also worth remembering that once established and successful, a name can be worth a lot of money.

In an ideal world, your business name should do all the following:

- Explain what sort of business you run
  - Be really, really clear about this; I see lots of businesses with names that sound very traditional, often involving family members, but it is not clear what the

business actually does! The word 'consultant' is used so often as part of a name, but on its own it really doesn't mean anything to anyone. If you want people who come across your business name to understand what it is that you do, make that *obvious* and *unambiguous*.

- I love food, and eating out. One of my favourite restaurants is called A Cena, an Italian restaurant; I had lived close to it for years before trying it, because I had no idea that it existed, even though I'd driven past it many times – its name didn't tell me instantly what it did. And instant matters, in our society where people spend much less than a second glancing around generally, whether it's at a shelf in a shop or signs on a street. In fact, I have since learned that *a cena* is the Italian phrase for 'to dinner', but I didn't know that.
- Another restaurant I love is called Chez Bruce. While this is still a foreign language, it is French, which most of the restaurant's target customers will speak a little, and the phrase *'chez'* (a French name) is taught early on at schools. The name stands out, because one doesn't normally expect to hear the very un-French sounding name Bruce after the word *chez.*

■ Help potential customers remember you
- How often have you experienced a really great product or service and wanted to find it again, but couldn't remember the name? It happens to me frequently. Let me use another food example. There are three basic Indian restaurants near my home which deliver food. All three are pretty standard in type, though varying in quality – one is good, the other two aren't, in my opinion. They also have fairly generic names, and similar looking menus/logos. This makes it very hard to remember which is which, especially as I don't order from any of them often enough to have this information locked away securely in my ageing mind! So recently I wanted to order from one, resorted to the local phone directory – and ended up with food from the wrong one. The restaurant I prefer lost business that night, directly because its name was not sufficiently distinct from its competitors.

■ Work well online
- Potential customers will often end up searching for your business using the internet, local directories or industry-specific directories. A name they can spell easily will make it far easier for them to find your business.
- One company who was a finalist in the Startups Awards recently had to change its name after two years of trading because searches for its name, i-magine, bought up more references to John Lennon than the iPod accessories it sold.

■ Lend themselves to an appropriate, helpful logo
- Logos need to come after choosing a name, but some names lend themselves more easily to creating a logo than others. I have seen countless businesses whose names begin with the word Vision, which is a good, if over-used, word; but trying

to think up images which imply vision is far from easy. This might or might not matter to your business, but if you think it will, then choose a name which works more easily as a logo.

■ Allow room for expansion

- I have lots of admiration for Mike Clare, who started Dreams, the UK's leading bed retailer, from scratch many years ago. It's one of the UK's biggest retail success stories. Yet when he started the business, he called it The Sofa Bed Centre. This was fine for a while, when Mike's company sold mainly sofa beds, but people wouldn't naturally think of going to a Sofa Bed Centre to buy a normal bed. It's also why British Telecom PLC changed its name some years ago to BT PLC, so that they could launch into other markets more easily.

- Having said that it is not a hard and fast rule; another of Britain's retail success stories arguably should have changed its name, hasn't, and has flourished anyway. Today, Carphone Warehouse is thriving, even though it doesn't sell car phones and isn't a warehouse!

- Some businesses set out to grow into a variety of product areas; if yours is like that, it will be more important to choose a name which can work for all your planned areas. After all, it is expensive and time-consuming to change a name and develop customer awareness for it.

Most of all, remember to keep it simple. At Impressions, we launched a computer game called *Renaissance* (meaning 'reborn', which we thought was very appropriate, and quite a smart name for the product); we were pleased with the product, which featured both classic and modern versions of four well-known arcade games. The game came out, and sales were really, really poor, even though people loved the game. After lots of discussion and thought, we ended up renaming the product *Classic 4* and re-launching it – it sold like hotcakes. The lesson I learned? Not to try to be too clever, and to follow more of a 'Ronseal' approach to product names, based on their well-known 'it-does-what-it-says-on-the-tin' approach.

Some real business names

Funny, unusual names can often make smaller businesses stand out. Here is a list of names of real businesses, courtesy of some research by Alliance & Leicester recently.

Battersea Cods Home (fish and chip shop in Sheffield)
Mad Hakkers (hairdressers in Leven, Fife)
Mr Bit (window cleaners, Derby and Coventry)
Spruce Springclean (window cleaners in West Byfleet, Surrey)
Tree Wise Men (tree surgeons in Wallington, Surrey)

Vinyl Resting Place *(second hand records shop in Croydon, Surrey)*
Walter Wall *(carpet sales in Exeter, Devon)*
Plaice Station *(fish and chip shop in Manchester)*
William the Concreter *(concrete suppliers in Hastings, East Sussex)*
Give Us A Break *(window fitters in Leicester)*
R Soles *(boot maker in London)*
Floral and Hardy *(gardeners in Hayes, Kent)*
Sarnie Schwarzenegger's *(sandwich shop in Liverpool)*
Abra-Kebab-Ra *(kebab shop in Dublin)*
Wok This Way *(Chinese takeaway in Glasgow)*

CAN YOU USE THIS NAME?

When you have settled on a name you would like, you need to check whether or not you can use it. There is a list of words you're not allowed to use without specific permission (for example the word 'royal') or without your business meeting certain requirements (words like 'institute', for example). This won't be a problem for you at all unless you are trying to claim to be something you're not, which I wouldn't recommend for starting a long-term business anyway. See startups.co.uk for a complete list of these 'sensitive' words.

Secondly, it needs to be available, which simply means to check that nobody else is using it. Twenty years ago, this was simply a matter of doing a company search, a trademark search, and checking in phone directories. Now, you need a website – and probably don't want to choose a name if there are no sensible websites left for that name (though it is often worth checking if there is something close e.g. flybmi.com is such because bmi.com was already taken, and this works for them). There are lots of websites which let you check to see if a name has been taken; it isn't enough just to type in a few names and see if a website comes up. The one I tend to use is www.simply.com, though there are plenty of others that will do a similar job. It's free to check any number of names – these sites will only charge you if you want to register a name, which they can do easily and cheaply for you.

Whether a name is 'available' or not can get a bit confusing. There are probably hundreds of shops all called The Village Store or similar, but they get away with it. The reason is that location matters. If your market is normally national, then you have the right to protect your name from being used by someone else – basically on a first come, first served basis. But if your market is pretty local or regional, then someone using the same name in a different region can't stop you using the same name in your own region. Unfortunately, the law is a bit of a grey area here, so if you are in any doubt, you should talk to a lawyer for advice. While using lawyers can rapidly get expensive, most lawyers could give you some useful advice on this topic in less than one hour, so it shouldn't cost too much.

To do some of these basic searches, try other websites. The government's official website for the department which holds information on every registered company in England and Wales, www.CompaniesHouse.co.uk, is very good, easy and cheap to use. But most businesses don't ever form limited companies (and some limited companies have more than one trading name, such as my own company, Crimson, which uses trading names such as www.startups.co.uk and www.growingbusiness.co.uk); so doing a Companies House search is helpful but not enough.

You can do a trademark search (see below for more on trademarks) if you want to. The easiest way to do this is by going to www.patent.gov.uk which is a government site that lists all registered names and logos ('devices').

The reality is that there is no single, comprehensive way of searching all possible other uses of your chosen name. But if you have tried all the above methods, and can't find anything which is too close to your own name, you're probably fine.

MAKE SURE NOBODY ELSE USES IT

Of course, once you have found a name that works, that you like, and is available, you want to protect it, so nobody else can come along and use it. There are several things you can do to protect the name. The most useful ones are wonderfully cheap and easy, too.

Websites

The first thing to do is to reserve your website name, using a service such as www.simply.com. It is probably wise to reserve several versions of the name – for example ending in '.co.uk', '.com' and '.net'. Above all, this means that if your business takes off, nobody else can take the other versions of your name and try to trade on the back of your success, or try to sell you these other versions for lots of money when your own business is up and running.

Trademarks

English law, which applies to England and Wales, is somewhat vague about protection for 'intellectual property' which is what a business name is classed as. There are two precise and formal types of law here: copyright and trademark.

Copyright law is what protects music, writing, and computer software, but it doesn't protect business names. Copyright is designed to protect creative work, and business names are not deemed to fit that.

Trademark law is the main formal legal protection for business names. If you register a trademark (which usually consists of both a name and a logo or 'device' together) then you can prevent anyone making unauthorised use of that mark. This still applies even if you registered the trademark after the other business started trading under that name. You can learn how to register at www.patentgov.uk. It costs around £200 to register an initial use and then £50 for every additional use, or 'class', thereafter. It can be fairly time consuming since you have to wait a while for anyone to lodge a complaint, but after about six months you can be pretty sure you will be ok using your chosen name. When a mark has been registered, you can use the little symbol ® next to the trademark so everyone knows it is registered.

Most people instead put the letters TM, very small, next to their name and logo (™). These letters signify that you are claiming trademark protection. In fact they are designed to mean that you have applied for trademark protection but it hasn't come through yet, though many people use the letters without applying to register it at all. This is powerful because if the trademark does get registered, then your protection is automatically backdated to when you first claimed the TM protection by using the letters.

Another thing to note regarding trademarks is that you can't register anything too generic – you couldn't register the phrase 'food shop' or 'supermarket' or 'fish and chip shop', for example, otherwise the registered owner would be able to have far too much power over usage of very common terms, which would be daft.

In reality, many people reading this book probably won't need to bother with registering your trademark; in all my businesses, I think I have only ever registered two or three trademarks. Using the letters TM is probably enough.

That's not fair!

The main protection for business name disputes (which you need to understand when selecting a name, to make sure you don't fall foul of it) doesn't rely on trademarks. It is called 'passing off' and is designed to protect a business against another business pretending to be it. So if you wanted to start a new business selling vacuum cleaners, and thought the name 'Dison' sounded good, Dyson, the established vacuum cleaner manufacturer, would be able to claim that you were 'passing off' and trying to trade on their good name in the vacuum cleaner sector, and they would most likely win.

CASE STUDY
IN MY EXPERIENCE

In my computer games business, we published a game in 1994 about the D-day landings, marking the 50th anniversary of the event. A French company sued us, claiming it had registered the trademark for D-day in France, and that by publishing this game in France, we were infringing its rights. (Trademark law is international, but you need to register separately in any country where you want protection.) But I thought that the term D-day was too generic, so defended us in a French court – and won. The court decided that the term was too widely used to allow anyone to hold a trademark of it.

It's a useful lesson, because it shows that not all registered trademarks stand up to challenges in court. It is easier to register a trademark than to win an argument about it in court. Crimson used to publish a magazine called *eBusiness*. We launched it in 1999, at the start of the internet boom, and we did the usual searches I describe above. The trademark search revealed that IBM had applied for a trademark over the term 'e Business' but that it had not been approved yet. Our lawyers advised that the term was sufficiently generic that it probably wouldn't get approved, and that we were probably best letting IBM know of our plans, but continuing.

We approached IBM, told them of our plans, and they were fine about it – they even ended up advertising in the magazine. Another key lesson: where there is scope for a dispute, often the best solution is to speak to the other side early on and see if there is a way of resolving it sensibly. If it ends up going to court, it will cost considerable sums of money, taking up lots of time, and even if you win, you will probably feel like you've lost!

One useful thing to note is that you are normally allowed to use your own personal name for your business even if someone has got that name. But you need to be careful. Some years ago, a Mr Dixon opened a small electrical goods shop, and called it Dixons. He thought he could get away with this because it was his name, even though the large chain Dixons was already very well known. They sued him and he lost. Why? Because he had not only used the name Dixons, but had also used white lettering on a red background which were remarkably similar to the sign used by the national retailer. So

Mr Dixon really was trying to make his shop look as if it were part of the bigger business – courts don't like that sort of thing.

The real test is whether or not a reasonable customer in the market would be confused. If the court thinks a customer would be confused, there is passing off, and they would order the newer business to change. So be careful not to try to get too close to another successful business. Besides, there's so much opportunity, you're probably far better putting your efforts into building something unique and worthwhile.

You should think carefully about what your market is. If you run a small shop, its market is probably very local – which is why it is easy for there to be so many shops, cafés, pubs and so on with the same name but in different towns. But if your product is sold all over the country, let alone internationally, you need to select a name which will work well everywhere. The real test is whether consumers would be confused because your name is too similar to an existing name in a similar market; if a court thinks they would be, it would require you to change the name.

Other than trademarks, company names, and website addresses, there really isn't any other form of registering your business name. It surprises lots of people when they set up, but subject to the above searches, you can literally decide to use a name, and that becomes yours from then on (unless challenged by one of the processes above).

IN MY EXPERIENCE

In 1989, I named my computer games business 'Impressions'. I felt that it was a good word, in a pretty vague sort of way. While the business thrived, my staff and I often felt in later years that the name was a hindrance. It was a bit soft, which didn't suit the very young, male customer base, and didn't actually mean anything.

We never really defined the font of the logo, which varied occasionally. This never hugely mattered, but I believe this vagueness restricted the brand's strength.

When I came to launch my second business, I wanted a logo which would be more striking. I also had plans for several divisions of the business and therefore wanted a name and logo that were versatile.

I decided that animals, fruit and colours were strong topics to find inspiration. There have been two highly successful businesses named Apple, while other fruit has also been used to good effect. There are plenty of animals that make you think of speed and strength; colours, too, have been used extensively in different products.

I went through many options, and found what was available and what else existed. We toyed with Gazelle, which in some countries means fast-growing business – until we discovered that Gazelle.com was a Canadian lesbian website. I also liked slightly unusual fruit such as Mango (now a women's clothing business).

I had learned along the way that red is one of the strongest colours for logos, and thought about all sorts of variants, such as vermillion, scarlet, and eventually crimson.

When I came across Crimson it passed all the tests we set it. It was unusual in a business context, and therefore memorable. It also lent itself very easily to a logo.

We decided to go with it, and I'm pleased to say that I think it has worked. We use it in all sorts of ways: online, in print and at exhibitions, and it has worked well for all of them.

ACTIONPOINTS

1. Choose a name that will help your business get started
2. Check you're allowed to use it
3. Register a domain name
4. Consider registering a trademark

CHAPTER 10

Your business identity

What's this all about?
- Creating a logo
- Business stationery
- A look and feel for your business
- Your brand

(?)

I remember just recently watching an episode of the excellent BBC programme *The Restaurant*, where a number of couples were competing to run a restaurant with Raymond Blanc. The couples had to design some cooked food to be sold in supermarkets, and had to create packaging for their dishes as well. The packaging for these dishes was really well done, and the looks on the faces of the couples when they first saw it was very familiar – they were blown away by just how good the packaging looked for their creation. That first moment when you see your dream look professional and finished is wonderful.

Getting the right look and feel for your business is more important, and more enjoyable, than choosing a name. I have always loved this stage: seeing your business come to life makes it start to feel real. It is the same whether that be packaging for a product or the look and feel of a shop or a website. I'm going to call the way your business looks and feels a 'corporate identity'. Basically a corporate identity is a visual look for a business, which would define the appearance of everything the business does. This would include a core logo, but also how the logo is used on business cards, letter headings, adverts, and so on.

There are two things you need your corporate identity to do for you. Firstly, you want it to help attract potential customers (and possibly also suppliers and staff) to you. Secondly, you want it to be sufficiently easy to remember and spot again so that it helps people who've dealt with you once to find you again.

THE LOGO

For many people, the first step will be to turn your business name into a logo. Logos matter to people, as the outcry over the new logo for the 2012 London Olympic Games showed. The logo won lots of media attention because so many people didn't like it. It was a very young, modern, bold approach. The London Olympic body commissioned Wolff Olins, one of the world's very best brand consultancies, to come up with the 'brand identity' including the logo. It cost a significant sum of money, much of which I imagine will have gone on research during the process to try to test people's reactions to it.

So what? Well, it shows some of the process that a top consultancy went through. We can all, as small business founders, learn from what the brightest people in different fields do for their very substantial clients. So to learn from the Olympic logo outcry, maybe you should try out the draft logos for your business on some potential customers.

As for the Olympic logo, what do I think? If it were a small business, I think it would be poor – because it is very hard to read. I have spoken to a number of people who didn't even know that the logo was trying to be a series of numbers (2012). The 2012 Olympics will have a sufficiently large advertising campaign that they can probably get over that hurdle; by the time of the games, we will all have seen it enough that we'll know what it is, so it could well work for them. But a small business wouldn't have anything like big enough budgets to make this work.

Above all, why make life hard for your new business? If there are easy things you can do which will make it easier for people to find you and use you, why wouldn't you do that? So bear this in mind when you're designing your new logo from scratch.

Lots of people have asked me, and I remember spending ages wondering myself, whether a business should have some sort of graphic symbol as well as text for its logo.

Mercedes have their three-point-star in a circle; McDonalds have the golden arches symbol; Penguin books have an oval with a picture of a penguin inside it. Yet Sony don't; Google doesn't; Coca Cola doesn't. Instead, these three brands all have a very distinctive text style. My conclusion is that a business doesn't need a symbol, though some founders may want one. Symbols have the advantage that they don't need to be translated the way that words might, I suppose, but for most of us that is a small factor. If you can come up with a symbol which is reflective of your business and will help people remember you, then use it. If you can't, I wouldn't spend any time worrying about it.

What look do you want – and need?

For almost all small businesses, logos should be easy to read and promote an image which is appropriate for the sort of business it is. So a chic, high-end fashion logo would probably be crisp, clean, simple and straight, whereas a clothing brand aimed at surfing teenagers would need to be wild and energetic and a little anti-establishment. The font and colours that you use and the way you use them will give out very clear messages about your business, very subtly.

It's a good idea to collect pictures of your competitor logos and any other logos which have elements that you think might work well for your business. It will be really helpful to whoever gets the task of turning your wish list into a logo if you can show them visual examples; most of us are pretty poor at expressing the way we want things to look in words. I know I still really struggle with this, even after doing it a lot over 20 years or so. It's a good idea to show a number of different images, and write notes showing what you like and don't like about all of them. With your competition, while you may need to be similar so it's clear that you're in the same line of work, you also need to ensure yours stands out from theirs.

Think about where your logo will be used. Common places to use logos include: business cards; letter headed paper; shop signs (and bags); commercial vehicles like vans; websites (and increasingly in 'email signatures) and within advertising, whether posters, leaflets, within newspapers or magazines or at exhibitions. Some logos work well in some environments but not in others. Something very intricate will be hard to reproduce very small, such as on a business card or on a website. Draw up a list of the uses you expect to need for your logo, and then check any draft designs against this list to see if you think they would work well. Some of our early logo designs for startups.co.uk involved silver, which looks great if you print it with special and expensive paper and ink, but pretty awful when photocopied or scanned in onto a computer screen.

Next, you should decide how many colours to use, which will mainly be an issue of cost. Typically, business stationery is either one colour of ink on one colour of paper, two colours of ink on one colour of paper, or four-colour. Four-colour is a printing process which recreates almost any colour you want using just four colours – so there's really no point in printing in more than four colours. (There are exceptions to this, but they're not important for most people setting up a new business; if a printer or designer ever suggests using 'a fifth colour' then ask them what that means when it crops up.)

There are several considerations when selecting the number of colours. The more you choose, the more expensive your stationery will be. While it might seem OK to have fancy stationery when you start, if you need a reprint at some stage, or you add an employee who wants a business card, the extra colour will really bump up your cost. (The reason that you rarely see three colours is that it is usually cheaper to print using a four-colour process than a three-colour process.)

Certain industries have 'norms' for stationery. It is unusual, for example, to see a lawyer with a very colourful business card. Other professional service sectors tend to be similar – investment and private banks, headhunters, management consultants, and so on often have very simple business cards with black ink on a white or cream background. Done right it can look very high quality; if more colours doesn't always deliver a higher quality image. Creative industries, though, such as design firms, often want to show off their talent with brighter, more colourful designs, as you might expect.

There are some really high-profile logos and corporate identities built around one or two colours; they needn't appear cheap at all. The innovative bank First direct launched with a whole series of white on black adverts, which made them really stand out as different from all other banks; Virgin's brands are always red and white.

Lastly, I feel strongly that you need to love your corporate identity. You need to be passionate about your business, and the way it looks has to fit your vision; if you're unhappy with the image, it will affect your passion and, ultimately, therefore, the business.

Moving from ideas to the logo

Once you have a sense of the sort of image you want to create, how do you go about creating a logo? I remember spending ages with my first business trying to work out how to do this without spending a fortune. If you're a designer, you can create your own. For the rest of you, you probably need to find a designer. Most local print shops will do something simple for you for not very much money. If your image is very important, you probably need more than that, and should find a graphic designer to do this for you.

There are lots of designers around the country, ranging from freelancers working alone to agencies.

The best way to find a designer is to ask around. If your friends and contacts don't know anyone, try asking someone at a business whose logo you like – business people will often tell you all sorts of information if you simply ask them to, even though it's not very British. If you flatter them by telling them you like their logo, they're all the more likely to want to help you.

You can of course search on the web or through a phone directory but my experience is that you have to sort through huge amounts of people who aren't what you're after before finding someone who is. It can be very time-consuming, and more than a little frustrating. www.britishdesign.co.uk is a website which lets you search for designers with specific sector experience.

How much should you spend on this? You can spend as little as £100, using a local high street print shop to design something very straightforward, and that might be quite sufficient. My first logo, for the computer games business, cost me £40, in 1988, and was fine. I eventually had another one done, for several thousand pounds, and was actually no happier with it. Large companies spend tens and hundreds of thousands of pounds; the larger sums including more research and presentations. I would advise not spending more than £10,000 even if your image is very important and you're well funded. I think most new businesses should spend something between £50 and £5,000.

When you find a designer, you will need to give them a 'brief', telling them the sort of thing you want. The more specific and unambiguous this is, the easier it will be for them to give you what you want, though you may well struggle to find words to describe the visual elements you want. As I said before, the best thing to do is to give them pictures of the sorts of look you want; it's quite OK to give them several pictures, telling them what you like from each.

Your designer should give you several draft designs for logos and ask you to select one or two to work up a little more, tweaking it according to your comments. As soon as you are close to having something you like, your designer should use it within mock-ups of the main uses for it, such as your business card, letterhead, shop front and website. If you are starting a shop, the shop front look is far more important than your letterhead or business card; if your business is a website, then the website is the most important thing; if your business is a recruitment agency or similar service business, the letterhead might be the most important. You will need to decide this and give that information to your designer.

At the end of this process, you should ask your designer to give you the logo, together with any designed items such as letterheads etc, to you electronically.

Consultants for ambitious businesses

If you have more ambitious plans, it might be worth spending more money at this stage and using a brand consultant rather than a designer. The brand consultant would use a designer, but would work hard to get the brief right, find the right designer for your business, and then help review what the designer comes up with. I would expect you to end up with a more professional identity this way than just by using a design firm. The biggest brand consultancies include Wolff Olins, mentioned previously, Interbrand, and Landor; these are more appropriate for large companies than for most startups. There are some outstanding smaller consultancies which would be a much better bet for even ambitious startups, offering the same expertise at a reasonable cost – for example Brand Catalyst (www.brandcatalyst.com).

BUSINESS STATIONERY

Once you have your designs, you need to get them turned into stationery and, in due course, websites, shop fronts, or whatever else is needed for your business. You probably need a business card and letterhead first, though, especially if you need to raise some money – it will be important to bank managers or potential investors for you to present the right image for your new business.

Business cards are fairly straightforward; you have probably seen hundreds in your time. It is worth spending time on them, though, to get them right. It never ceases to amaze me how many people clearly haven't done that, and miss out key pieces of information.

You should include:

- Your name
- Your position (proprietor, managing director, chief executive, partner, chairman, or whatever)
- The business logo (which should be sufficiently legible for people to read)
- Your preferred method for people to contact you. This usually means telephone number, physical address and email address.
- Your website address
- A fax number used to be important, and they are still on most cards I see, but fax is really not that important any more, and I probably wouldn't bother now unless fax is

likely to really matter to you for some reason. The less on the card, the better it will stand out.

Some people put a mobile phone number on their cards. I don't, since I want to control who I give my mobile number to. Many people are suspicious of businesses which only have a mobile number, so if you possibly can, put a landline down as well as a mobile number. If you don't have your own landline, it might be worth your while taking on an answering service who would take messages for you, providing you with a landline number.

Some people print cards portrait, some landscape; I really don't think it matters – whatever you prefer. Arguably most business card storage devices work better with landscape, but these days most contact information ends up being stored and accessed electronically, so it won't matter anyway.

It is worth making sure that your card can be photocopied easily. Partly this is so someone could give your details physically to another potential customer; partly, it ensures that it will also work well in a scanner – more and more people scan business cards in as a way of entering the information swiftly onto their computer. Some colours don't photocopy very easily, particularly yellow highlights, and light colours generally. The more colours in your logo, the harder it will be to scan in and photocopy. Use nice, thick card for your business cards. It adds very little to the cost but makes your business seem higher quality at a stroke.

Letterheads are different – most people don't know this, but there are laws governing the information which goes on here. Registered companies need to have the formal registered company name and number and registered office address on the letterhead. Partnerships need to have a list of partners or, if there are too many, a statement saying that a list of partners is available at the partnership's office, and details of that address. I've never heard of anyone being prosecuted for not doing this, but it is possible. More importantly, potential customers, and even more so potential suppliers, will expect this information and be concerned if it is missing. These details are needed for them to carry out credit checks on your business, which some people will want to do in due course.

Most small businesses use a local print shop, such as Kall-Kwik, to produce their business stationery. These can be very good, but they can sometimes also prove quite expensive. There are an increasing number of deals on the internet which offer to print your stationery for a significant saving. The internet firms usually have a larger factory somewhere, at a cheaper cost than a high street shop. They will be able to pass on considerable savings to you and are unlikely to take much longer to deliver the stationery.

OTHER TYPES OF CORPORATE IDENTITY

In addition to corporate stationery, almost every business will want a website; see Chapter Seventeen for more on how to set one up. Otherwise all businesses will vary in their needs. Here are a few other specific types which will help you.

Shop fronts and fittings

Shop fronts vary enormously, but typically independent shops look very distinct from chain stores. Some independent stores have excellent images, but many look terrible. Most people prefer shopping at a better-looking store, but that doesn't mean it's necessarily a smart decision to spend a fortune on the way your new shop looks. I strongly recommend using a firm of professional shopfitters – there are many around, and it's easy to find some via the web, or indeed by asking impressive non-competitor shops who they used. It is interesting to note that most large retailers expect to get a significant rise in sales after they do a refit on their stores, showing that the way a shop looks can have a direct effect on sales.

Often less well-fitted stores don't carry the look and feel of their logo through to their store fittings – and it really shows.

Signs

Many businesses need signs, whether it's outside an office or warehouse (where there is a legal requirement to have the name of the business occupying the premises) or above a shop. Again, frequently I see signs using different typefaces than the business's logo, which sends out a 'we don't care about our image' message to anyone seeing the sign. I also see too many signs just crammed with information. Make it clear, simple, and in keeping with your logo. If being seen at night is important, remember to get the sign well lit. The right sign can be your best form of marketing, so if it matters to your business, do it properly.

Business vehicle liveries

Lots of small businesses use vans, and it seems to me that this is the biggest single missed opportunity. If your van will be seen frequently by actual or potential customers, it's an outstanding opportunity to impress them. It's easy enough to create a look and feel for your business vehicle which will promote your logo and image. These days, depending on your business, I might not bother putting the phone number on your van – it's too much to expect people to write down; instead, I'd make sure to include a very prominent website address. And make it clear on the vehicle what your business does. Just look around the next time you are out and about, and watch all the vans – most make it actually quite hard to find out how to get in touch with the business by having tiny wording for key contact information. Keep it simple for people to remember.

Product packaging

If your business is going to sell products, you'll need some sort of packaging, and that is likely to be far more important than your logo. You need to get an idea of where the decision to purchase your sort of product is made, and then spend your money where it can do the most good. For many products, that will be on packaging. People usually decide which food products to buy, for example, when they're actually in the supermarket, so the right packaging is critical.

James Averdieck, founder of ultra-successful pudding brand Gü Puds, took samples of packaging for his new product into Waitrose and put it on shelves to watch how customers would react to it – without permission and before he had launched. It worked, and the success of that business is easy to see.

However, if the decision to buy your product is made at home or the office, by way of research, then spending ages and lots of money on the packaging is likely to be less worthwhile.

WHAT IS A BRAND?

I've already suggested that you might want to use a 'brand consultant' to help you develop the right corporate identity. Just what is a brand, and why should you care? Certainly there are many business owners who would say they don't care.

Your brand is everything to do with what you offer customers; if you are a retailer, it's your store's name and image; if you're a manufacturer, both your corporate name and certain products could be brands. Tesco is a brand, as is Coca Cola, Google, Gü Puds, Volkswagen and Golf; arguably many celebrities have become brands, too.

Marketing people talk a lot about brands. Why should you spend any time at all on it? The simple truth is that you have a brand, whether you want one or not. People will have an opinion about your business as soon as they encounter it. That might be positive or negative, of course; and it will certainly affect whether they want to encounter your business again. And those people could be existing or potential staff as well as customers. Not bothering to set up your brand doesn't make other people not form an opinion about your business – it merely means that you're not spending time trying to affect the experience they have and therefore what opinion they form as to what your business is about.

Increasingly, brands are worth very significant sums of money. If Google and I both separately come up with a wonderful new website tomorrow, and spend the same amount of money promoting them, more people would try the Google website before mine because of the association with the Google brand.

Corporate identity and your logo form a substantial part of your brand; they are what people will think of when they think about whatever it is that you do. So you should think carefully about what you want people to think about your brand when you design your business identity. But brands go way beyond that: the way your products work, or your staff behave, even the way your vans are driven can affect what people think about your business. And all of these thoughts get wrapped up into a collective opinion about your brand, which determines how weak or strong your brand is. Often you could use the word 'reputation' instead of 'brand'.

If your ambition is to open up one small shop, get it working quite well, and that is about it, you probably don't need to think too much about your brand specifically. But if you want to open a chain of stores, your brand will matter more – you will want potential customers to know what you're all about when you open, saving you time and money trying to educate people. Focusing on your brand can achieve that.

OK, that's all fine, but so what? If you follow the other main advice in this book (give your customers what they want) then you should automatically start to gain a good reputation, and grow a strong brand. That's true, but by understanding more about how people think about brands, you could grow it further and faster.

Only a few years ago, there were two new businesses selling bottled blended fruit drinks, called smoothies. One was called PJ's, the other innocent. Today, one is a much stronger business than the other (larger and more profitable), largely because of their brand.

What I would love you to do is to think about what your brand values are – the qualities you want people to think your business has. Then try to think about all areas of your business, and how you can use them to promote those values. It's really important that you don't have any areas of your business which detract from the values you want to have, too. Innocent drinks have taken this a long way, so that everything they do has a certain look and feel about it – especially the wording they use on packaging, advertising, and their website. It stands out, and everything you come across from the business supports our image of them as a wonderful, caring business that is totally committed to providing the best fresh fruit drinks.

It matters, because a stronger brand will be able to make more money, and provide a barrier to entry, making it harder for anyone else to compete with you. Think about a supermarket: the strong brands are always more expensive than either cheap brands (if there are even any on the shelves any more) or the own-brand.

Most small businesses don't focus much on their brand. Some won't have thought about it, others won't think they have the time right now, others might not even think it's a good idea. Great, as that makes it far easier for those who do concentrate on these issues to stand out, and really impress customers.

ACTIONPOINTS

1. Gather other logos that you like
2. Find a designer or consultant to help create a logo
3. Include all legally required details on stationery
4. Apply a consistent look to all materials you'll need
5. Test these on potential customers
6. Create a list of brand values
7. Apply these values across your business

CHAPTER 11

The right structure for your business

What's this all about?
- What options are there?
- Which is best for you?
- Can you change after you have started?
- Registering for VAT

W hen you start your business you need to register it somewhere – just where will depend on what type of structure you use. Yes, it's a pain, and yes, it's dull, but there are financial penalties if you don't, so you just need to accept it.

I'm using the phrase 'business structure' to mean what legal form your business takes. You can choose from these options:

SOLE TRADER
This is the most common type of business structure, and is simply an individual operating a business on their own. (Though despite the name, sole traders can employ

people.) You would own all the business assets personally, and owe all business liabilities personally.

ORDINARY PARTNERSHIP

This is where you start a business with one or more other people. You should have a legal document called a partnership agreement which sets out the basis of your partnership; you will need a solicitor to prepare this and advise you about it. The partners between them own all the business assets and owe all business liabilities.

LIMITED COMPANY

Limited companies are very different from the first two options in that they are separate legal entities to the founders. A legal entity can own things itself, can sue and be sued. Companies are owned by their shareholders, and run by directors. Shareholders appoint directors, and directors have a legal duty to manage the company for the shareholders' benefit. Shareholders own a share of the company, but they do not own the company's assets or owe their liabilities; directors can own shares but don't need to, and again, directors do not own any of the company's assets or owe its liabilities.

By far the most common type of limited company is a private limited company, which uses the letters 'Ltd' after its business name. (The main other type of limited company is Public Limited Company; these companies are usually larger, and use the letters PLC after their name.)

LIMITED LIABILITY PARTNERSHIPS

These are fairly new, made possible by a law passed in 2000. A limited liability partnership (LLP) is taxed the same way as an ordinary partnership, however it is a separate legal entity which owns assets and debts. It needs to be registered at Companies House (a Government department) and must file accounts in the same way as a limited company. It does not need to have a board of directors, though it could choose to have one, and it doesn't have any shares or shareholders – instead it has partners who own the business between them.

There are some major differences between these, so it is worth thinking carefully about what is right for your business, at least for now. You can change from one structure to another in future if you want to, but that will cost money and admin time so if you can, it's worth getting it right the first time. There are five major factors which will affect your choice:

1. Personal liability

It is never nice to think about what might happen if your business fails, but it is something you should think about here. If you are a sole trader or a partner in a normal partnership and the business becomes unable to pay its bills, you will need to pay the shortfall yourself. That could be a huge personal tragedy, possibly forcing you into bankruptcy, depending on your circumstances.

Even basically successful businesses could be affected by this if, for example, they lose a major liability lawsuit. Just recently there has been a mass recall of many toys from stores because these toys had defects which could have made them dangerous. Had a child been hurt by such a toy, the manufacturer might have been ordered topay significant damages. This is unlikely, but it is possible. It's not very many years since McDonalds was ordered to pay a very substantial sum of damages to a customer who spilt some hot coffee over herself and blamed the restaurant. I am not trying to scare you – these cases make the news because they are unusual. But you should realise that if things go wrong, as a sole trader or partner you have full personal liability.

I know a business which had grown to turning over about £4m. The founder had started it as a sole trader, and never changed the structure. Sadly, the business went bust, owing millions of pounds – and its founder went from feeling rich to being bankrupt within about eight months.

Limited companies, on the other hand, are called 'limited' because the law limits their liabilities to their own assets. So if things do go wrong, the company will have to use everything it owns to pay off its debts, and might itself go bust – but you, as founder, are legally separate, so anyone owed money by a company you have set up and own cannot come after your assets (your house or car, for example) even if your company can't pay the bill. This is the huge benefit of setting up a limited company.

It is open to abuse – you have probably come across companies which go bust one day then set up again very soon afterwards with almost the same people doing almost the same thing under a slightly different name. There are laws which require directors of a business to act in certain ways to avoid this; in fact if someone can prove you knew that the company was going to be unable to pay a bill but carried on and bought the goods or service anyway, then you could be made personally liable for that bill. In practice it is hard to prove, but you should take that risk seriously, and act responsibly.

2. Tax and national insurance

Tax is treated quite differently for sole traders and partnerships than for companies. Profits are taxable at both, but what constitutes 'profit' is different depending on the structure.

Because a sole trader or partnership is not a separate legal entity, when it pays any money to its owner, it is called 'drawings' and does not lead to any tax charge. Essentially, you would just be moving money from one account which you own to another. Companies, though, are different. Even if you own all the shares in a company, it is a separate legal entity from you; so while you own the shares in it, you do not own the assets within the company directly. Whenever the company pays you any money, it then leads to a tax charge.

Companies normally pay salaries to their staff, and dividends to their shareholders. Salaries need to be paid using the PAYE system, and all salaries paid out are costs that reduce profit. Dividends are different – they are not costs, and so are not deducted from profits; instead, they are a way of giving some of any profit back to shareholders. The company needs to deduct some income tax from any dividends it pays, and pay this to HM Revenue & Customs, and shareholders need to declare those dividends as part of their tax return.

As a sole trader, then, you would pay personal income tax yourself on the profits made by your business. As a director of a company, you would pay personal income tax on any salary paid to you by the company. As a shareholder of the company you would pay personal income tax on any dividends you received. The company would pay Corporation Tax on any profits it made.

Companies pay low rates of corporation tax on much higher figures than personal income tax – profits up to £300,000 a year are currently charged at a rate of just 20%. So if you expect to make profits of more than about £50,000, your business will be able to hang onto more of that money as a company than as a sole trader or partner, leaving more money in the business to grow. But note that any money in the company belongs to the company – and for you to get it, at some stage you need to pay it out as either salary, or bonus, pension contribution, or dividend; all of those (other than pension) will incur a tax charge. So you could end up paying less tax overall, but you could also end up paying more – it will depend on your specific circumstances.

National insurance varies, too. Again, sole traders and partnerships work the same way – you need to register with the HM Revenue & Customs within three months of starting to earn income or incur costs. HM Revenue & Customs will send you a booklet as soon as you register explaining remarkably clearly, actually, what you need to do. Note that you do need to register yourself as self-employed, even if it is just a part-time business you start while still working as an employee elsewhere.

Sole traders and partners will need to pay class two and class four national insurance contributions. Class two contributions are fixed regular payments you make monthly or quarterly. Class four contributions are a percentage of your annual profit.

Companies work differently: they pay national insurance on employee wages, through the PAYE (Pay as You Earn) scheme. Companies deduct the employee's NI contributions, and then also have to pay an employer's contributions as well, at about 13% of the employee's salary. This can add up to more than the class two and class four contributions. When you first pay someone (including yourself) through a company you need to register with HM Revenue & Customs.

3. Ability to raise money

All business structures have a similar ability to borrow from banks and asset-based lending forms such as factoring.

To raise venture capital or business angel funding, though, it is better to use a limited company structure. This is because a limited company is owned by shareholders, and it is both possible and easy for lots of different people to own shares in a company. People become shareholders by buying shares – sometimes new shares issued by the company (when the money goes to the company to use in the business) or else from an existing shareholder (when the money goes to the shareholder, not to the company). Because sole traders and partnerships are effectively the same legal entity as the founder, it is not possible for a third party to buy a share of you!

If you expect to raise money from venture capital or business angels, you will be better off setting up a limited company from the start.

4. Ongoing filing and training burden

There is no question about it; limited companies have a bigger administrative burden than sole traders or partners. Companies need to file an annual report at Companies House, as well as an annual tax return with the taxman. Companies also need to file details of any changes in their board of directors or shareholders.

It is easy to find someone to take care of the filing for you, but you must remember to tell them when something happens which needs to be filed, and make sure they do the filing on time – there are financial penalties if you file documents late.

The law also requires company directors to act in certain ways, and what this means changes from time to time. So as a company director, you would need to keep up to date with what is expected of you, both now and in the future as the law changes. Companies House will send you a booklet explaining this when you first become a director. It sounds worse than it is – most of it is common sense, but you ought to read the booklet when it comes, and act according to its rules.

5. Disclosing results

The documents you file with Companies House are all available for anyone to search. This means that anyone who wants to is able to find out quite a bit of information about you. This is not true for sole traders or partnerships, which don't have to file accounts or other documents with Companies House.

WHICH STRUCTURE IS RIGHT FOR YOUR BUSINESS?

All this is not obvious or easy for most people to grasp. It does make sense, but it is complicated. I really recommend you go and see an accountant and get specific advice about your own situation, unless you are very confident that you know the right way to go. If you use a small firm of local accountants it won't cost very much, and you then have someone you can go back to for bits of advice later on, which will be useful.

Here's a summary of the advantages and disadvantages of each business type:

	ADVANTAGES	DISADVANTAGES
Sole Trader	Easy to set up Simple to run Minimal ongoing filing	Full personal liability Harder to raise money
Ordinary Partnership	Quite simple Minimal ongoing filing	Full personal liability Harder to raise money
Limited Company	Limited Liability Easier to raise money Can pay less tax	Ongoing filing burden Need to disclose information Directors have obligations May have to pay more tax
Limited Liability Partnership	Limited liability Minimal ongoing filing	Harder to raise money Ongoing Filing Burden Need to disclose information

HOW TO SET UP A LIMITED COMPANY OR LLP

All you need to do to set up a limited company is to complete some official forms and send them to Companies House with a small registration fee (currently £20). The company will then be 'incorporated' for you within two weeks. If you are in a hurry, you can get a company incorporated the same day for the higher fee of £50. The Companies House website is very helpful: www.companieshouse.co.uk.

In reality, most people don't do this. There are plenty of companies who will do this for you, and more besides. When you set up a limited company, as I have said already, there is a fair bit of paperwork ongoing; some of this needs to be made using a company seal, for example, which you need to buy separately. These companies will sell you a blank company (they set up lots just waiting for people like you to come along and buy them) and will also give you a package of other papers and items that you need in order to actually use the company. Things that you would need, for example, to open a bank account. Startups.co.uk has details of some good company registration agents.

The process for setting up a limited liability partnership is almost the same, though you will also need a partnership agreement and really ought to consult a solicitor for this. By far the best way to find an appropriate solicitor, if you don't know one, is to ask for recommendations. The *Yellow Pages* (and similar directories) and The Law Society will both give you lists of names but it could still take you ages to find a firm which is right for this sort of work and won't charge you an arm and a leg. Your accountant, if you have one, or bank manager are good people to ask as they should know people in your area.

REGISTERING FOR VAT

VAT is often misunderstood by people. In fact it is fairly straightforward and easy to get to grips with, so long as you keep records properly, including VAT invoices, of all the purchases and sales you make.

You need to register for VAT if your quarterly turnover is larger than the level set by HM Revenue & Customs (currently £16,000). You can register online at their website www. hmrc.gov.uk; registration is free. You are also able to register even if your turnover is below the threshold.

Once you have registered you need to charge VAT on all sales you make to UK based customers, and you can then reclaim VAT on almost all purchases you make within your business. Usually once a quarter, you tell the VAT office how much VAT you have invoiced to customers, and how much you have been invoiced by suppliers. Normally established businesses invoice more VAT to customers than they pay to suppliers, and they then pay the difference to the VAT office.

If you are buying more than you are selling, as often happens early on in the life of a business, then registering for VAT will be beneficial as you will be refunded the excess of VAT that you have been invoiced for over the amount you have invoiced.

Your accountant will be able to help with advice and questions about your particular VAT situation.

ACTIONPOINTS

1. Understand what 'personal liability' means
2. Think about which business structure suits you best
3. Take advice from an accountant
4. For a partnership, take advice from a solicitor
5. Register as a sole trader or partnership, or set up a limited company or limited liability partnership
6. Register for VAT
7. Register as an employer

CHAPTER 12

Raising money

What's this all about?
- How can you raise money? (?)
- Borrowing from a bank
- Leasing
- Invoice finance
- Business angels

J ust about every business you might want to start will need some money to get going. Just how much you need, and precisely what you plan to spend it on determine where you might go to get it. The best place to get £20,000 from is unlikely to be the best place to get £200,000 from.

Before you even think about approaching anyone for money to help you start your business, you will need some sort of business plan, showing clearly how much money you expect the business to need (see Chapter Seven for more on how to work this out).

Basically, there are two sources of money for businesses. I'll call them 'banks' and 'investors'. Others will call them 'debt' and 'equity', but let's stick to where you get it rather than what they are.

'Banks' don't normally take risks when they lend money – they are happy to let you borrow some of their money for a while, but they need to make sure they will get it back (usually by making sure they have some form of security such as a mortgage on a house). In return, they charge a fairly small rate of interest on that money.

'Investors' are willing to take more of a risk, but in return, they expect to get much more of a return; this return needs to cover the times when they won't get their money back at all from other investments they have made, and still make it sufficiently attractive to them to want to do it again. Investors will typically get their money back when a business gets sold – it would be difficult for most businesses to generate enough cash to repay their investors. This means that if you don't think it likely that your business will be sold within a few years (say three to five years) then an investor probably won't be able to get his or her money back, and therefore probably won't invest.

IS IT A GOOD IDEA TO RAISE MONEY?

Let me also say that startups are risky. Extremely risky. I have started a number of businesses, and expected them all to work – of course, why start them otherwise? Quite a few of my businesses have done well, but a number have failed. I am also an 'investor' in other people's small businesses. I have invested in half a dozen startups run by other people – and I have invested in several funds which invest in other people's businesses. These funds are run by people whose sole job is to invest in such businesses. One of these funds is a 'fund of funds' which means that the fund I put money into invests in a series of other funds, managed, in fact, by some of the best regarded names in the investing world. I have been amazed (and somewhat disappointed, it must be said) by how many of these investments have gone wrong. It is not one or two, but many. One of the funds I invested in, invested in about 10 startups. All had good business plans and appeared to be run by good people or teams of people. Yet all but one of these businesses failed.

So what? The message is simple. Investing in small, young businesses is highly risky. Investing in startups is by a long way the most risky thing to do. This means that there are not many organisations at all which will even consider investing in startup businesses. And those that do expect a very handsome return – they expect a high proportion of their investments to fail altogether, so the ones which succeed need to pay for all the ones which fail.

So if you possibly can, try to avoid raising money from 'investors' when you first start out. It will be much, much easier, and considerably cheaper, to raise money to grow, if you need to, once you have established that you can make your business idea work.

This might well mean that you need to adjust your plans and start in a smaller way (with less money) than you would really like to, which is probably a really smart thing to do anyway. I have found for myself, and heard many other entrepreneurs saying the same thing: that if you've got money you spend it, and if you don't, you find another way.

⟶ STARTUP TIP

Be stingy early on! When I started my first business, I started it with £12,600, and grew it to turning over about £1m without any extra investment. When I started my next business, I wanted to grow much faster, so I started it with £2m, and with hindsight wasted quite a bit of that money. Worse than just the waste was the mindset I helped create in my staff that they could spend almost whatever they wanted without thinking about making a profit or where the money was coming from – this took literally years to change. I wish I had started much more frugally second time around, even though it would have been harder initially.

BORROWING

Most small businesses will borrow some money from a bank at some stage. After taxes and employment laws, banks come next in the list of complaints by small business people. I understand where many of these complaints come from, but think that most of it comes from not understanding what a bank's job is. So let me say again that banks aren't there to take risks. They don't charge enough to take bigger risks, nor do their shareholders and depositors want them to.

It's also convenient for people who are rejected for finance to blame the bank rather than their business plan or idea – while history is littered with rejected businesses that have gone on to prove the banks wrong, I'm sure the banks get the majority of decisions right.

What this means in practice is that if you want to borrow some money from them, you need to be able to show them how they will get it back, and have some sort of safety net, which they call security.

There are several ways in which you can borrow from a bank. The main two ways are an overdraft facility, and a fixed term loan. These work precisely the same way for businesses as they do for consumers, with overdrafts being 'repayable on demand'. This can be dangerous for a business. I know of one business which recently closed down after its bank required it to reduce its overdraft substantially within a month; it couldn't manage that, and ended up closing down. In that instance the surprise wasn't that the bank reduced the facility, but that it had made it available in the first place, but its lesson is clear: it is unwise to rely on an overdraft for very long.

How easy is it to borrow from a bank?

In fact, it is very straightforward. If you have what they are looking for, all the banks will be very pleased to lend you money – after all, they make a profit from doing just that. Banks will want to see a plan for your business showing how you expect the cash flows to work, in order to see that you should be able to repay the money from the business within a few years. If they believe in your business after looking at the plan, they will be keen to lend you money, but they will almost certainly then want some security for their loan. In most situations, they will want a personal guarantee from you, the founder, supported by a legal right to sell your home, assuming you own it, if your business cannot repay the money you owe them. This legal right is called a 'charge' or 'debenture'. Sometimes I come across people who have borrowed from their bank without having to give a personal guarantee, but very, very rarely, and with no clear pattern to it. It's safest to assume that you will need to give the bank a personal guarantee.

When I ran my first business, we had an overdraft and later on, a factoring facility (these are explained later this chapter). I had to give personal guarantees to both – in the end, I was personally guaranteeing about £500,000. This seemed very strange to me, since I had literally £2,000–£3,000 of savings. If the bank had ever called in its loans, there was no way I could have paid them – I would have been made bankrupt, and probably spent years paying them off. So what was the point of the guarantee? I think it was mainly a sign of commitment. The banks certainly don't want to use the guarantees – it's a lot of work for them, as well as being expensive and unpleasant. What they really want is for you to work through any problems the business might encounter, and ultimately get the business to pay them back, rather than just walking away from a business which owes them money. I also think they have got tighter about making sure there is proper security to back up personal guarantees.

GOVERNMENT HELP

Something called the Small Firms Loan Guarantee Scheme is one of the best government aids for small businesses. Basically the government provides a guarantee to the bank that if your business borrows money and is unable to pay it back, the government will pay it back instead. Actually, the government only pays 80% of it back, so the bank is taking some of the risk itself. Most banks will lend money under this scheme, but small businesses often find that their bank managers don't suggest it.

For a long time after the scheme was first set up, banks really didn't like using it, and many businesses that applied for loans using the scheme were turned down. A friend of mine, Teresa Graham, looked into this on behalf of the government and produced a major report into the scheme, which has picked up significantly since its early days. At the moment there are lots of lenders willing to use it, so if you find that the first bank you speak to turns you down, it is well worth trying one or two other banks.

You need to be eligible for the scheme – which you won't be if you already have enough money personally to be able to provide security to the bank. (This is pretty reasonable, it seems to me; why should the government take a risk that you're not willing to take yourself?) And there are a few types of business which don't qualify, such as certain investment companies. But most businesses and most people will be eligible.

Under the scheme you can borrow between £5,000 and £250,000. Typically this will be repaid over about five years, but you can have a 'repayment holiday' so that you don't need to repay capital for a period of time, the first year of the loan for example. This is perfect for startups, giving you the chance to build up your cash flow before having to pay the money back. The only downside to the scheme is that you need to pay a small amount of additional interest (2% more) which goes to the government to fund the scheme. Although every pound counts when you're starting a business, that's a small price to pay if it enables you to build your business.

You should expect rejection. Not because your idea isn't good, but because most entrepreneurs get rejected before they find someone to back them. It happened to me, and to Bobby and Sahar Hashemi, the founders of Coffee Republic, and to the founders of innocent drinks. Sahar Hashemi says that they received 22 rejections from banks before they found one to lend them the money to start.

It is gutting to be turned down. If you're passionate about your idea, then all you want to do is to get on with setting it up – and every rejection delays that and puts doubt in your mind as to whether you'll be able to get there. I got angry, and also wondered whether I really was onto such a good thing after all. You have to be realistic; at some point you might need to consider facing the fact that you might not get your idea funded. But if you read James Dyson's story, he carried on despite all kinds of rejections; his passion and conviction that he was onto something really worthwhile carried him through. You need to weigh up your conviction with the harsh reality of how you can carry on without funding.

ASSET-BASED FINANCE

Most businesses have some 'assets', which might be desks and chairs, or computers, maybe a van, occasionally even premises. It is pretty straightforward to borrow against these assets. There are three main types of 'asset finance' for new businesses: commercial mortgages on property, leasing, and factoring.

Commercial mortgages

These work very much the same way as personal mortgages. So if your business buys a property, you will be able to borrow a high proportion of the cost using a mortgage. Typically you won't be able to borrow quite as much as with a personal mortgage (75% is more typical than 90%) though if you search around you might be able to find a better deal. You will also need to show that the business should be able to repay the mortgage. This type of finance is primarily for property-based businesses, such as hotels or property development, where property purchase and possibly renovation is crucial to the business.

Leasing

Leasing is a great way of funding certain types of assets for new businesses. I leased computer equipment in my first company, which is still common today. Leasing basically means you rent the equipment you use from a finance company, spreading the cost of the equipment over its useful life to your business. It is often quite an expensive way of borrowing, with leasing companies charging a higher rate of interest to help pay for the extra costs of managing their schemes. It is very suitable for IT equipment, furniture, and company cars or vans as these are large and expensive items with a predictable and reliable second hand value, thus reducing the lender's risk.

Factoring

This is a way a business can easily borrow most of any money it is owed by its customers. This can be fantastic for businesses which send customers an invoice, then wait to get paid. (This sadly won't be helpful for retailers, mail-order businesses, bars, cafés, restaurants or hotels, though.) Before long your business could be owed quite a lot of money. Typically you should expect it to take about two months to get your money from other businesses – in some circumstances, though, it might take three, four or even more. As your business grows, you will need to pay more money out while waiting to get paid for the work you have already done.

When you use factoring, you technically sell your debtors (the amounts your customers owe you) to a finance firm, who pay you a large chunk of the invoice value in advance. They then collect the full invoice value on your behalf. When they have been paid, they pay you the balance of money due to you, less their fee. They charge a processing fee, which is typically 1%–2% of the value of the invoice, and also charge interest on the money you have borrowed from them. It is much easier for a startup to get a factoring facility than an overdraft because the factoring company doesn't need to take a risk that your business works – its risk is whether your customers pay their bills, which is almost always a much lower risk.

The big banks all have their own factoring companies and often when a business asks its bank for an overdraft facility, the bank will ask them instead to use a factoring facility. Banks like this because they can make more profit from your business this way. It is also a very good way to fund young, growing businesses, mainly because it can grow automatically as the business grows, unlike an overdraft, which is for a fixed amount.

HOW TO CHOOSE A FACTORING COMPANY
Factoring has grown so much over the last 20 years that there are now lots of companies offering it as a service to businesses like yours. Some of them are only active in some regions, others are national and several specialise in helping small businesses; they all vary a little bit as to what type of business suits them. Furthermore, factors vary more than you might think. There are three major things to look out for.

HOW GOOD ARE THEY AT COLLECTING DEBTS?
The factor will collect all the money you are owed from your customers. If they are good at it, they might do this far better than you would yourself, and this could really help you. If they are bad at it, it could really slow down your cash flow. Though I have never met a factoring company which didn't claim to be good at collecting debts, I have certainly come across some that are very bad at actually doing it. The worst firms focus mainly on sending out statements by post, without doing much telephone chasing (which is extremely effective and almost always needed). Check by asking several client companies of the factoring company you are considering.

STABILITY
Because your factoring company will own your invoices, you want to make sure that they don't go bust themselves. It sounds daft to be worried about whether a moneylender will go bust, but if they do, then they would own your invoices. It doesn't

happen often, but it has happened – in fact it happened to my first business, and lost us £60,000, – a significant loss for a small business. The larger factoring companies are probably the most stable, especially those owned by major banks, but it's well worth checking how profitable and well-financed your chosen supplier is. Your accountant or bank manager can help you with this.

COST

Cost varies quite a bit between factors. You need to look at several elements of the cost: the interest rate you will get charged on any money you borrow, the percent of turnover you will be charged for the service element, and any minimum fees. Try to work out what the overall charge will end up as at different levels of turnover to see which ones will work out the cheapest.

There are a number of factoring brokers around who will advise on the best invoice finance firm for you. They don't normally charge you anything, but will receive commission from the factoring company you end up using. You can also get factoring quotes from a variety of firms via one-stop-shop websites. Startups.co.uk offers this service, for example.

WHEN FACTORING MIGHT NOT BE A GOOD IDEA

Factoring is fantastic for companies that are growing, that sell on credit, and that can afford the cost. It is important to be growing because otherwise you should not need to borrow this way – if you do it suggests that the business is not viable. Factoring is designed specifically to help businesses fund growth. Factoring tends to be cheaper if you have a small number of high-value invoices (say invoices for several thousand pounds or more each) so if you have high volumes of low-value invoices you might find it too expensive.

INVESTORS

Most businesses will need some starting money which doesn't need to be paid back, and which the business won't need to pay interest on. This is called 'share capital' (or, for partnerships, 'partners' capital'). Banks will often lend money to top up the needs of a new business; therefore you'll need some initial money from somewhere else – either from you, or from other investors.

It is possible to start a business without any money at all yourself, but this is very unusual. Most investors would expect you to put up some money of your own to invest in the business – after all, if you are asking them to put their own money in, they want to know that you believe in the business as a great investment, and that you will look after it as well as you can. They usually assume that if you have a significant amount of your own money invested, you will do everything you can to look after it – and would worry if you weren't prepared to put money in yourself.

Once you know how much money your business needs altogether, you can talk to your bank manager about how much they might lend you, so you know how much you will need to raise from investors.

Friends and family

People who know you are your best bet by a mile. Dramatically more money is raised for small businesses from friends and family of founders than from either business angels or venture capital funds. Note that sometimes this might be more distant friends or family than you might initially think.

It is very easy to be relaxed and informal about taking money from friends and family at the start of a business. It can rapidly turn nasty, though, if the terms of the deal are not agreed very clearly to start with and written down so that everyone understands exactly what they are. Whether things go well or badly, there is scope for disputes if you don't have clear written details about what was agreed in the first place. This does not need to be at all complicated, but it should be unambiguous. The key points to agree are:

- What percentage of the business the investors will own
- How much they will invest for that, and when
- When they might get a return on this investment
- How much say they will get in important decisions about the business

You should also make it very clear to anyone who is thinking about putting some money into your new business that it is a startup and, as such, is very risky.

Business angels

Many people simply can't raise enough money from their friends and family, and so they look at other ways to raise the money. The popular TV programme *Dragons' Den* is all about people such as this, trying to raise the money their business needs from wealthy entrepreneurs. There are several thousand people like the 'dragons' on the TV programme who do invest their own money in small businesses run by people they don't necessarily know. These people are called 'business angels'. Businesses can raise anything from £10,000 to over £1m from business angels, although it is unusual to raise much more than £250,000 from them.

One big advantage to raising money from business angels is that they can often help you get where you want to go. If you take on an investor with experience in your industry, he or she will be able to provide lots of contacts and advice which could transform your business. Some businesses, like restaurants, often raise money from groups of business angels, partly to provide a group of people in the local community who will come to the restaurant as customers, and also tell their friends to do the same. I am a business angel and invested in a restaurant called The Cinnamon Club; I only own about 1% of it, but I still like going there because I feel it is partly 'mine', and I have encouraged many friends to go there, too.

Not all businesses are suitable for business angels. This is because the angels are investing almost entirely to try to make a financial profit, so they need to see that anything they invest in will be worth lots of money in a few years time. This means that the business needs to succeed, grow, and be sold for a high price; some businesses might be successful but quite hard to sell for a high price. Of course, the smaller the business, the harder it tends to be to sell for a decent price. Business angels would not be keen to invest in a business unless it had strong potential to be sold for a decent price. Other businesses might be suitable, but if the founder is not keen to commit to selling in a few years time, the business would be unsuitable for business angels to invest in.

Running your business will be very different if you have other people's money invested in it. The investors won't exactly be your bosses, but they will expect you to tell them what is happening, to work very hard, and to succeed; and they will give you a hard time if things don't go well, so you might not feel quite like you're running your own business. Ultimately, depending on the deal you do, the business angels might even be able to fire you. I don't want to scare you off using business angels – it can be a wonderful way to raise the money your business needs, but you should be clear about what it might be like first.

✓ HOW TO FIND BUSINESS ANGELS

If you think that your business might be suitable and you're willing to take on outside investors, then the first thing you need to do is find some. There are a number of 'angel networks' around the country, which exist to try to match up businesses needing funding with people wanting to invest. Most of these networks are regional – most investors will only invest in a business based one hour's travel time from where they live, to make keeping in touch with progress feasible.

You should know that it is pretty difficult to raise money from business angels. Statistics vary, but the amount of money raised by friends and family for small businesses is probably 100 times higher than the amount raised by formal business angels. If you have watched *Dragons Den*, you will have seen this on TV – for every business which gets an offer of funding, there are many turned down. Even then, many of the deals you see agreed on screen break down when the founders and investors try to put a written agreement together.

There is plenty of money around, and investors often say that they have more money to invest than opportunities they like to invest in. That is basically true. Yet at the same time, there are plenty of opportunities turned down, which can't raise money. The reason for this basically boils down to differences in expectations: every founder expects their new business to work, while almost every investor expects most of the opportunities it sees not to work well enough to meet their criteria.

Most angel networks have a few hundred investors; there are two that have considerably more. I belong to some of these networks, and have done for over 10 years. I have got to know quite a few of the people who run them, and what amazed me was how few of their members actually invest – typically these networks have just a few tens of investors that have actually invested through them.

This shouldn't put you off trying to raise money this way. But you should expect to try several networks rather than just one. It may be that the right investors are out there for your business, and you just need to keep trying until you find them. Innocent drinks was turned down by the government's Small Firms Loan Guarantee Scheme three times but raised money from a business angel who they found by sending out an email to everyone they knew with the subject 'Does anyone know someone rich?' A typically unconventional approach, which worked for them.

There is a list of angel networks in Sources of Satrtup Funding. This can be found in the Reference section at the end of the book. They do change quite frequently and startups.co.uk has the latest information on them. The two which consistently raise money for the most businesses are Beer & Partners (www.beerandpartners.com) and Hotbed (www.hotbed.uk.com). It's well worth looking at the website for any network before you approach them, to learn as much as you can. The network will decide whether to present you to its investors, so you do need to impress them, and doing your homework before making contact is an important first step there.

AGREEING A DEAL

The network will expect you to send them some brief details about your business, including how much money you need. If they like that, they will probably ask you in for a meeting, and will go over a more detailed business plan with you. After that they will decide whether to put your opportunity to their investors or not. If they do, they will typically charge you a small fee up front, and require that you will pay them a percentage (usually 5%) of any money that you raise from their investors.

They will then either send out information about your business to their investors, or ask you to attend a meeting where you will need to talk briefly about your business. They will probably help you with the presentation. After that, the investors will work out whether to invest or not. It's unusual to find just one investor committing to an opportunity – every investor will feel more comfortable if other people also want to invest in something, so you will tend to find either nobody interested, or a few people.

You will then need to negotiate with the investors, who will also poke around your plan, and might want to take references on you. If they make an offer, you should put any deal in writing so it's extremely clear what has been agreed. The investors will usually want a 'shareholders agreement' which will give them more power to control the business than their shareholding would give them on its own. If they do want something like this, you really ought to find a lawyer to advise you on it; that could cost quite a bit of money, but it would be dangerous not to take advice about something as important as that.

If you don't get offers of investment, don't let it get to you – remember that most businesses don't get funded this way. My own first business was rejected for investment by all sorts of people early on; they would all have made a very handsome profit had they invested, too. The fact that some business angels don't want to invest does not mean your idea isn't worth pursuing, it merely means that they don't want to invest now. Business angels tend to invest in projects that interest them, so finding an investor, providing you've got a viable business, can actually be as 'simple' as finding, someone who likes your market sector. Always ask why investors you speak to, but who don't invest, turned you down. Listen to any reasons they give – there might be some useful information there which could help improve your business or your next pitch to potential investors. But if you're passionate and committed, keep going.

EIS

The Enterprise Investment Scheme is a sort of tax relief given to private individuals when they buy new shares in qualifying companies. It is designed to encourage private individuals to invest in young, growing businesses. The scheme works very well for investors, by giving some income tax relief straight away, and so long as the investor holds the shares for long enough, currently at least three years, then there is no capital gains tax to pay if the shares are eventually sold at a profit. This has worked well, mainly by reducing the risk of investing in private companies. So an investor who puts £100,000 into your new company could get £40,000 of that back straight away as income tax relief, meaning that the true investment has only cost the investor £60,000. As I write, the policy is rumoured to be under review, so if you want to use it, it's best to check online or with an accountant for the latest information. Startups.co.uk has the latest information on this.

Venture capital

Venture capital is money which is invested in risky businesses by companies specialised in doing it. People who work at these companies are often called 'venture capitalists'. It is easy to get confused between business angels and venture capitalists; it doesn't matter very much, but the main difference is that business angels typically invest their own money, whereas venture capitalists invest other people's money from a fund. Venture capital companies raise these funds typically from pension companies; each fund will be set up to invest in a particular type of business, and will need to invest in a number of businesses, usually between eight and 20.

Venture capitalists typically have more money to invest in businesses than angels, but are rather more formal about how they run their investments. Most venture capital funds won't invest less than £1m, and most of these also would not invest in startups – they want to help existing businesses grow larger. There are some which specialise in smaller investments (still usually not less than £100,000) and who will consider new businesses. If your new business needs more than £1m to get going, venture capital funds are almost certainly the best place for you to raise it.

A few years ago the government launched a series of regional venture capital funds (RVCFs). These are run privately, using mainly private money, but they have some government support. There is one in every region of England.

These RVCFs are fantastic. They are focused on investing in businesses too small for the average venture capital fund, and in fact they are only allowed to invest a maximum of £250,000 initially in any business. The government's scheme has very effectively filled a gap in the funding market. These funds are there to invest money in businesses based in each region. They understand the state of younger businesses, too, and won't be quite as scary to approach as the more formal, larger funds. I have seen the London fund in action, and think they have helped the businesses they invest in considerably, beyond just providing money. If you need to raise between £100,000 and £250,000, your RVCF is the first place I suggest you contact.

Most venture capital funds, though, avoid investing in startups like the plague. I have seen the statistics for a fund's track record in investing in startups, and it is rough – lots of money was lost entirely, so the decision not to invest in startups is very understandable.

There are, however, some funds which do invest in brand new businesses. The best place to seek a list of funds which might invest in businesses like yours is at the British Private Equity and Venture Capital Association's website (www.bvca.co.uk). Here you can put in a few criteria – such as how much money you want to raise, what stage your business is at, whereabouts in the country you are and what business sector you are in – and the website will give you a list of funds which might invest. Another great (and free) site to find potential investors is www.vcrdirectory.co.uk.

You should approach these much as you would an angel network – as confident and prepared as you can be, having read the fund's website first. It's best to ask for an individual by name, too, when you ring; you can usually get the name from the fund's website. I think it is much better to ring first than simply to email or post something; when your email or letter arrives, you want to make sure it is expected, which should mean it gets attended to faster than if it is entirely 'cold'.

VCs, as the funds and people who work at them tend to be called, will expect a better standard of business plan than most business angels, and they will expect slicker presentations while at the same time providing you with less help. If you want to raise serious money, you need to be well prepared. If this is all new to you, your best bet is to find a firm of chartered accountants who can help you with this before you make contact. The accountants might just agree not to charge you unless you raise the money, too.

Grants

Grants are fantastic: they're free and you don't need to pay them back – what's not to like? The problem is, there aren't very many of them, and so they don't help very many people. I've never met a successful entrepreneur who cites a grant as being a significant source of funding for their business. The exceptions are in certain regions and certain sectors. Grants are a government's way of influencing social behaviour, for example they might want to encourage businesses to take on staff in a certain region to counter unusually high unemployment. If you happen to want to move to a region where there are grants available, that's great.

CASE STUDY
IN MY EXPERIENCE

When I started my first company with friends, we all put enough money in to get us through our first year, but after that we needed to raise more. Our bank turned us down for a loan, twice, until I threatened to withdraw both my business account and personal account. They agreed to lend us £15,000, requiring a personal guarantee from me.

The business grew, but didn't make any real profit for its first few years. We used factoring to help fund it, and this worked fantastically. We were able to reach a turnover of £1m without raising any more money, so we didn't have to dilute our share capital.

To make enough profit to survive, we realised we needed to launch in America. It was late 1991, and I wanted to raise £50,000–£100,000. None of the venture capital funds were interested and business angel networks weren't well known.

Getting rejected when you know you're running out of time is terrible. I put on a brave face to our customers and suppliers, while having sleepless nights over our financial situation.

In the end I asked family and friends, and one of our suppliers and got about £47,500 – which we made do with.

We launched in America in 1992 and also used factoring over there. In one year, we had a turnover of £2m, which made the whole business nicely profitable. We then started to get approached by American venture capitalists. I had a phone call one day offering to invest $5m!

Instead of relinquishing shares to VCs, I chose to keep control and instead switched to a distributor that paid us much sooner than our previous customers, therefore releasing capital.

When we sold the company in 1995, the investors received their investment back tenfold. I was delighted – they had taken a risk and their trust enabled me to turn the business into a success. That's partly why I am now a business angel myself – to give others the same chance.

There are lots of different grants; some small grants are available to help develop new technology, regardless of where you are located. Grants in Britain mainly come from the Regional Development Agencies – look at their websites for more information. There are also increasing numbers of EU grants available, though they are hard to track down.

The startups.co.uk website has a grants section that is kept up to date and is probably the best place to start looking.

The Prince's Trust operates a fantastic scheme with a small amount of financial help for young entrepreneurs. See their website for more details: www.princes-trust.org.uk.

OTHER WAYS OF RAISING MONEY

Borrowing and using investors and grants are the three main ways a business can raise money. There are other ways which have worked for some businesses and might be worth a try, though be very careful.

First is supplier finance: you effectively get extra-long credit terms from a supplier in return for something, possibly a small stake in your business. This could be a great help if you buy a lot of supplies from one source, though be wary of getting tied into just one supplier; your negotiating position would not be strong when it comes to price discussions.

The other way I have come across several times, but I must say I don't recommend at all, is to fund a business on credit cards. For some years it has been relatively easy for most adults to take out all sorts of credit cards. It would be possible for someone to borrow £50,000 or even more on credit cards, and use it to fund a business. One problem with this is that the interest rates on credit card debt are extremely high. The other problem is that if the business goes through a hard time, and you are maxed out on all your cards, you could very easily end up going bankrupt; this form of funding would turn the sad demise of a potential business into a real personal nightmare for its founder. I know people who have been tempted to do this – please don't do it. If your business is viable, there will be another way.

ACTION**POINTS**

1. Be clear about how much money you need to raise
2. Find out how much, if any, you might sensibly borrow from a bank
3. Be persistent – you will need to try, try and try again
4. Work hard to find targeted potential investors
5. Call for feedback after every rejection, and adjust your pitch accordingly
6. For as long as you continue to believe in the business, keep trying

CHAPTER 13

Where to start your business?

What's this all about?
- Which region is best for your business? (?)
- Where should you locate within that region?
- Negotiating the deal
- Serviced offices

There are two elements to this question: in which region, or even country, should you locate your new business, and where within that area. Most people don't even think about the first question – they simply start the business close to wherever they live.

WHICH REGION?

Starting a business from where you already are makes some sense – in fact, if you can possibly start from home, I would. But there are times when it might be wise to start somewhere else. The improvements in global communications mean that it is really easy to do most business tasks from anywhere these days. And there are several good reasons why you might want to move region to start up:

Labour availability and cost

When I first started publishing magazines I looked at a few other businesses to see how they did things, and realised that one reasonably successful business based in Bournemouth simply wouldn't have survived had it been based in London. The difference in wages and premises costs between Bournemouth and London would have wiped out all their profit and then some. Which makes you think. It may well be that your business will be viable somewhere cheaper than where you live now. I am nervous of businesses which are that tight, because they feel too vulnerable to me, although that business in Bournemouth is still going and so far as I am aware, still making profits.

Just about everyone I know who currently runs a business in London is finding it really hard to recruit good people. There are more jobs available than good candidates to fill them. If I were planning to start a new business that needed plenty of skilled people, I would seriously consider doing it away from London for that reason.

Certain industries often develop in certain areas. Cambridge is renowned as a centre for high technology, for example, and Oxford has built up real strengths in bio-tech. Setting up a business in an area which is already strong at your industry means that you should have a bigger pool of qualified people to recruit from.

Cost of living

More and more people are moving away from a high-cost area to somewhere cheaper. Often they can sell a home and release substantial money from the equity there. They can then use some of that money to fund a new business. If you are starting a business as part of a desired change in lifestyle, this could be significant for you. Equally, it may be that you have enough money to start your business but not to live where you do now, given its high cost of living; perhaps a move to somewhere cheaper could enable you to fund yourself for longer while you try to get your business to viability.

Grants and investment

There are good grants available in some areas to encourage businesses to set up there. These can help fund capital expenditure or the recruitment and training of new staff. Typically these grants are in less economically successful areas, but the benefits can be substantial. One of the businesses I invested in moved its warehouse from London to north Wales to take advantage of these; it achieved lower wages and rental costs, and received a substantial grant to subsidise the cost of setting up there.

Grants are typically managed in the UK by Regional Development Authorities (RDAs), though there are also some European grants. Some cities or towns have their own additional packages to attract businesses, too. All the RDAs have websites with information about what support they offer to new businesses; if you're interested in learning more, it's worth phoning up and talking to someone there in more detail as there may be more help they will provide than is detailed on the website.

It is not just grant availability that you should think about, either. Some areas have investment funds which can only invest in that area, as I mentioned brefly in the last chapter. For example, Karen Darby, founder of SimplySwitch, only got investment from venture capitalist Bridges after agreeing to move her business to Croydon. She did and later sold for £22m.

Tax regime

Depending on where you live now, you might be in a high tax region. When I set up my business in the US, I moved to Boston, in the state of Massachusetts. What I didn't know at the time was that locals often refer to the state as 'Taxachusetts' because it charges high state taxes; in the US, states, and even some towns, can charge taxes like income tax. They can even charge luxury tax, based on what assets you own. Had I set my business up just an hour's drive away, in the state of New Hampshire, I could have saved considerable amounts of tax.

Tax is a big reason why the Irish economy has improved so dramatically over the last 20 years. The Irish government made all sorts of low tax deals to encourage international businesses in certain industries, such as software, to locate over there. And the British government does something similar in areas it calls 'assisted areas', to which it wants to attract new business. These benefits can be very significant, and are worth considering.

WHERE SHOULD YOU BE *WITHIN* A REGION?

I don't mean which town or city, so much as what sort of position within that area. The cliché that 'location, location, location' matters is applicable to business premises. What you need to think about is what matters to you.

In general terms, I suggest that you work as hard as you can to find the cheapest premises you can find which meet the criteria your business needs and which are available for a *sensible time commitment* and at a *sensible capital cost.* I'll explain more about each of these.

The cheapest premises

It's not exactly rocket science to suggest that you find the cheapest premises you can. The only thing I really want to add to expand on it, though, is to plead with you to look at the whole cost of a premises. It is extremely easy to look at the rent that is being charged and ignore the rates or service charge. Sure, rates tend to be roughly one third of rent, but sometimes they can be considerably more. I have also seen service charges as high as 40% of rent for some buildings, which I hadn't expected. This made one office I thought would suit us turn out to be too expensive. The potentially hidden costs with renting premises revolve around repairs and maintenance, depending on the type of lease you have. If you need to take on the obligation to find repairs and maintenance (which I would really try to avoid) then you should get some sort of survey of the place before you take it on, to get an idea of what sort of costs you might be signing up for.

Your criteria

You should draw up a list of what you are looking for from your business premises. The actual size is a start; be sure to take into account all the space you'll need for filing, storage, meeting rooms as well as core work areas.

Think about how prominent your premises need to be. Prominent premises can be a wonderful form of marketing; if this applies to your business. For example, you might decide to reduce your marketing budget but spend more on premises in order to get a location where large numbers of potential customers will notice you.

How close do you want to be to other similar businesses? Depending on the business, it might not matter at all – or you could want to be miles away, or right next door. Car dealerships and certain other businesses sometimes cluster together, which can turn into a sufficiently attractive destination for customers of that type of business so that everyone gains. Hatton Garden is a great example of that for jewellery, and engagement rings in particular.

Other factors to consider include transport links, for you, your suppliers and your staff; how smart you need the place to be; and how close you need to be to your customers. My main company today is based in Richmond, which is great, but it means that every time we hold meetings in central London we need to allow two hours to get there and back. If that happened more frequently than it does, we would have been better off somewhere in central London.

Consider your own commute, too; I've been called out to my office at midnight more than once to investigate the burglar alarm which had just gone off. When it's your business, you need to go. The shorter the commute, the better at times like that.

This also raises another factor to take into account. For a while Crimson had some nice offices next to a park, including some on the ground floor, facing the street. These were broken into several times, which was a real pain. There is no question; some premises are more secure than others. Saving money by taking less secure space might appear sensible initially but could end up being both less pleasant and more expensive in the long run.

Sensible capital cost

By 'capital cost' I mean the sum of money you will need to spend to get the place ready for you to use it. This might be zero, or it could be substantial – and could easily be the deciding factor on a location. This has been the case with a number of possible shops for the retailer I am a shareholder in – several seemingly good potential stores would have cost so much money to fit out in the way that we needed that it made them unlikely to be profitable for us, so we decided not to take them.

It is normal, too, for you to be obliged to return the premises to the condition you found them in at the end of your time there. So if you do spend quite a bit of money making changes, take into account that you will also need to spend some money undoing the work. I got a shock when I first learned that the hard way...

Sensible time commitment

This has been the biggest challenge I have had with premises. Normally leases are at least 15 years long, which is far too long for a new business to commit to. If demand for your sort of space is weak, then you are in a better bargaining position, and can make an offer for a shorter length of time. I have done that and had an offer accepted for a considerably shorter time period than the landlord said he would take.

The hard part is that you may well have plans to grow, so that in a year's time you probably expect to need rather more space than you need right now – but you can't really afford either to pay for the extra space now or to move in a year. You might just be able to find places split up into a number of units, where you could add an extra unit or two as you do grow. That has worked well for me several times. Landlords are usually happy enough to let you get out of a lease at no penalty if you are taking a larger unit from them – this is especially easy with industrial estates, and also possible with shopping centres and larger office buildings split up into units.

My suggestion would be to sign a lease committing you to no more than three years, and ideally two. Often the way to achieve this will be to have a longer lease length, but to include a break clause, which allows you to get out before the end of the lease at no penalty. Or you could take over someone else's existing lease.

Premises selection usually involves compromise. You are unlikely to get the perfect premises for a low rent without a huge time commitment and without needing to spend big money doing them up. I hope you can, but don't rely on it. You will therefore have to decide where to compromise.

I invested in a business called Soup Works, which was a fast food business offering fabulous soup. It couldn't find the retail outlets it really wanted, but had to open up somewhere, and ended up choosing a couple of sites which were away from the main high streets. It thought that that was a better idea than paying much more money for the premium locations. What happened? The business couldn't attract enough customers to its stores, and failed. We will never know if paying the higher price would have made the business succeed. With hindsight, I think that the right decision would have been to continue to look a while longer, and widen the areas the business would consider. But it is a stark warning about how fundamental location can be to some businesses – retail and leisure businesses especially.

WHERE TO FIND POSSIBLE SPACE

It's a really good idea to see as many potential business premises as you can before putting an offer in on one. I suggest you view at least six, just to get a feel for how they vary. There are commercial estate agents who deal with commercial space just as residential agents do for homes. Occasionally the same firms do both, but rarely. I have found the best way to see what commercial agents are active in an area is to travel around and look at the 'To Let' boards for commercial space; these are usually up at first-floor level. If you see three or four boards from the same firm, they're probably good people to call. If they aren't active in the sort of space you're after, they will usually suggest someone else for you to try. It is common for retailers to appoint a specialist agent to look for possible store sites.

I am sure that in five years time there will be a master website which business people will have access to with details of all available commercial space, just as we can do now for residential property. That would make life far easier. There are a few fledgling sites claiming this, but none that I have come across yet which are comprehensive. Such a website would save you a lot of time and would make asking prices far more open, which would work to your advantage too.

Choosing premises frequently gets quite emotional – it's natural to like some places more than others, and all too easy to justify in your head why you really need more expensive space than you had set out to find. I will never forget an episode of *Risking It All*, the excellent Channel Four TV programme about people setting up their own business, where two friends were setting up a new hair salon; they started out looking for a sensible salon to rent, and ended up buying an enormous building which they turned into a salon and therapy centre. This consumed far more money than they had planned, and the business failed. Business space is likely to be one of your biggest costs: keep it as low as you possibly can while ensuring it still meets your criteria.

LEASES

When you have found the premises you want, you can start negotiating a deal to secure it. There are two types of agreement you can use for business premises. Leases are by far the most common type; the other is a license, which is normally used for serviced accommodation.

Leases are very formal legal contracts which need to be 'stamped', which means that when you sign, you incur a tax charge. Leases commit both you and a landlord to a set of obligations. These could be very significant, and you really should talk to a solicitor about this before you sign one. Make sure you find a solicitor who is used to handling commercial leases and has done some of a similar size to yours, so that they are up to date on what you should be able to get away with. Try asking other small, local businesses that have recently moved into your area who they used if you don't know someone already.

There are several key items to negotiate with regards to a lease:

- The rent you will pay per square foot or metre
- The size of the area you will pay this rent for (amazingly, is often debatable)
- Whether there is a rent-free period, where you occupy the premises and pay rates but no rent or service charge
- Capital contribution from the landlord – sometimes landlords keen to sign you up will make a contribution towards your capital costs

- Work to be done to the premises by the landlord before you move in – you can often persuade them to make the place look smarter before you move in
- Whether it is a lease 'within the Act' or not, which affects whether or not you have a right to renew. The Act referred to is the Landlord & Tenant Act 1954 which sets out the law governing leases; when a new lease is created, its wording will state whether it is a lease within the Act or not. For retail premises it is important to get leases within the Act so you have the right to renew, but otherwise it is not that important.
- The level of service charge (sometimes negotiable)
- Who pays for repairs

You should be aware that as a new business you will almost certainly need to stump up money for a rent deposit. The landlord will probably want six months rent from you as a deposit, but you might be able to negotiate them down to three. They are taking a risk by renting the space to a new business, so although it is a pain to have to tie up the cash, they're not being unreasonable asking for this.

The stronger you are as an attractive tenant, and the fewer other potential tenants there are, the more likely you are to win a good deal. It's well worth talking to enough local commercial property brokers to get a sense of how strong or weak the market is when you look; you could appoint one to act for you, but you may not need to if you can get several brokers talking to you independently, so you can compare what they each say.

I have been told frequently that it is usual for the tenant signing a lease to pay the landlord's solicitors bill. I find that really offensive as a notion: if two parties want to do a deal, why should one pay for both sets of legal advice? Especially when one is usually a cash-tight business trying to grow and the other all too often a wealthy pension fund or property company! Anyway, I am delighted to be able to say that I have never ever paid the landlord's legal costs when signing a new lease. And nor should you.

It is probably worth saying, in case you didn't know, that business premises that you lease will normally be empty. You will need to supply any furniture and equipment you need, and probably also wiring for IT systems.

SERVICED OFFICES AND FLEXIBLE SPACE

A serviced office is sometimes known as an 'instant office' for good reason – they are literally offices you can move into and start working in straight away. Typically these consist of a building split up into office units, ranging from tiny rooms to larger rooms; you rent them usually by the week or month, and they come supplied with furniture and telephones. They usually also have common photocopiers that you can use and meeting rooms you can rent by the hour when needed.

In short, they remove a large number of potentially high setup costs for premises, and let you sign up without a long commitment. They are also often friendly places, where the reception and admin staff can feel like part of your own team; sometimes they are available to help with your admin, as well. Even better, there are often some really interesting businesses there, which makes them great places to start to get to know other people running businesses.

The single best part about serviced offices is the flexibility they offer you, by not needing long-term commitments. You can easily grow by adding extra rooms or moving to larger rooms, and even shrink back if you need to.

There are several very large companies offering serviced offices – Regus and MWB are by far the best known, but there are also lots of individual buildings operated on this basis by independent local operators. An AIM-listed company called Workspace has lots of offices in and around London. In the last five years several online brokers dedicated to serviced offices have sprung up; they take your details once, and then send you details of all available properties which meet your needs. You can find details of them on startups.co.uk.

One thing to be wary of is insurance – most normal commercial insurance policies won't be valid at a serviced office because the security arrangements are not entirely under your control. There are dedicated insurance policies for clients of these offices.

While it is mainly offices that come in this flexible category, there are workshops around as well. Often local authorities manage some units like this – and Workspace (www.workspacegroup.co.uk) also has some light industrial units they let on flexible terms.

You can find very different levels of serviced offices – from the very cheap and grotty to the ultra luxurious. At the top end there are a number of operators who run buildings without signage so your visitors won't know that you're using a serviced office. I've never felt the need for that, but if you do, it's there.

As you might expect, prices vary enormously too – usually dependant on quality and location. You tend to get what you pay for in this market. It is worth negotiating rather than accepting the first quote you receive. The prices you'll pay will feel far higher than if you leased the same space. But then, you're getting flexibility and a load of services for that, and not having to pay out quite a bit of money up front. I do think these offices tend to be a good deal, but you should certainly still keep your costs to a minimum and not go with the swankiest office in the smartest part of town to start with.

ACTIONPOINTS

1. Decide the best region to start your business
2. Draw up a list of criteria for your new premises
3. View as many possible properties as you can
4. Negotiate hard on any deal
5. Use serviced offices or units if possible

CHAPTER 14
Working from home

What's this all about?

- why work from home?
- Is it right for your business?
- Ways to make it work
- Equipment and services to help home workers

(?)

P retty much everyone who starts a business does so from home, at least while they have the idea, develop it and consider whether or not to launch. If you can possibly stay at home for the early months, or even years, of setting up the business, I recommend it.

The most obvious reason is that working from home is free. Also, it has no commuting time, which frees you up to spend more time actually setting up the business. And if you do get inspired early one morning or late at night, it's very easy to get some work done.

Some people find it very hard to work from home. Specifically, it is easy for some people to get distracted, and not get on with work. If that is you, then you should really question whether or not you're right to start a business at all; when you're starting a business you should be so excited that it won't feel like 'going to work' but more like fulfilling a dream, or a hobby you love.

When I started my first business, working from home was talked about a lot, but still very new, with the result that there was a distinct drop in the respect given to people who ran businesses from home. That simply isn't true any longer; the world has moved on, and it is now perfectly accepted as a good place for work. The key is to ensure that the home atmosphere is conducive to your work.

MAKING IT WORK FOR YOU

There are a number of ways to help ensure your ability to work. If you possibly can, dedicate a room to your work which no other household members use. If there are any small children in the house, try a rule such as 'if the door is shut, they can't come and disturb you', while 'if it is open they can'. This gives you control and the ability to concentrate when you need to and ensures you don't get interrupted on an important phone call by children returning, very excited, from a trip that they're bursting to tell you about. If you can achieve this, I think having a room on the top floor of the house is best, out of the way of the various daytime family stuff which goes on.

It is also really important to be able to shut the door on your work, so that home can still be a place for you to relax and unwind. If you leave your work stuff in a corner of the living room, even when you're not working it will be very hard to completely stop thinking about work – and if you're working as hard as I suspect you will be, you will need to be able to stop properly to recharge your mind and body.

There is a growing trend for people to convert garages or even sheds in their gardens into workspace. This can be fantastic if you have the space and are happy to use it in that way. In fact this might make it possible to run some unlikely types of business from home. Jennifer Irvine, for example, founded the successful nutritionally-tailored food business The Pure Package from home, and used a huge walk-in fridge in her back garden to store all the food she needed.

Some home environments are so busy with non-work activity, especially small children, that they might make it impossible for you to get the peace you need. If that is the case, you could consider basing yourself at home but using other environments during the day when things get too noisy. Libraries are free, quiet places where you can probably tap into a broadband if you have a laptop; obviously mobile phones are the norm now, and while you can't actually have long phone conversations in a library, you could take the call outside. I increasingly see people working in coffee bars, too; this is even more the case in America, where people literally stay for hours with a laptop and mobile phone. Clearly you can have conversations there.

In fact, business people are increasingly using coffee shops for meetings, rather than using conference rooms at offices, so if you need to meet clients a lot it needn't stop you working from home. I also feel that these days people don't even mind coming to a home to meet someone – it's become sufficiently acceptable and frequent; I have had several business meetings at other people's homes, and expect more in future.

One of the biggest adjustments for anyone not used to working at home is the lack of social interaction. You might be completely OK with that, or actually really unhappy about it. Most of us are naturally social, and enjoy a little chat with people we work with. If you're spending enough time on the phone from home, you might have all the social interaction you need. If not, there are home working groups which meet for lunch from time to time all round the country. Ask around in your area, or search on the web, to find out what's going on near you. Social networking websites can help, and these are getting better all the time. But they're not the same as speaking to people face-to-face of course, so you should think hard about how important that is to you.

POST AND PO BOXES

One of the biggest drawbacks to working from home is sending and receiving bulky items of post. If you're out, or simply on an important phone call, you might miss a delivery of anything too bulky to fit through your letterbox. When I worked from home years ago I frequently needed to send things by post, and it would often take me an hour or more to go to a post office, queue up, pay for various parcels to be sent, and get back. It took a big chunk of my time, and was a real pain. Email has helped substantially, meaning far less needs to be physically posted any more. And being well organised, with a supply of envelopes and stamps, can mean that all you need to do most of the time is nip to a post box. But it would be much more of an issue if you were starting a mail-order business from home, for example.

The rise in numbers of people working from home has helped fuel a rise in the number of outlets which can help. Specifically there is a chain called Mail Boxes Etc, who will provide you with a Post Office Box, so you can receive deliveries regardless of whether you're on the phone or are out, and handle all sorts of delivery needs for you. If physical post is a reasonable part of your business, then find your nearest MBE (as they are known) and set up an account there for a much easier time. Another chain, called Fedex Kinkos, operate similar shops which are also quick-print shops, and these are open very long hours. They tend to be situated in larger city centres, but if you are working on something late, and want to bind a document in the middle of the night, they are just what you need. I remember using one to prepare a presentation for a venture capitalist at one stage in America; they wanted to invest in my business, too, so it must have worked!

If you know someone well who runs their own business, you might also be able to use their business address and even equipment, as a favour while you get started – it might not cost more than a drink or two!

EQUIPPING YOUR HOME OFFICE

What equipment should you have in your home office? The basics would include a PC, whether desktop or laptop, and a printer. I much prefer a proper keyboard and screen to using a laptop, but if you plan to move around lots with it then obviously a laptop is what you need. I really like the all-in-one printer-cum-scanner-cum-fax machines you get these days. For a long time Brother were the only make which offered a laser print version of these, though others now do too.

You are likely to need a mobile phone. Increasingly there are decent phone and email devices in one; if you get one you are comfortable emailing on, I really recommend it – the ability to keep various projects moving along when you're out of the office is a huge advantage when you're setting up a business. 3G mobile cards for laptops are another great way to keep in touch when out of the office.

I would invest in a decent landline phone for the office. We all use the phone so much these days that you want to get one which is comfortable; last number redial is an important time-saver, and not as standard as it should be, and a speaker phone is probably also useful. You should also investigate Skype or other 'VOIP' (voice over internet protocol) phones, which can save you big money if you do lots of overseas calling, although the main telecom companies have introduced really cheap call costs now too, so the difference is not what it once was. I don't like answering machines, and wouldn't recommend adding one – an answering service is a much friendlier, more proactive solution which tells the world that you're a more professional, serious business in my mind.

You really should also have broadband. There are loads of providers; the key is to get one which works well, so I'd pay a few quid extra if that's what it will take to get better service guarantees.

IT BACKUP AND SUPPORT

What you might not have thought about but is really important is some form of IT backup. An easy way to do this is to buy a few USB memory sticks or portable hard drives, and back up onto those. It is important to store one or, better, two or three copies of this at another premises. The simplest thing is a friend or relative's house. It needs to be somewhere you go often where they can look after these safely and easily. And ideally it shouldn't be too close – if there is a fire or flood, or even burglary, you don't want to risk having both houses affected! How often you keep backups really depends on how you operate. If you have a web-based email service, like Hotmail, then that service will back up all your emails anyway. If you do lots of documents, and don't want to risk losing a week's work, then you need to back up more than once a week. The key is to make sure you do it regularly – if you use Microsoft Outlook, or a similar online diary planner, then it might be worth setting up automatic reminders to back up.

If you aren't backing up vast amounts of data, then web-based backup services might be the best solution of all. These are businesses which simply store your data. You download it via the web, and you can set most of these up to back up automatically as often as you want. Then someone else takes on the task of keeping the stored data safe; most of these services have at least two storage locations. If you don't know whether you have lots of data or not, the real test is pictures, video and audio – if you work extensively with electronic picture, audio or video files, then you probably will have very large amounts of data. If it's more emails, spreadsheets, word documents and accounts information, you should be able to use online backup services easily.

Technical support for computer problems is another thing most of us take for granted at an office – which is suddenly missing when you're on your own. PCs are much more stable than they used to be, but unless you're an IT expert, you probably do want to find a service which will help you out. Even if your PC is new, the chances are that the manufacturer won't help you if they think a problem is to do with your printer, broadband, or anything not down to them. There are some good local freelance IT support people who you could find. I have seen plenty of small adverts for them in local papers and magazines; sometimes small independent computer shops will help support you, too. Whatever route you take, you should try to work this out in advance – long before you need it! And you will need a solution that can help you whenever you need it – not something where you have to take your PC back to a shop and then wait for hours or days while they fix it.

There are more and more remote technical support services available. These can set your computer up so that they can access it from their office. This lets them monitor it for potential problems, and do routine maintenance tasks; it also lets them try to fix any problems when they arise. The quality of these services does vary, but many are excellent. If you want to use one, find one which has other customers like you, and talk to them to see how well-supported they feel.

Something most people I know who work from home don't even think about is their work chair. If you're spending the majority of a day sat on one chair, it really does need to be well designed to help you sit at the right posture etc. I'm no back or chair expert, but if you go to one or two office furniture stores they will take you through the things that matter. Make sure you get a decent chair to protect your back – the last thing your business needs is to have to stop working for a while due to back problems!

Obviously most people working from home lack the sort of support they would expect in an office environment. Most people can easily do without administrative support in the early days of a new business. But there are 'virtual PA' services which will answer the phone for you, take messages, and so on. There are even typing services you can use where you would use a voice recorder, send the service your recording, and receive back an electronic version, all typed up. Depending on the nature of your business, some of these could really help you come across as professional, and mean that you don't miss important calls or deadlines. There are several good companies offering this (such as www.moneypenny.co.uk) and it won't cost you much money.

LEGAL AND INSURANCE ISSUES

You should check to see what you are allowed to do. Most home leases prohibit you from working from home. I'm not aware of any test cases, but I can't imagine a court letting a landlord throw you out because you were using a laptop while at the home you were renting. The clause is very much there to stop you using the home for commercial purposes which might not be legal under the planning laws. So if your business meant that lots of people were coming to visit, with a steady flow of vehicles, or if you started doing loud or dangerous work at your home, you would probably be breaking the law, and could be stopped. If you are sensible this really shouldn't be a problem, but it is important to check what you can and can't do. A simple phone call to someone at your local council's planning office should tell you what you can and can't do.

Then there's the matter of insurance. It is likely your home insurance policy will specifically exclude any business assets or equipment. So if your home was burgled, and your IT equipment for work was stolen, your domestic policy probably wouldn't cover it. Many standard small business policies would cover you, though some wouldn't – you need to ask before you buy. There are also some dedicated home worker insurance policies; www.theAA.com is just one good place to try.

ACTIONPOINTS

1. See if you can start your business from home
2. Create some dedicated space you can shut away
3. Get the right equipment for your business
4. Set up a system for IT support and backups
5. Don't skimp on a decent chair
6. Take out appropriate insurance

CHAPTER 15
Taking on staff

What's this all about?
- How to recruit the right staff
- How to get the best from staff
- Employment law
- Wages and PAYE
- Do you need staff?

F or most people starting a new business, the people you employ will make or break your business. However brilliant you are, it is your staff who will need to get most things done and talk to customers. One of my biggest shocks when running my own business was just how significant, and difficult, this is. (Of course, if you are setting up a business which you can run entirely by yourself, you can happily skip this chapter.)

People matter in any business, but they matter far more in a smaller business than in a large one, since everyone represents a much bigger proportion of the business's activity. If an employee at a large business such as Tesco doesn't show up for a few days, Tesco won't really suffer for it, and its customers won't notice; if one of three or four members of staff at a small, new business doesn't make it into work for a few days, a number of things probably wouldn't get done, and customers would definitely notice.

Starting a business is hard work, just like pushing a heavy cart up a hill. I compare staff at a new business to a group of people trying to push this cart up the hill. The good staff are putting their backs into it, helping push the cart; some are just casually walking along, with one hand touching the cart to look as though they are helping, without really making much of a difference; then there are sometimes a few who are actually sitting on the cart, making it far heavier and therefore harder to get that cart up a hill. Clearly, the more people you have helping and the fewer you have sitting in the cart, the better; the right people can make that task possible, the wrong ones could ensure that it never happens.

It's your job to hire the right people for your business, and to get them working together as a team. You need to lead, inspire, motivate, communicate, constructively criticise, develop, encourage and reward your team. That is a long list, I know, and it is a bit daunting. And there are times when leading any team is daunting. But do it well, and your team will help your business take off; do it badly, and your business could fail. Getting your team to work well is down to you.

HIRING THE RIGHT PEOPLE

I have personally hired hundreds of people to work at companies I have run. My companies could not have been built without the hard work of many of these staff; these days I can go on holiday comfortable in the knowledge that I have people looking after the business sensibly while I'm away. But at the same time, I have also had more anxiety, disappointment, and occasionally anger dealing with people than I ever would have imagined.

Recruiting and getting the best out of your people is important and you need to take it seriously as a task, and devote proper time, energy and resources to it. There is no question that many of my frustrating experiences have happened when I was in too much of a hurry to hire someone, or when I didn't take enough time to tell them what I wanted from them. It's a common fault among founders – because we know what we want, we often assume it is also obvious to everyone else, and because we're in such a hurry to get it done, we don't want to take the time to explain clearly to our team how it should be done.

So my first piece of advice here is to slow down when it comes to hiring, and take whatever time it takes to do it right. That really does mean thinking hard about what each position you want to recruit really entails. Job descriptions sound like bureaucracy, but it is really key to make sure all your new staff know what they are supposed to do, and what they're not supposed to do. It's also essential for you, to make sure that you hire someone who can do all that you need.

Sourcing candidates

It is hard to generate a short list of good quality applications. The internet job sites typically generate vast quantities of mainly inappropriate applications; and to find the good ones you need to read the rest, which takes ages. Advertising in newspapers and trade magazines can work very well, but I have found that it generates considerably poorer responses in the last few years, as more and more people switch from newspapers to the web. Advertising in newspapers for a job vacancy can also be expensive. Asking around within a sector can sometimes lead to some good people; I have asked some of our customers if they know of someone who might be a good sales person and who would consider moving, which has produced a few good results.

Business owners typically regard recruitment consultants in the same light as estate agents: overpaid, necessary evils. I'm not sure it's entirely fair; I know several recruitment consultants who work very hard and deliver good people to appropriate jobs. But I have also used some who were utterly useless. Recruitment agents will usually charge something between 15% and 25% of the starting salary when they find you someone you take on; always try to negotiate them down from the starting rate – most will move a little – which is all pretty standard. But the key thing is that if the new employee doesn't work out, it can prove really expensive. You usually get a refund if the person doesn't work out within three months, but most of that typically has to be within the first month; so if you do hire someone through a recruitment agency, you need to understand quickly whether the person is right for you. Otherwise, it's a wasted expense.

⟶ STARTUP TIP

I hire people who are friends of friends whenever I can. If someone works for me and suggests someone they know for a job, I will leap at it. I have consistently found that they work out better than 'raw' people that are entirely new to the business, perhaps because they knew more about it before they started, or perhaps because they were more committed to doing a job because their friend also worked there. So I now encourage people to suggest their contacts for roles by paying staff a bounty if we hire someone they introduced to us.

Attitude

Good people will take your business further than you could ever do alone, and they can make your working life far more enjoyable, too. So how do you go about finding them? What I look for when I hire people, above all, is the right attitude, full of enthusiasm. And if there's a sales element to the role, I look for hunger.

When I was a director of Watford Football Club, we signed many players, some very talented and experienced at the top flight of football, some younger with plenty to prove. My belief is that in the Championship, while talent is important, desire to play as a team and to win is even more so. Young, small companies are a bit like a Championship team in this way – of course staff need a good level of skill, but above all they will need the right attitude. You need people who will do what needs to be done when you ask them, not people who will say that task isn't part of their job description. It won't be possible for you to write fully comprehensive job descriptions for your staff early on, because you won't know everything which needs doing. New businesses have to evolve and, especially to start with, you need staff who understand that and want to help you build the business.

Experience

Depending on your business and what help you need, you should probably try to hire someone with reasonable experience of your industry early on, giving you more details of what has worked or not worked at another organisation in the same trade. I look to try a combination of sector experience and 'discipline' (type of work, eg sales, marketing, accounts etc) experience. When a business is trying to bring something new to a sector, you don't want to hire people who don't understand that, as they might tell you it can't be done, or resist trying to do it. Sahar Hashemi says that when building Coffee Republic early on, they hired staff who had been at Pret A Manger, since they understood the attitude that Coffee Republic were looking for. That is smart, saving the job of educating people who might not understand.

I like to try to hire people who have had one job before coming to work for me. That way, they will have had some basic training, and will also appreciate the difference in culture at my businesses, which tend to be happy, hard-working places. Someone straight out of school or university won't know whether we are a good place to work or a bad place to work, which can sometimes lead to them incorrectly thinking the grass is greener elsewhere.

INTERVIEWS AND SELECTION

For middle to senior positions, I really recommend at least two interviews. Sometimes someone you thought was just right for a role simply doesn't perform as well at the second interview. I like to see around six candidates at first interview, and then three for second interviews. The role of the first interview is to see who, if anyone, is worth considering properly, which is what happens at the second interview.

At the first interview you should check that the person matches their CV credentials, and try to get a sense of what drives them; are they really interested in your position, and if so for how long? Will their ambition match yours, or will they want to move on shortly after you have trained them? I try to keep first interviews to just half an hour, but they usually creep up towards 40 minutes or so. Any longer than that is probably a waste, though.

At second interviews, I like to have a couple of other senior staff sit in with me. That way not only do I get valuable second opinions; it also means that other senior staff can help integrate the new person when he or she starts. And of course it gives the candidates a better sense of our business – we want them to choose us, too. When you're just setting up, why not ask a friend or relative who has some relevant experience to sit in with you on any second interviews?

Above all in your new business, you need to decide whether the person you are considering is someone you would like to work with. You will see plenty of them, and be relying on them to help you bring your dream to life. You should be really comfortable that it will work before taking them on. This needn't mean that you like the person, but it does mean that you should want to work with them.

Of course in the real world you often don't have a great selection of candidates to choose from; there have been times when I didn't really want to employ any of the people that were available. The question then becomes whether someone who's not ideal is better than nobody. You will need to weigh up the potential drawbacks versus not having anyone – and whether you expect to be able to find more of what you are looking for in the future. This is just one of many areas where you'll need to make a compromise; one of the factors which will help determine whether, and to what degree, you succeed at running your business is how you manage through these compromises. My advice is to wait a bit longer to get the right person if you possibly can, rather than someone you're not comfortable about.

When you have found someone you want to take on, and agreed terms with them over the phone, you need to put the offer in writing. This usually involves a letter formally offering them the job, plus a copy of your terms and conditions of employment, and a job description.

References

It is always a good idea to take up references on staff. Usually job offers are made subject to references, so that if the references come in suggesting the person is not what you thought, then you can change your mind and take back the offer. I don't think I have ever seen a poor written reference for someone, and these days most references only confirm the dates someone worked at a particular place – companies have been successfully sued in the past for giving a reference that either the new employer or the employee disagreed with. What I therefore tend to do is to phone a previous employer, and try to chat to them about someone I want to take on. You tend to get a bit more information over the phone than you get in writing, and this can be really useful. Getting a new hire wrong can be extremely expensive for a small business, so it's really worth taking the time to get it right.

A few years ago I was given a glowing written reference about someone I had offered a job; but the written reference took longer than I really wanted to arrive, so before I saw it, I phoned up for a verbal reference – and was told the candidate was terrible. I thought the verbal reference might have been sour grapes because the candidate was leaving, and the written reference was good so I proceeded with taking them on due to their written reference – only for it to go badly wrong; it proved one of the poorest hires I've ever made. I won't take the risk again – if I get a poor verbal reference, I will listen carefully.

It also highlighted another key issue about hiring. Nice people aren't always the people you need. It's so easy to want to work with 'nice' people; but sometimes the world is a tough place, and you need some toughness in your staff. If a member of staff is so nice that they don't want to let you down, they might not admit to not being able to cope with things, which ends up letting you down far more than had they owned up to it. I'm not saying that you should set out to hire mean people, just that you should be aware that it's easy to hire people you like and that sometimes they may not be the best candidate.

INDUCTION AND TRAINING

Once your employee has started, you will need to introduce them to the business, train them to do their job, monitor and review their performance, and motivate them.

Larger companies usually have a fairly formal 'induction programme' which all new staff go through to learn about their new employer. As a new business I strongly recommend that you do as much as you can here. You should give your new staff an overview of the company and its aims, and let them know things like your policy for taking lunch breaks, smoking breaks, use of the company phone for personal calls, security procedures, and so on. Introduce them, make them part of a team. And of course you'll need to let them know clearly what you expect them to do in terms of work, and how you want it done.

You probably then want to give some more specific job training. Even when you are recruiting people with experience, they will need to know how you want them to work – every business will have slightly different approaches to things. This might matter a lot, or not very much, depending on the sort of business you run. Most new businesses will give training pretty informally and over time. You should probably expect your first few staff to need several days' pretty intensive training from you when you first take them on.

There is quite a bit of government support to help smaller businesses train staff, subsidising the cost of sending people on formal training courses. There is a very wide range of training courses available, covering almost every type of business. You might not have thought about sending anyone on training courses, and I know it seems like a way to simply spend money, but the right course could really improve the value you get from people, so do think about it. You can find out more about the latest government training support schemes at startups.co.uk.

GET THE BEST FROM YOUR TEAM

After that, you need to monitor what they do carefully. You need to find the balance between breathing down their necks, giving them enough space to do what you've asked them to, and leaving them so alone that you're not sure whether they are really getting on well.

The reality is that everyone you employ will have weaknesses as well as strengths. Finding a way to improve or work around people's weaknesses is often a much better solution for many small businesses than to let that person go and then recruit someone new. Frequent staff turnover is disruptive, expensive and not good for business. The key is to try to get all the people at your business working well together, as a team, helping each other out rather than saying 'that's not my job'.

I often say of employees that 'leopards don't change their spots', by which I mean that on the whole people are pretty set in their ways by the time they hit the job market, and so it's hard to change bad habits. But I have been proved wrong enough times now that I always give people the chance to change. I just try to give them a clear message about what was wrong, the consequences if it doesn't get turned around, and then a fairly short time to show me things are different. Sir Richard Branson tells a story about an employee who stole from him early on, he gave him a second chance and that guy has now been with him 20 years.

Motivation

One of those annoying clichés that you'll hear from time to time is that there is no such thing as a bad employee, merely an unmotivated one. It is not what you really want to hear when you're dealing with employee problems, but it is worth listening to. The key to getting what you want out of your staff is motivating them to do that. Understanding what motivates each of your people is crucial; it will vary from one person to the next.

Money is far less of a motivator for most people than you might expect. Job satisfaction, feeling appreciated, being shown respect, and the overall working environment are consistently ranked as more important for most people than money. Saying 'well done, that's a great job' when someone does something well is free, easy, and goes a long way towards keeping that person motivated. Other staff, too, will feel better about working for the type of business which shows its appreciation for good performance.

I use an 'employee of the month' award to publicly thank one of my staff every month who has done something above and beyond the norm; other staff get to nominate whoever they feel deserves it each month, and I think it has worked really well. There is almost always strong competition for the award, which is great. I also hold monthly gatherings with all my staff at a pub; different managers talk a bit about what has been happening in their area, we announce the employee of the month, and then have a drink or two. We start this in company time, and expect all staff to come. It has worked really well in terms of getting people who don't work closely together to know each other better, which leads to much greater understanding and respect for each other's roles and challenges. Everyone also really appreciates hearing about how the business is performing.

It may be that there is nothing you can do to motivate someone to do what you want – in which case they really are in the wrong job, and the sooner you sort that out the better. If you tackle this right, making what appears to be a harsh decision can work well for both your business and the person involved.

Constructive criticism

Try hard to give constructive feedback. For years I tried to be nice when giving criticism, and sadly I got it wrong. I ended up sugar-coating some of my criticism, not wanting to be too blunt, with the result that often whoever I was speaking to didn't get the message I had wanted to send, yet I had thought they had. It is very easy to be ambiguous, and one of the hardest things for new bosses especially, is to be really plain about what you mean. But when you do give criticism, give it in a constructive way, saying things like 'you could do this better if you did it this way instead; do you think you could give it a try?' rather than 'you're doing that all wrong, do it this way'. It's often better to find something positive you can praise in a member of your team before and after your main message of constructive criticism, so they don't feel too downhearted.

EMPLOYMENT LAW

There is a heavy burden of employment law for employers in the UK, and it seems to be getting worse every year. While much of it is sensible, I feel that the dice are heavily loaded in the employee's favour now, and that smaller businesses in particular get treated badly. But you and I can't change that, and need to work with the system as it is. By far the best way to minimise the pain is to be aware of the key laws, and abide by them.

There is far too much employment law for me to cover here; you'd be bored stiff anyway, and probably wouldn't read it. There are a number of dedicated books you can get, and some print and electronic services you can subscribe to that will keep you up to date. Our startups.co.uk website has details of these. Here, I'll cover some key areas I think you should be aware of.

The law starts with recruitment, sensibly enough. In the UK it is illegal to choose or reject anyone for a job because of their age, race, colour, sex or religion/faith. Nor can you discriminate against any member of staff on these grounds once you have taken them on, for example by giving all the men higher salaries. The age item is a recent addition, and you should be careful about how you word job advertisements – asking for two or three years' experience might be deemed discriminatory. If in doubt, ask a lawyer or legal advice service.

It is a legal requirement to give your staff an employment contract, setting out clearly the terms of their employment. This should specify their hours, their normal place of work, their salary, holiday entitlement, and any other key details important to your business. If your staff are going to use expensive equipment, or drive vehicles for you, you probably should specify some sort of policy about how you expect them to drive and behave while driving. Not doing so could lay you open to lawsuits if there is an accident caused by bad driving.

You can download a very basic draft employment contract from (my website www. smallbusinessexpert.co.uk) free of charge. You'll need to fill in details such as name of the employee, job title, your business and its address, salary, holiday and other benefits, but it will get you started.

You should always have a probationary period in the contract. This makes it clear that you can end the employment relationship straight away during that initial period, rather than having to give a month's notice. In that time, which is usually three months, you should try hard to establish whether the employee is what you want or not, and therefore whether you want to keep them. Once the probationary period has run out, it will be much more difficult to change things. If you're still not sure whether the person is right at the end of that period, you can formally extend it, by talking to the person and then putting in writing to them that you are formally extending the probationary period, and for how long.

You also have an obligation to provide a safe place of work for your staff, reasonably enough. This now means that you need to get your electrical appliances checked every year, and have someone come and do a yearly health and safety assessment of the workplace. There is a small charge you will need to pay for this.

You should also take out employers' liability insurance; this is usually included as part of your standard business insurance, but many new businesses might not have that to start with. My advice is that as soon as you take a member of staff on, and ideally before, you should have that insurance in place.

EMPLOYMENT DISPUTES

When you, or an employee, are unhappy about something, it is always sensitive and awkward. You need to treat any problems really seriously and be sure to follow the procedures set out in your employment contract.

It is extremely easy for an employee to make a complaint to an employment tribunal; this will often cost them almost nothing, yet going there to defend your business against even a frivolous, groundless claim could cost your business more than £10,000. If you win, the tribunal probably won't award you your costs; your employee (presumably now ex-employee) probably wouldn't have the money to pay you anyway. Even in clear-cut cases where, for instance, an employee steals or strikes another member of staff, employers are automatically found guilty at a tribunal if they don't follow the exact procedure to the letter of the law for disciplinary action. This is a very real issue for all employers, and is highly unjust. It really is enough to make you want to think very hard before deciding whether or not your business needs its own employed staff. Know the law back to front and get advice as soon as a dispute crops up.

(Note that at the time of writing the government have reviewed the employment disputes mechanisms and found that it is unsatisfactory; changes are expected in due course which should make some improvements, particularly to help protect employers from groundless claims.)

Arbitration is a good solution, which is increasingly dealing with employment problems before they get to a tribunal. If you possibly can, I would try that route first. Acas are very active in this area, and don't charge for their services (www.acas.org.uk.)

WAGES AND PAYE

Obviously, you need to pay your staff. The first point to be aware of is that there is now a minimum wage in the UK; this means that you are obliged to pay people at least that amount. The basic minimum wage is currently £5.52 per hour, which equates to £10,764 a year for a standard 37.5-hour working week. You can pay 16–18-year-olds £3.40 per hour, and there is a 'developmental rate' of £4.60 for people aged 18–21. You should check online for the latest rates as these are likely to go up every year.

Employees need to be paid through the Pay As You Earn scheme (called 'PAYE'). This means that you are obliged by law to pay your staff the net amount they are due after deducting income tax and employee's national insurance contributions from their wages. You pay the deductions to HM Revenue & Customs on behalf of the employee. You also need to pay employer's national insurance contributions, which currently add roughly 13% to your staff's wages. As soon as you take on any staff (including yourself if you have set up a company) you need to register as an employer with HM Revenue & Customs. This is easy to do online at www.hmrc.gov.uk. You will then be sent details of how to report payroll information to the government, and how to calculate PAYE and NI deductions. You will be sent a really simple software package on CD which calculates the numbers for you. If you have quite a few staff you might prefer to use an agency to do it for you, where they give you payslips for your staff and work out all the amounts for you; or you could buy a software package to do this. You're probably best off getting an agency to do this, at least to start with, for a pretty small charge; your accountant can probably help you with this, and if not, then they will certainly know of local agencies who can. Internet searches will bring up lots too, in any case.

You might be able to get away with using 'contractors' – people that you don't employ but merely use for a specific project. One significant advantage is that you avoid the hassle and risks of employees, since the employment laws don't apply.

The other big advantage of contractors over employees is that you would not need to pay employer's national insurance contributions, although proceeding in this way often means that the tax man will be very concerned to make sure you aren't falsely claiming that some people working for your business are contractors when really they're employees. You should expect to get a 'PAYE Audit' when someone from the HM revenue & Customs will come and inspect your records, and decide whether they think you have got this right.

The key tests that determine whether someone is a contractor or an employee are:

How many clients

If your business is the contractor's only customer, the assumption is that it is more like an employment situation than a supplier one.

Where is the work done

If it always takes place at your business's premises, it suggests that the situation is more likely to be deemed employment.

Whose equipment is used?

The person using his or her own equipment or tools would help to show that they are not employed by your business.

Does the employer control the manner in which work is done?

In other words does the contractor have to do as you say to the extent that an employee would? Do they need to ask you when they take a holiday or lunch break; do they need to work certain hours every day for you? The freer they are to take their own decisions about when and how they carry out the work, the better chance you have of convincing the tax man that they are suppliers, not employees.

Certain trades have historically been notorious for getting this wrong, such as building trades. If your business is one of these 'high risk' categories, you should expect more frequent scrutiny by the tax man.

It's all a minefield though; if you aren't sure, ask your employment advisory service (if you have one), a lawyer, or accountant.

ACTIONPOINTS

1. Work out what sort of person you really need
2. Take time to hire someone right for that role
3. Put their job offer in writing
4. Check references
5. Provide a written employment contract
6. Make sure your work environment is safe
7. Take out employers' liability insurance
8. Train new staff properly and monitor their progress
9. Subscribe to an employment advisory service
10. Know the law, and take advice early about any disputes

CHAPTER 16

Marketing your new business

What's this all about?
- What is marketing?
- Your message
- How to promote that
- How PR can help
- What mix is right for your business?

M arketing is a word lots of people bandy about these days. Different people use it to mean different things. To me, marketing means working out what customers want, adjusting a product or service to make sure it delivers what they want, then telling these customers that you've got what they want.

I think this is absolutely crucial to the success of any business. It's the ultimate advantage for younger, smaller businesses, too – being closer to customers. As businesses get older and larger, it is almost impossible for them to remain as close to their customers as they did at the very start. You, however, have just decided to start a business precisely because you have spotted something which you have identified a group of customers want, but can't currently get efficiently.

There are two main points I want to make here, both equally important:

- If you continue to give customers what they want efficiently, you should do well.
- When you have something a group of people want, make sure you tell them!

If you have the best product or service imaginable for a group of people, but they don't know that you're offering it, they won't buy from you, and your business won't survive.

This chapter is mainly about getting the message out. For some businesses, that is relatively easy; for others, it's much harder. Imagine a small village in a remote part of the country, where everyone shops at the local village shop. If you open up a new store in the village, the local population will get to know of you quickly. So long as your message is clear from the shop sign and window, your target customers will all know your message very fast indeed.

Now imagine a new shop selling almost anything, opening somewhere in central London. London is so full of shops, and its streets change frequently enough that even people who walk or drive down the street regularly might not actually notice that there is a new shop there. And London, being as large as it is, means the chances of all the target customers walking down that street are fairly small, so the shop will somehow need to let its potential customers know that it exists, as well as showing what it has to offer, and where it is – a much harder task.

WHAT DO YOU WANT TO TELL POTENTIAL CUSTOMERS?

Your first step is to work out precisely what your 'message' is. You need to be able to put this very clearly, in as few words as possible. We are all bombarded with so many messages throughout each day that it takes a strong, simple message to actually break through the 'noise' of our world and get noticed. Think back to what I said in Section One about unique selling points and making your business different. These are the points to try to bring out in your message.

Ideally, you should have a single phrase that describes what your business is, and up to three points that describe what you do differently to, or better than, anyone else. There is plenty of research which shows consistently that people just don't take in more than three points, and that by offering four or five, the first three are less clearly absorbed – so stick to three! On the other hand, if you only mention the areas where your business is different, you might miss out the fact that you also do the core stuff really well too; you'll need to find the right balance there for your business.

To use an example, the children's shoe retailer One Small Step One Giant Leap has about five things it believes it does better than its competition: better range, faster service, more shoes in stock more of the time, more convenient locations, and a pleasant, brighter environment. It also offers quality feet measuring and shoe fitting services, and this is crucial to its business – but that is offered by several other competitors, too, so it is not unique. Parents are also very price-conscious, so it's important that the business makes it clear that despite its advantages it really isn't any more expensive than the competition. That's a lot to get across in a message; too much, in fact. So One Small Step's marketing tends to focus on only certain messages at a any one time, typically promoting the range or service as one major message with a secondary message along the lines of 'and of course we offer a free proper fitting service by our trained staff'.

The key with the message is to give potential customers enough reason to try your business out. Once they've tried you, their opinion of the experience will be the main factor in whether they come back again or not. For now, try to think about whether the message you have got will persuade someone to give you a try.

REACHING YOUR CUSTOMERS

You need to think carefully about who you want your customers to be. You probably know quite a bit about them already, but at this point you need to define them in more detail. They might be anyone in a given area, or anyone who shares a particular interest; it might be men or women; it might be people of a certain age, such as children, parents, students, or pensioners. Define your audience tightly enough that you can then work out how to reach that group efficiently. That group is often called your 'target audience'.

Reaching your target audience is very, very important, but also one of the easiest ways for new businesses to waste lots of money. The money might be wasted if the message is wrong, or if it is delivered to the wrong people.

Different types of target audience can be reached in different ways. If your audience is concentrated in a geographical area, local outdoor messages can work well, such as on shop fronts, vans, poster sites, or on buses and at stations. Phone directories and local papers or magazines can also work well. If your audience is more spread out geographically, other methods might work better, such as specialist publications or direct mail.

The internet is helpful whatever audience you are targeting, and it is important enough that there's a whole chapter on it next.

The following are types of promotion which small businesses often use.

Premises signage

This is a wonderful opportunity for any business which relies on local custom. You probably need to have some signage on your premises anyway, so why not make it really work for you by shouting out your message? I love the way that Pret A Manger get new shops ready – they have signs which fill every window, so passers by don't see the building mess inside, which are really simple and bold, saying "Pret opening here soon." Their stores usually take a few weeks to prepare, so by the time the store opens, most of their target customers will already know that the sandwich shop is there. These signs probably cost just a fraction more than plain signs, but mean that sales should grow much faster when the shop opens.

Vehicles

We all see hundreds of commercial vans and trucks every day. I reckon that at least half of them, probably more, are really badly done, and represent a real wasted opportunity. Of course, any plain van without markings is an opportunity wasted, too.

For most businesses which need vans, these can be a really valuable (and extremely cost effective) way to get your message out there.

What is wrong with most vehicle messages out there? Too much text, most of which is far too small. These vehicles move around a lot, so any message has got to be really short and sharp to get across. The biggest fault I see is huge type for a very long name, just one word for the sort of business, then tiny lettering for a website or phone number. Anyone who sees such writing will probably ignore it anyway as it's simply too dull, but even if they wanted to remember something, what is it? Such vans don't tend to put down any USPs, and getting in touch will be hard since the website address or phone number is too small to see easily.

Strong, unusual colours with simple, bold text works best. There are so many white vans out there; you need to work far harder for it to stand out than a bright pink van does, for example. OK, pink might not be the right colour for your business, but the point is that unusual and strong will stand out.

Do also ensure they are clean and well driven – both of which will add to potential customers' opinions about your business before they've even started.

In recent years lots of businesses have used very customised Smart cars to promote their business; I see lots of local restaurant delivery services using these, often very well done. If I see such a car out and about, saying clearly what type of food is being delivered and looking clean and interesting, I'm quite likely to remember it.

Leaflets

You can print leaflets pretty cheaply, and hand them out at stations, in high streets, or at exhibitions – wherever there are plenty of your potential customers. Or you can use local delivery services to put them through letterboxes at types of address you can select according to your customers.

Have a look through the leaflets you get through your own door, and you'll soon see an immense difference.

Sometimes the personal touch can work – like the letter in an envelope hand-addressed to the occupiers. We get plenty of pizza delivery service leaflets through our letterbox at home; many of these are from small, independent stores. Yet there is only one of these which even attempts to tell me why I might want to order from them rather than the others; most simply say 'here we are' which is nothing like enough if there are several pizza delivery services to choose from.

I think leaflets can work extremely well for new businesses; the key is to have a strong, clear message on them, and to get them into the right hands. Ideally, have some sort of offer on them so people bring them in to you – that way you can measure how many come back.

Posters

There are posters almost everywhere these days, but they can still work really well. In a small, local market, on the sides of buses, in bus shelters or on very prominent billboard sites can all work well. When I first started in business, I thought you needed to be a huge company to use this space, and while they are mainly used by large businesses, it is possible to take just a few sites locally and this can be very cost effective.

You would need to get the poster designed and made up, and then book the space. Most poster sites have details of who owns the site, so you could call them to find out how to book one. The site company will also give you details of a company who can create the posters for you if you need it.

Local papers and magazine advertising

In some areas, local papers are extremely well read and effective. A small, classified advert can be very cheap and yet if it is in the right section, could generate good business for you. In general, though, local newspaper advertising is suffering as the internet rises. My own opinion is that I wouldn't spend the money for a large advert in a local paper as a startup business – I think there are cheaper and better ways to get most messages out.

Local magazines can work well – I think better in many cases than local papers these days. This is very true for property adverts, but also for more specialist domestic services such as kitchen or bathroom shops where the magazines can often show much better examples of what the shops offer, given the higher paper and print quality of the magazines. It's also often possible to negotiate very hard with local magazines – certainly don't pay the first rate they ask for! I have seen small businesses pay less than half the asking price for adverts in these magazines. And often you can ask for an article to be written about your business, too.

You should think carefully about whether you think your target customers read the magazine you are thinking about. If you're not sure, ask the magazine for some readership figures (be sceptical – advertising sales people have been known to exaggerate from time to time!) and ask people you know whether they read the magazine or not.

National newspaper and magazine advertising

National newspapers still have enormous circulations. For a new business, you are almost certain to be limited to a smaller advert in the classified section of a newspaper, or one of the many colour magazines. I would say strongly to be cautious here – start small, and test; please don't spend your entire promotion budget on one large advert! The first business I ever invested in as a business angel did precisely that; the advert didn't work, and the company folded, despite having a great product.

Specialist magazines, covering subjects from cars to computers, weddings or whatever, can be extremely good ways to promote your new business if they have the right audience. Check that they are read by looking at their readership on the ABC website (www.abc.org.uk). The ABC is an independent body which checks how many copies magazines really are selling; if a magazine doesn't have an ABC at all, then be careful

– it means that they might be lying about their circulation (it is sad to say that more magazines do this than you would have imagined). Also check that the publication has 'an ABC certificate'. If you can't find a publication on their website, then it does not have a current ABC certificate. Even if it does, make sure you check how many of the readers on there want to be readers – sometimes publishers send magazines to people who haven't asked for it, and that is not worth very much to you as an advertiser; this circulation is classed as 'unrequested' or sometimes 'bulk'. And if the magazine doesn't have an ABC at all, be very careful before spending any money advertising with them. There are plenty of extremely good, worthwhile and honest publications that might be great places for you to advertise—just try to avoid those that aren't!

The internet is increasingly taking money away from both papers and magazines, so you should look first at whether the web would be a more cost-effective way for you to get your message out than either papers or magazines.

PR

PR stands for 'public relations' or sometimes 'press relations', but in this context what it means is getting 'media coverage' for your business. Twenty years ago, for most small businesses this mainly meant coverage in your sector's trade magazine, and maybe something in your local paper. These days the media is far more interested in covering small business stories, so there's a reasonable chance you could get talked about on the radio, on various websites, or even national newspapers or television.

It is widely thought that getting a recognised paper to write good things about a business is worth many times more than it would cost to buy an advert in the same paper. People still tend to believe what they read, or watch on TV. There is no question that good coverage in the media can lead directly to significantly increased sales.

How can you take advantage of this for your new business? The best way is for you to work out what the people you want to buy your product read or listen to, then approach those papers, magazines or radio stations. I wouldn't even think about TV at this stage – the great thing about PR is that if your story is interesting enough, it will often get picked up by bigger media after being covered elsewhere.

✓ BOOST YOUR CHANCES

When approaching anyone who you would like to write or talk about your product or business, give them a reason to talk about you. Give them a hook, or a story. It won't work just to say that you have launched a new business or product. Media want to talk about interesting things, so you need to make clear why their readers or listeners will be interested to hear about what you're doing. Also note that many journalists are under so much time pressure that they won't want to spend any time turning the message you send them into a story – either it is already in usable form, or it won't get picked up.

You should write a 'press release' with your story, which should ideally be no more than two pages long. It will need to get the attention of whoever you send it to; sometimes it might make sense for you to send different versions to different media, so that you make each version as relevant and interesting as possible for each audience.

Read the publication you're sending it to and make sure it's similar in style and content – if they don't carry features on your type of business or in the format you're sending it in, it's unlikely they'll change for you and it'll go straight in the bin.

If you are launching a new restaurant, for example, you will probably want your local papers (and magazines) to write about it. You might also want to get some of the national papers and food magazines to write about you. The local press will probably want slightly different information than the national press, so you should tailor what you send them according to what you think they will want to know.

✓ FOLLOW UP

It's always tricky to know how hard to follow up journalists when you have sent them something. When I have asked journalists how they like to be contacted, most say that they prefer email. That is all well and good, except that if they don't reply, what do you do? My rule of thumb is to give them a few days, but then email again, or phone. Don't leave lots of phone messages if you can't get through – you don't want to harass them. But do keep trying; eventually you should get through, and your enthusiasm will come across.

When you do get to speak to the journalist, you should be relaxed and confident, and show that you are very knowledgeable about your business – and their publication. Journalists hate people who clearly haven't gone to the trouble of finding out what they actually write about. Our website startups.co.uk is constantly receiving press releases, sometimes expensively typed and packaged, sent to three or more members of staff about content utterly irrelevant to anything we write about – what a waste of time and money!

Always be prepared. Think about what a publication might want to know in addition to what you have sent them; try to think up some difficult questions they might ask you and have answers ready. They won't be trying to catch you out, but they might need convincing that you are really worth writing about – the journalist will be inundated with requests to write about all sorts of products so you need to stand out. Try to understand their point of view, and develop a relationship with the people you speak to.

In some senses, PR is 'free'; in others, it is very definitely not. It doesn't usually cost money to get written about (though there are some unscrupulous publishers that might try to charge you to write about your new business – I would not recommend doing that). Occasionally, and especially with local magazines, you will find that the magazine will agree to write a nice profile of your new business if you agree to advertise. Although it isn't ideal, if you think the local magazine is read by people who you would like to become customers, then it might be worth doing.

The key to getting good press coverage is having a good story; much of that is down to how you pitch what you are doing. After all, there must be something good and new about your business, otherwise why will anyone want to buy from it? Turn those new points into a story.

Arguably less politically correct but nevertheless true, if you are attractive, make sure to include a photo with your press release – if there is a good picture to go with your story, it makes the journalist's job slightly easier; and editors like having pictures of attractive people in their publications. Have good quality high resolution images ready to email over – there's nothing more frustrating than losing a feature because you haven't got an image to go with it and gone are the days when papers and magazines would send round a local photographer. Make sure the images are professionally taken – spending a few hundred pounds on some professional pictures could be one of the best marketing investments you make.

You can also make a story out of who you are – if you have struggled, or are a husband and wife team, or are especially young or old; any of these backgrounds could help create a story.

It is also often worth applying for awards schemes, since even getting short listed can lead to quite a bit of publicity. There are all sorts of worthwhile schemes, from local business schemes, to national ones like the Startups Awards, which recognises great businesses that have started in the last three years. Winning an award like this should lead to plenty of press coverage which could really help your young business grow.

Phone directories

The *Yellow Pages* is a fantastic place to advertise for some types of business. I never advertised my games company in it, since nobody looks at the *Yellow Pages* to work out what computer game to buy. But if you are supplying a local service such as plumbing, electrical services or even a restaurant, it could be a great place.

If you think it might be a good place for you, have a look at the current edition of the *Yellow Pages*, BT's new local directory, and the *Thomson Local* directory. The key thing for your new business will be to stand out. If your category is not full of advertisers it could be easy for you to stand out strongly with a fairly small (and therefore cheap) advert, but you should ask yourself whether your competitors are staying away for a reason. If your competitors are advertising plenty in these directories, try to think about what might get you the best bang for your buck; it might be to have a larger advert, or to have an advert in one of the smaller directories (eg *Thomson Local*) where there are probably fewer advertisers.

When you advertise, you want to get people to use your business. Being more prominent in a smaller directory might deliver better results than being a smaller fish in a larger directory. You will probably need to experiment to find the best route. My advice would be to test gently, not spending too much money to start with. The people you talk to all earn commission from selling you an advert, and the more money they persuade you to spend, the more commission they get, regardless of whether your advert delivers what you want or not.

Remember too that, increasingly, people are looking to the internet for phone directories, such as www.yell.com. There are typically far fewer advertisers in the online versions of these directories, so you might be better off advertising on these instead.

Think about what phone number you use – having a freephone number will cost you money but will encourage people to call you and make you seem larger than you are. In turn, having a national rate number can work against you if your customers tend to prefer a local business and expect to see a local dialling code.

Bus, taxi and other similar outdoor options

Most buses and taxis carry advertising these days, and it can be very effective. Buses can work very well if a particular route covers the right area for your business.

Radio advertising (also TV and cinema)

Radio advertising is usually local, and can be very cost effective. It is probably cheaper than you think, although it is sure to cost at least £5,000 for even a very small

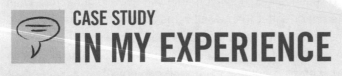

CASE STUDY
IN MY EXPERIENCE

When I launched startups.co.uk in January 2000, the dotcom boom was in full swing, and lots of people were thinking about setting up a dotcom to make a quick fortune. I wanted to get the website known fast so I decided to advertise on some London taxis.

We contacted several agencies, and after some haggling, agreed on a set price for a campaign. This was a reasonably large chunk of our marketing, spending roughly £50,000. Some taxis with our adverts on were driven over for us to see; they looked great.

There are roughly 15,000 taxis in London, and we had agreed to advertise on 150 of them, so roughly one taxi in every 100 would have our advert on it. I started counting the number of taxis I saw, as we were based in central London and saw hundreds of taxis every day. Before long, I began to get concerned, having seen just one taxi, out of around 3,000, with our advert on. We contacted the advertising company, who assured us that the 150 taxis were out there. We carried on counting, still seeing almost none of 'our' taxis.

After a while, I became cross; it was clear to me that there were nothing like the right number of taxis in London displaying our advert. It turned out that our suspicions were right – they had only put our adverts onto 15 taxis, despite billing us for 150. The advertising company refunded us the money, but crucial timing was lost and the adverts weren't seen when we wanted them to be.

The moral of this story is to be careful, and to check that you get what you pay for. There are sadly a number of unscrupulous media companies around, who will take your money and make all kinds of promises verbally. If you are relying on certain circulation details, make sure you get them in writing.

campaign. Plus, you will need to pay to create the radio advert. But radio adverts are extremely effective for certain sorts of businesses. Have a listen to your local stations, thinking about who advertises regularly. If a business advertises somewhere over a long period of time, the adverts are almost certainly working for that business, and so might do for yours.

Typically, radio adverts are 30 seconds long, in which time you need to get across what your product is, why it is different or better than whatever is already out there, and also how listeners can get it. Ideally, you should also include a reason for listeners to act straight away, such as a sale or limited-time special offer. Without this 'call to action' you could easily find listeners are interested but don't act on that interest.

Local cinemas also take advertising, and it is not unusual to see local car dealers or restaurants advertising there. Cinema adverts tend to be very slick, often featuring new, trendy campaigns before they hit TV screens. Be careful of seeming amateur – this might just do more harm than good. Creating an advert for a cinema can also be very expensive. I remember my father advertised his business in our local cinema some years ago, but it didn't work well. Try and speak to other advertisers with similar businesses to you but who aren't direct competitors, to see whether they are happy with their campaign. That might be people in the same sector as you, but in a different town, for example. The cinema advertising sales people ought to be able to get you some names to ring for a reference.

Amazingly, even TV advertising might be worthwhile. I don't imagine that prime time slots on ITV will be right for many new businesses, but there are increasing numbers of very specialist TV channels, and advertising on those channels can be much cheaper than you might think. You can select by region, demographic and time of day and pay per number of slots/views.

The biggest cost of any of these audio or video advertising campaigns might be creating the advert in the first place. The advertising sales people should be able to suggest agencies that could help you put an advert together, and searching on the internet probably would too. Something I have done in the past is ring a company which I have seen advertising, and ask them who made the advert. It is a little unusual, but I have found that when you explain who you are and why you are calling, most people are very happy to help, giving you contact details and also advice as to whether it worked well or not. Just make sure you don't call someone who is a direct competitor for your new business!

Direct mail

Often referred to as junk mail, the reality is that businesses still send out lots of it because it works for them. And it's worth remembering that we all only refer to the mail we don't want as 'junk' – if something you haven't requested arrives but you are interested in it, you don't think of it as junk mail at all.

Direct mail offers a number of advantages over other forms of marketing. It enables a business to be very specific about the audience it targets – there are so many lists of names these days that you should be able to find a very suitable list of potential customers for your new business. Secondly, it allows you to test your message on small portions of the total market, adjust it based on results, and then roll out a larger campaign when you know more about what works. You can literally start by mailing out a few hundred letters, for a small amount of money.

There are plenty of suppliers around now who will help you find a good list to mail, and who will help you create the letter or whatever else you might mail out. There is quite a bit of 'science' in this now, so many of the agencies and suppliers will be able to create something for your new business which learns from the vast experience that is out there. It sounds remarkable to me, but certain typefaces simply work better than others, and there are certain established techniques that work. Using a supplier who knows all this could save you time and money, and if you think direct mail is likely to be a significant marketing tool for your business, I would strongly recommend finding a local specialist to work with on it.

Direct mail can work very well for professional and service businesses. You should make sure that the letter you put together feels appropriate for the type of business you are running – if you are selling an expensive service, don't put together a very cheap letter on cheap paper. As with everything else you do, your direct marketing should fit in well with your brand, enhancing your business's reputation in anyone who sees the mailer.

Increasingly the internet is taking over from physical direct mail, saving on print and postage costs (and cutting down trees). But response rates are still considerably lower for this than for traditional direct mail.

Promotional merchandise and loyalty schemes

This means things like branded pens, mugs, T-shirts and so on. You probably own a number of branded merchandise already. Businesses spend vast amounts of money putting their logos and messages on all sorts of goods. They do this hoping to make you, the recipient of a free pen or whatever, feel good about the brand. And sometimes this works – though if the pen is cheap and nasty, it could conceivably make you think less good thoughts about a business than you did before. Of course businesses hope that someone worthwhile will see you using the pen, pad, mug or whatever in due course, which will help boost awareness of a brand, and ultimately boost sales.

One of the simplest and best forms of promotional merchandise is the humble shopping bag. If you are a shop, giving customers a bag with your logo prominently on it is a fabulous way of getting your message shown in your local area, as your customers go about their every day activities. But decent carrier bags can be expensive, while cheap ones might not give out the right message about your brand. As with so many things, you need to try to find the right balance for your business.

Unlike direct mail, buying promotional merchandise is almost always about branding rather than directly leading to sales. This means that businesses expect a much longer delay between handing out their branded pens and sales going up than they would from a direct mail campaign. This means that it probably isn't the best way for a new business to spend a small marketing budget.

There can be exceptions, though. I recall a highly popular campaign from Nescafé while I was at university: if you sent in a few coupons from Nescafé coffee jars, you got a free (or very cheap) mug. At the time, these mugs were highly desirable, which meant that lots of people wanted them, and bought more Nescafé as a result. Essentially this is a form of 'loyalty scheme' whereby a business rewards its customers for repeat purchases. Plenty of shops, even individual shops which aren't part of chains, have loyalty cards that give a discount or free product after a certain number of purchases. Coffee shops often have loyalty cards like this, giving a free coffee after you've bought eight or nine.

These schemes can really work, giving customers a reason to come back to your business. But they aren't for every business. If yours is the only coffee shop in town and customers really have little choice whether they come back to you or not, you might take the view that you want to reward loyalty, or that actually there is no need, so it would be a waste of money.

Introduce-a-customer schemes

Loyalty schemes can be great once you have a customer, but they don't directly help you get a customer in the first place. Some companies reward customers for introducing new customers, which can be a great way to build your business. Simple things like asking people who like your business to tell their friends can work well; some of this will happen naturally, but by telling customers that you'd like them to do this often persuades people who wouldn't otherwise have thought of it to go and tell a mate about you. You could then take this further by giving them an incentive to do so; I've often seen wine or discounts used in schemes like this.

The great thing about schemes like this is that they won't cost you anything in marketing budget, since you only pay money out if someone introduces a new customer. You do need to keep things in balance, making sure that the prize for introducing a customer doesn't cost you more than you know you will make from that customer.

Partnerships and affiliate deals

It can work really well to team up with non-competing companies who want to reach the same audience as you. The children's shoe shop I mentioned has done several joint promotions with a childrenswear businesses, for example. Web retailer CD WOW! sends a staggering number of mailshots every month by partnering with similar companies such as Firebox or phone and credit card companies to include each others' fliers. One advantage here is the cost saving, another is sharing lists of target audience with each other, and a third is that you can often learn from the other business's own experience.

There are many forms of affiliate partnerships on the web which can promote your business for free, if you pay a commission to the website when a sale gets made. Amazon used this extensively to build their business, and you still see 'click here to buy this on Amazon' boxes all over the web.

Launch offers

A new business might be sufficiently newsworthy to attract some local newspaper and magazine coverage, which would encourage you to hold a launch event, with balloons and an official opening – possibly including the clichéd ribbon cutting. Mike Clare, who started Dreams, the bed retailer, says that for their shop openings they invited the local mayor and had a cake in the shape of a bed, generating decent local media coverage from that.

New businesses often start with a special promotion or offer. One well-known building supplies firm used to open up with an offer of 50% off the price of sand for the first month, just to break local customers' habits and get them to start using the new store. New restaurants can do tasting events in local high streets, offering bits of food handed out for free to get potential customers to see how good the food is. Other offers might be buy one, get one free (now delightfully known as 'BOGOF') or, for services, the first session or hour might be free. Think about what might work for your target audience.

DO YOU NEED TO SPEND MONEY?

Getting your message out is going to cost some money, but it needn't be enormous. In fact I would say that for almost all of you, you should keep this amount as low as possible. It is extremely easy to spend vast amounts of money getting your message out there, and even then not to get much response. As a new business, you should keep your spending to an absolute minimum.

I wish I could be more helpful about what that really means, but it varies enormously from business to business. If I were launching a conventional coffee shop or fast food restaurant, I would try to spend no more than a few thousand pounds, which would almost all go on leaflets handed out or distributed in the local area. If I were launching a website I would spend a small amount on search engine promotion. For a new consumer product, I would focus on PR and possibly advertising in niche publications read by consumers of that type of product. If I were launching a new business service, I would spend money on a brochure and website, and do small direct mailshots to potential customers.

It is really, really easy to waste money on advertising. One of my companies makes much of its income from advertising. I have spent years looking at it and its competitors, and have seen new businesses starting to advertise in the sector lots of times. What is so sad is that many of these new companies make the same mistakes others have before them, spending quite a lot of money without really getting what they wanted from it. When I was a boy, I took out a classified advert in a local paper to try to sell my skateboard, which I no longer used; I paid for the advert, and then waited eagerly for the paper to come out and the phone to ring. The paper came out, with my advert in there looking good – but nobody rang even once to enquire about the skateboard. Why not? I will never know, but I still had to pay for the ad, so ended up worse off than before I started.

The cliché that you know half your advertising is working but you don't know which half need be less true today than in the past. By trying a few things out, and measuring and analysing the results, you should be able to get a good sense of what works for your business. Even very simply, just doing one thing at a time will give you a better chance of working out what works well than doing four different things at once.

It is often said that we need to be exposed to a message three times before we remember it. So get your strong, simple message out often to maximise its effect and don't keep changing the message, which would dilute the effect. Don't be surprised if the first time you put a message out there, the phone doesn't ring; you might well find that it does after a few more messages are seen.

Getting the marketing mix right

You can see that there are many ways to get your message out to potential customers. There are even more than I have covered here, such as corporate hospitality, but they tend to be better for more established businesses.

One of the things you should think about regularly is what mix of these devices to use; you probably should do a number of them, rather than just one. Repetition of a message is important for it to really sink in, and trying several different options gives you a better chance of covering your target audience properly.

Don't spend your entire marketing budget in the first week. Try to spread it out over several months, so that if something doesn't work the way you'd hoped it might early on, you still have enough money to adjust things and try again later. Remember, it is far easier to spend money than to boost sales. Lots of young businesses spend lavishly to launch their business, and rely on the launch marketing working well to generate the money they need to survive into month three or four – when that doesn't happen, for whatever reason, the businesses often can't carry on.

You need to decide what the right mix is for you: spend too little initially, and you won't get your message out there to enough potential customers for your business to survive; spend too much, or get the message wrong, and your business won't survive. Running a business involves making all sorts of decisions like this; good business people will get enough decisions right to make a profit. But nobody gets them all right, so don't worry if you do something that doesn't work, just try hard not to put yourself in a position where everything relies on one thing working.

Once you're up and running, there are various other things you can do to try to retain customers and grow your business further – things like newsletters, loyalty schemes, reminders before a customer's anniversary and building communities. But they are less useful when you're starting out. For now, focus all your time, energy and money on getting the business launched well.

CHAPTER 17

The internet

What's this all about?

- Internet basics
- Your own website (?)
- Online promotion
- Customer relationships
- Making money from your website

I n 1997, most people outside the USA hadn't even heard of the internet. Literally, it was just starting to take off. Now most households have access to broadband, most young and working people spend more time online than they do watching TV, and most of us use the internet for all sorts of things without giving it a second thought – from shopping to email to research.

I believe that in 10 years' time the internet will play an even larger part in our lives than it does now. I think it is going to continue to make substantial changes to our lives, and to certain industry sectors in particular.

It has already changed the face of business – killing some traditional businesses but giving birth to thousands of new ones and reviving a whole load of others. Indeed, sites like eBay have burst the entrepreneurial doors wide open to a host of people that would never otherwise have started their own businesses.

So what? The point of this chapter is to make sure you understand just how much the internet could help your new business, and how. This chapter is very much for normal businesses; if you're setting up a great new web business, wonderful, but you probably won't get as much from this chapter as the others.

INTERNET BASICS FOR SMALL BUSINESSES

There are some really good, simple basics that the internet can do for you.

To start with, you need to have internet access and an email account. Then you can carry out all sorts of research into your business idea. You can find out about how much competition there might be, and learn quite a lot about any businesses that you might compete with. You can search for suppliers, and potentially find suppliers much further away than you might otherwise have considered; this might well lead to better quality or better pricing, which could really help you get started.

Of course, there is plenty of help available online about running a business with the site I publish startups.co.uk being a great place to start.

SHOULD YOU SET UP YOUR OWN WEBSITE?

I still meet people who don't think that their business should bother with a website – there was a scary piece of research recently claiming that something like 40% of small businesses in the UK still don't have a website. I think that is largely because while they know the internet is 'big' they don't really understand just how big it has become, or how it could help them. There are also many business owners who know that there might be some benefit in doing something online, but they are scared that their current lack of knowledge means that doing something about it would be a huge task. I know someone whose business could get a real boost from the web, but he thinks it is too remote a prospect to justify taking the time to do it.

At one of our startups.co.uk events recently, someone told me about a small tailor's business. It made very high quality suits, but wasn't selling enough to survive, so the owner had decided to shut the business down. A friend had persuaded the tailor to carry on for a little longer, and to launch a website and a blog. (I'll talk more about blogs later.) The result was astounding – the tailor suddenly won lots of new business and ended up having to turn some away. His business had gone from being unviable to a tremendous success. Yet a traditional tailor is not most people's idea of a business the web would significantly affect.

I'll give you two more examples now to illustrate how powerful the web can be for a small business. The Book Depository was a tiny online business started in 2004 with just a few thousand pounds by Andrew Crawford. It set out to make available every book that is in print, and many more that are now out of print – more, even, than Amazon. This would only be viable on the internet. The latest figures available as I write show that its turnover has grown to over £24m, more than double the previous year – and it is still growing fast. This, in a field most people thought wasn't worth bothering with because of Amazon's dominance, is a fabulous achievement.

My main company today is Crimson. We have only recently got into book publishing by buying two other publishers and launching some books of our own (like this one). So no consumers know the Crimson Publishing name yet. Yet within one week of putting up our Crimson Publishing website, people were buying books from it; we hadn't spent any money at all to promote the site – search engines had led people to it for us.

So whatever business you are in, I think you should have a website for your new business. This site should explain what you do, and make it easy for anyone reading it to contact you. The site should give as accurate a sense of your business as it can, so it should look and feel very much like the rest of your business.

You should ensure you keep the website up to date. There are thousands of businesses who have thought of a website as being a one-off project – once the website is launched, the owner can tick the item off their 'to do' list, and move on. What a waste! I'm sure you have seen sites like that; you probably don't spend very long on them. Please try to build your website into part of your ongoing strategy, keeping it fresh. That need not mean updating it every day, or even every week, but it probably should mean updating it at least every few weeks and of course the more often, the better.

HOW TO SET UP A WEBSITE

Unless you really want to build a website yourself, I think the best way to develop your website is to look at similar sites that you like, and approach the people who built them. Usually you will find a link to the website developers at the bottom of the webpage.

Prices for developing websites vary enormously, and it is not fair to assume that you always get what you pay for. There are often several ways of doing some things, and most web developers have a set way of working – it might well be that the way they would develop the website you want might cost far more than another method. I would get at least three or four rough quotes from developers before selecting one. I would also make sure that the sites the developer has built rank well on the search engines – that's the best way of seeing if they really can build sites which are optimised (which most developers seem to claim these days). If your web developer does a good enough job of building the site, and you do a blog or otherwise update the site regularly, you shouldn't need to spend money using a specialist search engine optimisation agency.

You should write a document describing the way your website should work, both now and with anything you think you might like to add in the future. You should also try to get some sort of visual representation of how you would like it to look, which you can do in Excel very simply if you are worried about your lack of drawing ability. These will help potential web developers know enough about what you want, to come up with an accurate quote. It will also enable them to implement it the way you want them to.

There are all sorts of web developers out there, from the amazing to the terrible. So long as you use someone whose websites you have seen and liked, and whose references you have checked, you should find a decent one. That does not mean that you should expect it to be put together precisely on time – websites usually run slightly late.

Your web developer will probably offer to host the site for you, as well as just building it. (Hosting it means making the site available on the internet.) That is likely to be a good idea, since they will then be able to do the regular behind-the-scenes maintenance and backups that websites need. You should check, though, and find out what that will cost before you agree to use a developer – you don't want a nasty shock when you see what they want to charge you for ongoing hosting once they've already started building your site.

Depending on how tight you are for cash, you might want to see if the developer will do you a deal taking shares in your business instead of some or all of the cost. This has happened enough in the web world for it to be a very fair question to ask, and if it reduces your initial funding requirements you could have got from selling shares, while at the same time incentivising the web developer to make the site work, it could work well for your business. Either way, I would make sure that most of the money you pay them is paid after they've delivered the site, not before.

PROMOTE YOUR BUSINESS ON THE WEB – FOR FREE

Five years ago, people thought that simply having a website was enough. Now it is clear that to properly promote your business using the internet, you need to work at getting your website easily found by your target audience.

By far the best way to get lots of traffic to your website is to get the search engines, such as Google, to send people to you. The way to do that is by building your website in such a way that makes it easy for the search engines to understand what your site is about. Most web developers today can do this, but make sure you push for it. This mainly involves having lots of 'key words' which describe your business in various parts of your site; you can also add things called 'meta tags' which are electronic descriptions of each webpage which visitors to your site don't see; the search engines but look at them and these help them classify your site.

Search engines also look closely at how active a site is – how frequently it is updated. The more often it is updated, the higher up the search engine rankings it will be, which means more people will find it. Search engines also count how many other sites link to yours, and how popular those sites are; the more popular sites that link to yours, the better the search engines think your site is. There are plenty of companies which specialise in improving your website's search engine rankings.

The thing to aim for with all this is to be at the top of the list on the first page of results when your target audience searches for your sort of business using a search engine. You will find that the first search terms you come up with are very popular already. The key is to define your market more tightly, coming up with more specific terms. While these are likely to be searched less often, when they are searched, they are more likely to deliver people who are really interested in your specific area – and there will be less websites in that category, so it will be easier for you to be higher up the listings.

If you want, you can get very into this stuff yourself. There are books you can get dedicated to improving your search engine ranking, and there is plenty of information found online, of course. But most of this will be done by whoever builds your website, or possibly by a dedicated 'SEO' (search engine optimisation) agency. Most new businesses won't need a dedicated agency just for this; they're really for the very ambitious websites.

BLOGS

Writing a blog about your new business is one of the very best things you can do to kick-start your marketing. I really can't recommend doing it enough. And it's easy to get going – you don't need to be a technical genius, or a great writer.

Blogs have emerged in the last few years. A 'blog' is really an online diary; people who write blogs tend to write about a certain subject, but they do so frequently. The tailor in the example above started writing about his passion for making great quality suits. And by writing a blog about suits maybe twice a week, the search engines started to place his site higher and higher, which meant that more people found his site. Enough people visiting the website liked what he was saying in his blog and revisited to read more – they then carried that positive feeling and respect into buying suits from him.

People who read blogs understand that they are predominantly casual writing, rather than formal literature. What should come across is what your business is about, just how passionate about the subject you are, and what great quality your service or products are. Be topical, and comment. Don't be afraid to be controversial – blogs grew out of a frustration with the sanitised, politically correct, corporate world; people want to hear real voices. You can't simply write about how great you are, of course; it needs to come through as a feeling, rather than from bragging. Ideally you should come across as being an expert (or at least passionate) in your subject – people love buying from the experts in a field.

ADVERTISING YOUR BUSINESS ON THE WEB

There are two main ways to advertise your business online: pay-per-click advertising on search engines, and display advertising on other websites. Pay-per-click advertising is a way of paying to be at the top of the list of results when people use search engines. It is the main reason Google has turned into one of the most profitable businesses on our planet. Google worked out that internet search engines are wonderful ways for companies to promote themselves. Businesses choose a number of key words, and how much money they are willing to pay if someone clicks on their link after searching for that word. The search engine then works out which advertisers are paying the most money for each word, and whenever someone searches for that word, they display the adverts which will earn them the most money. This is wonderful for advertisers, who only pay when someone clicks on their advert, and they know that their advert will only appear if someone has searched for a term they have set.

This works really, really well in practice. For you setting up a new business, it means that you have the ability to buy an advert appearing next to the results whenever someone searches for terms which might include your competitors. That gives you the chance to tap into your competitors' brands from day one of your new business, which is unique. (There are some legal cases challenging whether this is legal, but at the time of writing it is still OK to do this in the UK.)

Better still, a number of companies have set up systems which will automatically check all the other bids for advertising for your selection of keywords, to make sure that you pay just enough to stay where you want to. So if someone else pays a little more than you for an advert, they might bump you off the crucial first page. These systems would automatically check this, and increase your bid to get you back to the position you wanted. All you need to do is to set the maximum you are willing to spend.

When someone clicks on your advert, the click takes them to your website – so your website needs to be ready for them whenever your advertising starts.

As it works on an auction system, prices for popular keywords can rise extremely high, though, and so it could become more and more difficult for startup companies to justify the cost. With this in mind it might be wiser to focus on organic SEO – which most people trust more anyway. Most businesses active on the web use a combination of both paid and natural search engine promotion, in practice.

Banner adverts and other forms of web advertising

Since the early days of the internet, businesses have been buying adverts on websites. There are various types of 'display' advertising, such as the common banners (wide, shallow horizontal strips) and 'skyscrapers' (tall, thin strips). These are usually animated, and increasingly creative. People click on these adverts far less often than they do on an advert next to search results, but that also means that the adverts are usually much cheaper to place.

There are also more 'intrusive' adverts which appear over the top of a webpage, blocking your view so you need to click on it to make it go away. Although many people say they hate these ads, they do tend to work very well for the advertisers. They cost more to put on a website than a more discrete ad.

The great thing about advertising on the web is that you can start with very small sums of money – literally just a few hundred pounds. You then get the results really quickly, and can measure how well it has worked. If your business is new, most of the traffic to your new site will have come from any online advertising you run. You can then tell from your own site whether people who clicked on one of your adverts go on to contact you or buy something. That is wonderful information for you to analyse to see what works best for potential customers. And of course if it works well, it is easy and quick to do more of it (unlike printed magazines, where you sometimes need to book three or four months in advance).

By advertising on the websites your target customers use, you have the opportunity to put your message across to those potential customers. The different types of website advertising give you loads of ways to get your message across – meaning advertising is much more flexible than the simple pay-per-click text adverts on search engines. Even small and simple advertising campaigns using banners and skyscrapers can be very cost effective. The key is to pick the right websites, and produce good adverts.

There are lots of agencies which can help you work out the best way to promote your business online. Most of them have technology and access to information which makes it easier for them to work out where your business should advertise. It's a good idea to try three or four different agencies before you select the one which you think fits your business the best.

DIRECT EMAIL AND VIRAL MARKETING

Just as businesses can buy lists of addresses and post them a letter to promote a product or service, so this can be done online. I'm sure you are well aware from your own inbox that there is a vast amount of unrequested email sent out to try to promote something. On the web, this often has particularly negative connotations due to a high number of distasteful subjects being touted aggressively. Nevertheless, it can still work well for some businesses.

If you can get or buy a good email list, sending out an unsolicited email is likely to generate some sort of response. As with everything, you need to get the target audience right and the message right. You should expect most of your emails not to get opened by recipients; many of them might not even get through due to the spam filters that so many people use these days.

Viral marketing was a huge buzzword a year or two ago, but the concept remains strong. Basically this involves sending something so compelling to a group of people that they send it to their friends, who send it to their friends, and so on. I'm sure we've all received these sorts of things from friends – and because the email is usually forwarded to you by someone you trust, there's a much higher chance that you will open it.

One of the best campaigns like this I have come across from a small company recently, was from an Irish natural cosmetics company. They created a video clip purporting to show their technicians at work in a laboratory; the difference was that everyone in the video clip was stark naked (without being in any way lewd or pornographic). They sent this out to an email list, and it was sufficiently interesting that these people sent it onto their friends, and generated vast numbers of people visiting their site. And best of all, it worked – it led directly to an immediate and substantial jump in sales of the cosmetics.

DEVELOPING CUSTOMER RELATIONSHIPS

The web offers you lots of ways to develop your relationships with customers. For example, you could send your customers a regular email newsletter that people could sign up to on your site. Alternatively, ensure you take every opportunity to collect data at point of sale or by running competitions, special offers etc. It's then a great way for you to keep people up to date with what is happening with your business. It enables you to be proactive; going to them with news, rather than waiting for them to come back to your site. It also means that if they sign up with you, you're not relying on them remembering your site.

A good e-newsletter should always offer information people might want to receive – rather than being too brash – by introducing a special offer, for example. Quite a few very large web retailers use their e-newsletters to clear out old stock at the end of a range, which can be very handy. If you put really useful information in your newsletter, there's also a better chance that people might forward it to someone they know who might be interested – a fantastic way of you growing your customer base.

You could try to build a community within and around your website. This would work especially well if your business involves something a particular group of people feel passionate about; that could be anything from Italian food, fashion and photography to sport and property development. If you think there are a large number of people, either nationally or internationally, who might get some pleasure or value from talking to each other online, then there is scope for you to start something. You could start this easily enough as a forum – see the forum on startups.co.uk to see the sort of thing I mean.

Another great thing to do is to get involved in existing, substantial online communities, such as Facebook or MySpace. They already have literally millions of people, and by taking an active role in your specialist area, you could develop a following and increase brand awareness. That's very much the sort of thing I did with my computer games business. There is no doubt that talking in depth to customers online turned my business from being so-so to being highly successful.

MAKING MONEY DIRECTLY FROM THE WEB

Of course much of this activity is aimed at getting your business to make money. You can do this most directly simply by selling your goods or services on your website. I am sure you will be surprised by just how much business you will do this way, even without making much effort. As people use the web all around the world, you will start selling to people online that simply couldn't come to visit you in your area. If your other website activity works and drives the right sort of people to your site, then it's a great idea to make it possible for them to buy while you have their interest.

Your web developer should be able to talk to you about the latest ways to accept payment online – the choices are growing at the moment, and there is more on this in the Taking Money chapter later in this book.

There are other ways to make money from your website. The easiest way is to build some search engine advertising space into your site, or at least into some of the pages within your site. This is very easy to do, whether through Google or other search engines. Once this is set up, the search engine company adverts appear on your website, and they pay you money whenever a visitor to your site clicks on an advert. You literally get sent a payment every month. Your website developer can easily incorporate this if you would like them to. This can be a great way of funding marketing to drive more people to your site.

Alternatively you could become an affiliate partner of other websites, whereby you send some of your visitors to them, and if they buy from these other websites, you get a commission. The Amazon scheme is the best known, but there are others, which are all really easy to start. Don't expect to make huge money from these unless your site gets very large numbers of visitors, but a little money coming in regularly is still very worthwhile.

WEB 2.0 AND FUTURE DEVELOPMENTS

The web is evolving all the time. There is a lot of media coverage at the moment about 'web 2.0' which is a name people are giving to a new generation of website functions. These centre around harnessing the mass of people on the web to generate content for sites or to rate other people's content; this includes blogging and sites such as wikipedia.com, an online encyclopedia written by millions of web users. Social networking is the other big trend that forms part of web 2.0, as sites such as Facebook, Bebo, YouTube and MySpace have attracted many millions of people looking to communicate with each other over their sites. It's well worth looking at these sites to see what is happening, and then think about whether there is a sensible way for your business to get involved.

Already more and more websites offer browsers the chance to see video clips or hear audio files, whether music or speech. There is no absolute need for you to, but if you do, you could make some of these free, and put them up on other popular websites like YouTube, giving them a chance to get seen or heard by lots of potential customers.

The web will continue to change, and I am not going to even attempt to suggest what tomorrow's big trend will be. But it is worth keeping an eye on what is happening, since it is sure to threaten more established businesses while opening up new opportunities for other startups. It could even help you grow your business further.

ACTIONPOINTS

1. Use the internet for email and research
2. Set up a website for your business
3. Ideally, start writing a blog
4. Promote the website
5. Start selling from your website
6. Talk to customers and potential customers online

CHAPTER 18
How to sell

What's this all about?
- Do you need to sell?
- Before you start to sell
- Sales conversations
- Powerpoint presentations

Ultimately, however good your product or service and however good your marketing, you need to sell what you do or the business won't work. Selling scares some people. All sorts of people think they could have a go at marketing or human relations, but most people will try hard to avoid sales. I certainly did. I never thought of myself as a sales person.

Yet if you have what it takes to set up a new business, you will have what it takes to sell your product or service. Many businesses don't need a sales person at all – shops, for example, arguably don't; nor do cafés, bars, restaurants, bed and breakfasts, mail-order businesses, and more.

In fact, when you speak to your bank manager, potential staff, or potential suppliers, you're actually doing a sales job on them: selling your business to them in order to persuade them to work with you. Yet most people I know who think they have a problem 'selling' have absolutely no problem 'promoting' their business.

Sales are in many ways the most important aspect of any business. Without income, you won't have a business for very long. I used to think that a sales job wasn't all that important – and that sales people were overpaid. After all, if a product is good, it sells itself, and if it is no good, the sales people won't expect to take the blame for low sales levels. But I was very wrong. I have since seen that in all sorts of businesses sales people can, and very frequently do, make businesses with average products perform much better than they arguably 'should'. In most businesses, simply having the best product or service is not enough – important, still, but not enough on its own.

If your business is an online retailer, or an organisation like a bed and breakfast, then although you probably won't need sales people as such, you will need to deliver the same sales strengths to your potential customers. Your website needs to have plenty of 'calls to action' encouraging people to 'click here to buy'; or, for a bed and breakfast, your advertising or directory entries or website should provide very obvious reasons to book now.

No matter how much many of us dislike very direct sales approaches, they tend to work very often. The reason you get cold-called by people offering you cheap electricity or telephone services is because enough people buy from these approaches to make them keep going.

Ultimately, though, if you're not cut out to do the selling, and your business needs sales people, then you need to hire someone who is good at it. It is a critical position, so it's worth spending time getting it right from an early stage.

BEFORE YOU START SELLING

You should start by doing your homework, and build up a list of potential customers. This list should consist of the types of people or businesses that you think should buy from your business. Very often buying a list of names that meet the criteria you set will be a good place to start. There are lots of list brokers around who literally just sell lists of names for businesses. You should be able to find some suitable ones easily by searching on the internet.

Once you have a list of target customers, think again about why they will want to buy from your business. You know why you want them to buy from you, of course, but that is not the same thing at all. When you first decided to set up the business you will have had lots of reasons why people ought to buy from you. Now it's time to go back to that list and set out the main reasons why your target customers ought to buy from you now. Very often you will find that things have moved on slightly by this stage, so the reasons might have changed.

The sales story/pitch

You should work on your main pitch. First, think about it; write down all the major points, both those that explain what you do and the points which set you apart from the competition. Whittle the good points down to the best three (or maximum four) and then try to work out the most sensible way to tell this story. Once you've got that, write it out, and then practise telling it to friends or family – try a few people who know a little bit about the sector if they don't need to be experts. They should be able to point out which bits are clear and which bits you might need to make clearer, as well as giving you a few tips on your delivery. Ask them to be honest! Far better that you hear any negative points from a friend than lose business because they were too kind to tell you where you could have improved.

When you're ready to start contacting people, I always like to speak to someone, if at all possible. You get interaction that is simply not possible with a letter. If you send an email and don't get a reply it's hard to know how to interpret that, whereas if you speak to someone you can at least learn more, even if they're not interested.

The first hurdle is trying to get through to the right person. There's usually a 'gatekeeper' in between you and the person who makes the decision to buy whatever your business is selling. This will vary a little bit from customer to customer, so the best thing to do is to ask whoever answers the phone. When I make a cold call, I make a point of being friendly and polite, and always tell the receptionist that I just have a few questions, and really won't take very much time. Gatekeepers are trained to not put 'sales people' through, so you don't want to come across overtly as a sales person. If you befriend the gatekeeper, you can usually get through after a few calls.

HOW TO SUCCEED AT SALES CONVERSATIONS

This advice is primarily for people selling by phone or at specific sales meetings. These might be at an exhibition or at a specially set meeting. Much of this, though, applies equally well to a retail situation.

✓ PREPARE WELL

Firstly, this will make you feel better as you go into the conversation. Secondly, it will impress whoever you're speaking to. Preparation has two elements: preparation of your own sales story, and preparation about the potential customer. Very frequently if you can demonstrate that you understand your potential customer's needs and can provide them with a product or service which will work well given those needs, the customer will be impressed and you stand a good chance of getting the business.

✓ TAKE A DEEP BREATH, AND SMILE

Ok, not like an idiot, of course, but enough to set a friendly tone. When you smile, it physically releases endorphins into your bloodstream which make you feel better – which will help you set off on a positive note. And everyone prefers to deal with happy rather than grumpy or desperate people, so it will help relax your target customer, too.

✓ LOOK PEOPLE IN THE EYE

Not continuously, but much of the time. It makes an enormous difference to how well the person you are talking to feels – they will feel more important, more listened to if you do this, which makes them enjoy the conversation more. Of course this isn't practical on a sales phone call, but use positive, encouraging noises/comments while the other person is speaking to let them know that you are listening and taking in what they are saying.

✓ SPEAK SLOWLY AND CALMLY

This is the point I need to work hard on. When I'm tired or under pressure, my natural weakness is to speak very quickly. It's subconscious, but I've been told about it enough times now that I make a point of telling myself to slow down. And it really does make a difference. For a start, whoever you are speaking to has a better chance of understanding what you're saying. You will come across as being far more relaxed and confident. And a little confidence is attractive – buyers want to think that they're getting something that's in demand, not that you're desperate and nobody else is buying anything from you.

✓ BE ENTHUSIASTIC

You are passionate about your business, and that is very compelling. Try to get this across in a measured, planned way rather than with too much aggressive energy. Often people who are running new businesses are so enthusiastic about it that they rush through their pitch, focusing on a few details, without properly explaining what it is that they do.

✓ WATCH THE PERSON YOU'RE TALKING TO

It's critical to see what they're thinking of you (or listen hard if you're on the phone); if they're bored or angry, adjust what you were going to say. I have been in a meeting

CASE STUDY
POWERPOINT PRESENTATIONS

Some people don't mind it, some hate it. Should you create a powerpoint slide presentation? It depends on the situation and how much time it takes. I would advise against it initially unless you think it will really add something. The danger is that it takes ages to set the laptop up, and that is your valuable time with a potential client. Nobody looks good fiddling about waiting for the laptop to start working – and most people get flustered if something doesn't work. It's also too easy to use powerpoint too much, so that you're really dependent on it. If you do use it, keep the number of slides to no more than six or eight, and don't have more than three points on any slide. Try not to put all the information you want to get across on a slide – you want people to be listening to you, not reading. If you have a copy of the presentation printed out, I suggest not giving it to them until the end of the meeting, for the same reason.

Powerpoint is a great tool, though, and it is easy for your business to look really professional when using it. In the early days of Crimson we used powerpoint quite a bit; we often created customised presentations for potential customers, and used a designer we nicknamed 'cheap as chips' who charged us £100 to create a really impressive set of slide templates. There are plenty of freelance people who can do this; if you do decide to use powerpoint, I think it's well worth getting a decent slide template put together.

where the sales person lost a really important client pitch by continuing with his pitch while the potential customer was very obviously getting more and more angry. I have seen sales people witter on through every slide of their presentation, not noticing the fact that the potential client is bored stiff. If you are losing the customer's interest, stop what you were doing and try a different approach.

✓ SAY YOU DON'T KNOW
Don't be frightened of admitting you don't know something; you can always say that you'll need to look into it and can come back to them later. This gives you a reason to get back in touch – and the more conversations you have, the more likely it is that you will seal a deal.

✓ CLOSING

Remember to be clear before you end the conversation what the next steps are, and ask for the business. Be relaxed and confident, but make a point of asking. If the reply is 'I'm not sure yet' or something similar, then follow up with 'I understand; what can I do to make sure I get the business/order?' or, 'what factors will you be assessing this decision on?'

Depending on how the conversation has gone, it can be a good idea to ask whether they have any concerns about you or your product. This gives you a chance to address any concerns head on, and is a sign of someone who is confident in themselves and their business. If someone doesn't tell you any concerns, it is harder for them to use any as a reason not to give you business.

LEARNING FROM REJECTION

If you don't get the results you want, don't be too disappointed. I've been in meetings where I knew that we hadn't won the business, or where I didn't know but it felt unlikely. It's not a great feeling. If you get a 'no', try to learn from it. Ask as much as you can about why you haven't got it, how you could improve, and whether you might stay in touch and pitch again some time in the future.

One thing to note is that people will often lie to you about the reasons they're not giving you business. Why? Usually because none of us like delivering bad news or hurting people's feelings, or because they don't want to end up in a debate with you. People often tell you a reason they think will be hard for you to argue with that won't hurt your feelings too much. It's never easy to get through these sorts of answers to find out what the real reason is, but do try. Being positive and friendly with the customer is the best route to getting at the real reason. It's also worth explaining that you're a new business, and it would really help you to understand all the reasons why you didn't win, so that you can improve your business.

Remember that there are plenty of customers, and we're all slightly different as people. So one person turning your business down doesn't necessarily mean that other people will. Expect to get turned down quite a bit – it happens to all businesses, but especially to brand new ones. When it happens, go back to the basics of why you believe in your business and you should find the passion returning. Plenty of highly successful people have gone on to become successful as a direct result of being turned down by someone as they were spurred into action to prove them wrong. Emotion is a powerful force, and I've learned to try hard to turn any negative feelings into positive ones like this.

As I write, the last Harry Potter book has just been published. It is clearly a huge success, selling many millions of copies. Yet it was rejected by plenty of publishers, and even Bloomsbury (the UK publisher which eventually signed it up) was sufficiently unsure about how it would do that they didn't pay a few thousand pounds more for worldwide rights. Instead, an American publisher bought the rights. Dyson's vacuum cleaner, The Beatles and Post-it notes are just three other famous successes that were rejected countless times. It just proves how easy it is for good products to get rejected. Being turned down, even lots of times, doesn't mean that your business isn't good enough.

Ultimately, if your product or service is delivering what some customers want, in the right way and at the right price, providing you get your message across to those customers, you will succeed. Keep trying, adjusting the way you present your message if you need to.

MAKING YOUR FIRST SALE

It's hardest to get the very first customers. Once you have a few, you can use them as references and gather testimonials; you can talk about them, and you will be more confident naturally since you know people out there have bought into your ideas. Getting the first few customers is therefore really important. It might be worth trying some very special deals, just to get started. If you're a consultant, or selling very expensive products, sometimes doing something at cost or even free can be worthwhile, or maybe try a 'pay me what you think it's worth' basis. This gives potential customers a great reason to use you, even though they will be taking a risk by using a brand new business.

ACTIONPOINTS

1. Decide who will do the selling
2. Draw up a target customer list
3. Prepare for any conversations
4. Make the phone calls
5. Close the sale if you can
6. Analyse the response, and adjust as needed

CHAPTER 19
Taking money

What's this all about?
- Invoices and credit control
- Issues to consider when handling cash
- Credit card payments
- Online payment systems
- New payment systems

G etting paid by customers feels fantastic. This could be in various ways, though, and you'll need to decide on your preferred method of payment. The main ones are obvious: cash, cheques and credit cards. You will need a business bank account for this. It is very important to set up a dedicated business account rather than trying to run your business out of your existing account, so that you keep the business distinct from your own money.

INVOICES AND CREDIT CONTROL

Almost all sales to businesses are paid for using invoices. When you make a sale, you send the customer an invoice, which is a request for payment. The invoice should have the name of the customer, the date of the delivery, the nature and quantity of what was bought, and the price. It should add VAT if appropriate, and state how and when your customer should pay you. 'Net 30 days' is a common credit term, which in practice means that customer pays you at the end of the month after the month they bought the goods. Make sure you include your bank sort code and account number on your invoice, as increasing numbers of businesses like to pay bills electronically.

Or at least, they should. The average length of time it takes to get invoices paid for the whole of the UK is just under 60 days. Some people take considerably longer than that, too. If you will invoice most of your sales, then credit control needs to become an important function at your business.

The best ways to make sure you get paid as early as possible are:

1. Send out invoices with accurate details on the day of the sale.
2. Send proof of purchase with the invoice (this might be a purchase order number or a copy of an email ordering the items).
3. Call within a week of sending the invoice to make sure that the customer's accounts department (more specifically the purchase or 'bought' ledger department) has received the invoice and got it in their system.
4. Call a week before the invoice is due to check that the customer is on track to pay it on time. This is typically when you might encounter some delays – such as someone needs to authorise it but hasn't done so yet. Try to resolve any issues promptly.
5. Then call if you haven't received it within a day or so of it being due. Ask for a specific date when you can expect the payment. Stay polite and friendly (you are likely to get paid far faster by befriending the person at the other end of the phone, who you will speak to several times each month for regular customers) but firm.
6. If the date you were given passes without the payment, then make another phone call explaining that the payment is now late and you require payment promptly in order to avoid further action.
7. If nothing happens for a week after this, send a Letter Before Action. This is a letter from you, ideally nicely printed out with very large letters saying Letter Before Action in red type, looking somewhat official. This letter should state that unless you receive payment within 10 working days of the date of the letter you will be forced to take legal action to pursue the debt. These letters are pretty effective at collecting most debt from honest businesses which have the money but were trying it on with you or just being a bit inefficient.
8. If this doesn't deliver the payment, then you are probably faced with a customer who can't pay the bill, at least easily, or simply doesn't want to. It's worth finding out

which category you think the customer is in – there's no point in spending time and money chasing a debt if the customer simply hasn't got any money to pay.

9. If you believe the customer has got the money and is just paying other people first, or being awkward, then send a solicitor's letter. There are a number of law firms specialising in debt collection who will send a letter like this for you for a pretty small sum, such as £25, and then advise on the best steps to take next. Some of these firms will also offer a no win, no fee service to recover money owed to you. You can find firms like this on startups.co.uk.

Statutory interest on late payments

A few years ago the government introduced a new law entitling anyone who is owed money that is late to statutory interest. While I applaud the government for wanting to do something to speed up payment, I don't think this is the answer. By and large, you will really antagonise a customer if you invoke this clause – and customer relationships matter far more than a few pounds of interest. You are entitled to it, though, and if you have late paying customers with whom you have no interest in prolonging a relationship, then why not use it.

Credit insurance

You can buy credit insurance which will give you typically 80% of any bad debts you incur. If you think that there is a reasonable risk of some of your customers going bust, then this could be a really good way for you to reduce your exposure. It can be expensive, and the insurers won't take on any of your customers that they view as a serious risk. But at least you then know the score, and can decide whether to take the risk of continuing to do business with them or not. A web search for credit insurance should get you enough leads to get a couple of quotes.

ACCEPTING PAYMENTS

Cash

Physical cash (notes and coins) is so easy and tempting to steal, for both staff and general thieves, that if your business handles much of it you should think carefully about how to deal with it to keep your business protected.

If your business receives a lot of notes and coins, you'll need a float so that you have change available to give to customers. Not all banks are happy to provide this, especially now that physical money is being increasingly replaced by 'plastic' and other forms of electronic money. If physical cash is important to you, make sure that you choose a bank which can give you what you need.

If your business receives very large sums of notes and coins, you could become a target for crime. As a teenager, I used to work at a petrol station my father ran, and we used to take enormous amounts of cash; because the station was open quite late, it got targeted pretty often by local criminals. This is obviously unpleasant and also expensive. One solution is to use a company to come and collect the cash from you frequently.

Another thing to watch out for if you get paid in physical cash, is counterfeit money. I used to think that this was something which was really rare except in films, but there is more around than you would think. Your bank will give you advice on how to tell whether or not notes are genuine, and you need to make sure any staff who handle money know to check. If you do receive 'funny money' then the bank or police would take it, but it is worthless, so you would effectively lose that money.

Cheques

Cheques used to be far more common than they are today; debit cards have really taken their place. Be careful accepting cheques today, since most people no longer have cheque guarantee cards. Without a cheque guarantee card, there is a risk that the cheque will bounce. It's a good idea, therefore, to wait until a cheque has cleared before you hand over any goods or service if you're running a shop. Most petrol stations and restaurants won't accept cheques these days.

Debit and credit cards

Of course debit and credit cards are the most common way to pay for most things in shops now. You will need to set up a merchant services account for your business if you want your customers to pay you using a card. The way these services work is that your business pays a fee, usually a percentage for a credit card, and a fixed sum for a debit card; the merchant services company will then pay the money you put through its machine into your bank account a few days later, after deducting its charges.

The main banks have their own companies offering this service, but you should shop around – rates do vary considerably. It might be worth joining a trade organisation which offers cheaper rates for merchant services; the Forum of Private Business, for example, has a deal offering its members cheaper access to credit cards. You should expect the merchant services company to be quite wary before they give you an account. They are at risk if a business puts through false transactions, so their concern is justified. They are especially wary of mail order and internet firms; sometimes they might ask you to put up a deposit to balance their risk.

Accepting payment online

Taking payment over the internet is very widespread these days. There are a number of major payment services you can use, such as PayPal, owned by eBay and widely used, or WorldPay, owned by the Royal Bank of Scotland. Google and Amazon have both recently launched services for other websites to charge using their systems – and both are currently offering highly attractive terms to encourage businesses to start using them.

It is important to use a well-known payment service to convince online customers that they can trust paying you online. The charges for these online payment services are usually a little higher than for normal credit card merchant services.

Electronic bank transfers

Increasingly businesses are using direct electronic payments; the two UK systems are CHAPS and BACS. The first is a same day transfer, which costs the sender a fee; the second takes three working days, but is usually free to senders. You will need to check your bank account regularly if you expect customers to pay you electronically; most banks have internet facilities now which you can use to check your account, which is pretty much essential if you are using a lot of electronic transfers in or out.

New payment systems coming soon

There are more and more new forms of electronic payment coming up. Some businesses already charge money to mobile phone accounts. If you think you'd like to be able to get people to pay your business this way, contact one of the larger mobile phone operators to find out how this works.

There is also at least one new system which works a little like the Oyster cards used to pay for transport in London. These are plastic cards which customers pass in front of a 'reader' and the money is immediately deducted from the customer's account – no need for either a signature or PIN. These are expected to be widely used to pay for small items such as papers and magazines within a few years. Your credit card merchant services supplier will offer this service.

ACTIONPOINTS

1. Send out accurate invoices promptly
2. Give priority to firm but polite credit control
3. Take legal action early if you need to
4. Set up policies to handle cash carefully
5. Set up credit card merchant facility
6. Set up separate online credit card receipts service
7. If relevant, keep an eye on future developments

03

SECTION THREE
Once You've Started

CHAPTER 20
Cash is king

What's this all about?
- Why money is key
- How to hang on to your cash early on
- Track cash flow
- How to improve cash flow in a hurry

(?)

It is such a cliché, I know, but one of the biggest things to grasp about running your own business is just how much money matters. You might make a loss, but as long as you have enough in the bank to pay your bills, you will be able to survive. For most new businesses, surviving is what it is about initially, while you try and get things up and running properly.

There are plenty of things you can do to keep more money in your own bank account for longer. Some of these might cost you more in the long run, but in the short run they will save you cash. Once your business is established and profitable, you can easily switch to cheaper long-term options.

Choose a business which fits your available funds

Some businesses don't need you to buy any stock at all. Others need you to buy stock six months in advance. Obviously, once you have started a business it can be very hard to change this – though there may be ways to add a new activity which helps this. Fashion clothing shops are pretty bad from this point of view: you need to buy the stock long in advance, and pay for it before you have had a chance to sell much of it. Coffee shops, on the other hand, are fantastic: if you buy your supplies on credit, you will have the money from sales before you need to pay your suppliers (assuming the business generates some sales).

Don't spend money you don't really, really need to spend

It is amazing how little you really need to set up a business. I have seen founders of a new business convince themselves that they really need to spend £100,000 fitting out their new premises, before they have sold a thing, while someone else achieves a different look, and opens the same business for less than £20,000. When you start, challenge yourself about everything – do you really need to spend it, or not. Don't make the mistake of not spending anything, just make sure you only spend on things that are really important. Remember – once the money has been spent, it's gone forever.

Buy second hand, especially furniture

Sometimes it can make sense to buy new equipment and furniture; but often you can get great deals on second hand stuff which will do you just fine. There are a number of business equipment auctions; there are always businesses ceasing trading, so sometimes you can get a whole load of pretty new kit for much less than if you bought all new equipment. If you need equipment, such as catering or IT appliances, make sure you get a maintenance agreement from someone who will fix it if it goes wrong.

Don't buy new equipment – lease it

If you decide you really do need to buy something new, then see if you can lease it. This will spread the cost over a few years, normally three to five. You will pay more over the long term, but it will significantly reduce the amount of money you need to set the business up, which is most important for the early stages. Banks have leasing companies which might help, but many equipment sellers will also help you find a leasing company that is comfortable leasing their particular type of equipment.

Negotiate long credit terms with suppliers

Sometimes you might be able to do a really good deal with a key supplier. Petrol companies and brewers, for example, have been known to pay a new business a lump sum when they start, in return for you agreeing to buy from them for a period of time, say five years. It can be a great way of funding your new business, so long as you are happy to buy exclusively or primarily from that supplier.

Pay with a credit card

Typically when you buy something from a supplier, they will expect you to pay them within 30 days; this usually means 'the end of the month after the month you bought the supplies'. If you then pay the bill by credit card, you could have another 45 days of free credit before that money actually needs to leave your bank account. So you effectively don't need to pay for supplies you received in early January until mid-May. Not all suppliers will be happy with you paying by credit card; some might even charge you a surcharge for doing so; but many that don't advertise it will still accept a credit card if you ask them.

Please note that this can be dangerous. If you want the extra time so that you can earn money from sales that haven't happened, and something goes wrong, you are effectively building up a larger debt. You should also be careful about wrongful trading, which is when you buy supplies knowing that you might not be able to pay for them – it's against the law. There are plenty of stories of successful entrepreneurs who have done this and got away with it; there are plenty more stories you tend not to hear about, where the founder didn't get away with it. Be careful.

Don't take on staff – use freelance people or agencies

Hiring staff can be really expensive. You need to recruit them, give them a contract (which might cost you money in legal fees early on), pay for their equipment, and so on. You then need to pay national insurance on top of their wages. If things don't work out, you might need to pay the person to terminate their employment, then pay again to hire someone new. Often you might be able to find a freelance person to do the work you need – they will take care of their own national insurance, buy their own equipment, possibly work from their own office, and cost you far less in the short term. You will probably get some credit from them, too, so you don't need to pay them quite as quickly as you would with an employee. If you're not sure whether there are freelance or temporary staff available for your business, ask around.

Don't pay yourself a salary to start with

This is only useful if your business is set up as a limited company. If you pay yourself as an employee, you will pay standard PAYE tax, and both employee and employer national insurance. So, for every £1 you need to live, your company will end up paying at least £1.40. Instead, don't put money into your company to pay your salary; just hang on to what you really need to live on, and avoid 'earning' it at all (which means you don't need to pay any tax or national insurance). At some stage, your business will need to be able to pay you properly, if it is to succeed, but in the short term, paying yourself as an employee simply sends some of your precious starting funds straight into the government's pocket.

Think about what you really need to spend to live; I know one person who used to earn £100,000 a year before he started his own business. The business took longer to get off the ground than expected, and in the end this person cut back on personal spending, and found he was able to live on just £6,000 a year, releasing money to help get the business into profitability. Rumour has it that Peter Jones saved money on living costs by sleeping in his office in the early days – he wouldn't have been the first.

Request part payment in advance

If your business is supplying larger companies, you might well be able to get part of the payment in advance. Just put 25% or even 50% payment in advance as part of your standard terms and conditions of sale. Many businesses you deal with will simply accept that, and pass the request for payment to their accounts department. At large businesses, the people you are selling to probably won't think about cash flow at all, so what matters to you won't matter to them. When selling to smaller businesses you might get away with this, too – especially if you explain that you are new and need to work this way in the early days. With smaller customers this also helps reduce your risk if the customer goes bust.

Invoice as early as you possibly can

When I set up my first business, at times I was doing just about everything. The task I often left till the end of the month was sending out sales invoices. This was a terrible thing to do: it gave customers a reason to pay me later than the due date. So if you sell to customers on credit, make sure you send out your sales invoices as fast as possible – ideally the same day you make a sale.

Chase your debtors

If you are owed money by customers, unless you make managing this a priority, it can get out of hand. Lots of businesses out there are trying to improve their own cash flows, and therefore don't pay their bills unless they get chased, and in some instances, chased hard. I know of one company which has a policy of not paying its suppliers until it receives a court order to do so! Try to look at who owes you money at the start of every single day. That way it shouldn't take very long, but you will know who has paid you and who hasn't. Phone people regularly, being friendly and polite rather than aggressive, but just make sure they know that you are watching them and are anxious to get your money. It's a good idea to phone them to check that they have received your invoice, then again a week later to check that there are no queries with it. Then you can ask when to expect payment, and make a point of ringing again a few days before the date given to make sure that they are still on track to pay you on the agreed date. This sort of friendly, regular contact should see you getting paid as on time as your industry normally accepts.

It is always hard to know just when to get tough with people that haven't paid you. On the one hand you don't want to upset a customer by being too pushy over an invoice that is one day overdue, on the other you don't want to get taken for a ride. Many businesses give lower priority to paying suppliers which they can do without if they need to – often small new businesses won't be 'essential' to them, and so can suffer. A friend of mine who was owed money 120 days' late by a major customer went in to see their finance director, and laid photos of his children on the table during a meeting, saying 'unless you pay my bills faster, these children won't be able to eat'. He got his money that day.

Delay payments to suppliers

Basically, do to your suppliers what you are trying hard not to let your customers do to you. It sounds tough, but it really can help. The best thing to do is to establish credit terms in the first place that are generous enough for you to be able to meet. But sometimes circumstances change and it is no longer practical to pay people on those terms. If you have developed a decent relationship with a major supplier, talk to them about your issues. Ultimately if you haven't got enough money to pay them, they need your business to be able to work through its issues until it earns enough cash to be able to pay them. Most businesses don't want to lose a customer. Try to tell the supplier that you can't make the current payment schedule, but give them a schedule that you think you can make; pay them less but often to assure them that by continuing to supply you they aren't risking a larger bad debt. With my first business I always found enough suppliers to be flexible to help me through difficult patches. But keep paying your smaller suppliers as close to on time as you can – otherwise they can tell credit ratings agencies, which would hurt your credit rating, and your ability to start using other suppliers in future.

Occasionally, you can even delay a VAT or PAYE payment. HM Revenue & Customs are generally the last people to delay payments to, since they can and will shut a business down rapidly if they don't get their money on time. But if you phone them and explain that you have a short-term issue and ask for extended terms as a one-off, they will often be helpful. But they have great records, and will know if you try to do that every month, which won't go down well.

Be careful

Cash flow problems can be a sign of growth and success, or of fundamental problems. Try hard to understand what is going on in your business, and seek advice if you are really struggling, before the business ends up bankrupt.

ACTIONPOINTS

1. Always know how much money you have in the bank
2. Always know how much you expect to pay out and receive in each week for the next few months
3. Prioritise collecting money owed to you
4. Be stingy! Always delay payments when you can
5. Talk to your accountant early if you foresee problems

CHAPTER 21

Is it working?

What's this all about?
- How are you doing?
- Are customers happy enough?
- How can you improve?
- Common issues early businesses face
- What help is available?

Many new businesses find that once they have started, some areas of what they are doing are working well, others perhaps less well. It's easier for customers to make a real decision about a product which they can actually buy than it is to say whether they might buy a theoretical product. So once you are up and running, you soon find out what real demand for your business is.

Don't get carried away on the back of great or terrible news; one swallow does not make a summer. In other words if you have a really fabulous first month, you might then experience a lull later on. This often happens if your friends and family make an effort to use your new business when it first opens; they can't keep that level of interest up for ever, so after a while, it will dwindle, and you need to replace them with customers you don't already know. Or if business is lower than you had hoped to start with, it might well pick up.

OBSERVE, CONSIDER, ADJUST

The key for all founders of newly launched businesses is to monitor progress, then to work out what is happening, and decide what to do differently, if anything. One of the clichéd 'definitions of madness' is to do the same thing tomorrow as you did yesterday but to expect different results. It may be that you need to alter your core product or service in some way, or simply adjust the way you present your message.

It's important to measure how you are actually doing, and compare this to your initial expectations. The best way to do this is to produce monthly management accounts, showing revenue and costs, and the resulting profit or loss. I don't think many startups do this, though. Realistically, you need to keep very good track of sales to know in detail what is happening, and what you expected to happen. You also need to keep a handle on costs. Excel can help you do all this pretty simply, assuming you don't have a bookkeeper doing monthly accounts for you (and for the record, if you can get that going, please, please do!).

It is not possible to predict exactly how well your new business will do, so expect to find that actual results are different to your expectations. Most founders predict that sales will be higher, sooner than it really happens. This is usually because founders have so much passion for their business, they find it hard to understand why other people don't, or at least fewer of them than expected.

This is sensible – if you didn't think there were good reasons for people to buy from your new business, you would either have changed something before opening, or not bothered, right? What matters once you have started is that you try to understand what is happening, and why.

If sales are less than you had expected, why might that be? Do your target customers know that you exist, what you offer, and how to find you? For many new businesses this is the main reason why early sales fall short of expectations – it takes longer than anticipated to get the word to the right people that you are there. If you find that people try you once but not again, that suggests that they weren't as pleased with your business as you would like them to be. Try to learn what the reasons might be; by talking to both returning customers and people you think ought to be customers but aren't. Market research businesses can do this for you, but small businesses can get most answers by doing this informally themselves.

FIND OUT WHAT YOUR CUSTOMERS REALLY THINK

Focus on your customers; if you give them what they want at a sensible price, you will keep them happy. The larger the business, the harder it is for the management to stay in close touch with customers; as a small business, this is a huge advantage for you. In fact, once your business has been launched, learning what customers really think is arguably your most important priority. If you need to make any tweaks to what you do, the sooner you learn this and implement the adjustments, the better.

By far the best way to find out how well you are doing is to talk to actual customers in depth. Find out what they think about your business; has it met their expectations? What could it do better? Does it need to do anything better, or is there simply an opportunity to improve from an already good base? How does it compare to any similar suppliers out there? What do the customers really like about your business? Do they plan to buy from you in future?

As with all feedback, you will need to interpret what they say; sometimes language can be ambiguous, so make sure you really understand what they are getting at. Then you'll need to decide what to do about any of the constructive points received. We used to get lots of suggestions for computer games; people would ask for certain things to be put in. Often, these things sounded great, but would have really upset the balance of our games, so in fact would have made the product worse. We started to tell people that, explaining why we were not proposing to implement those changes, and we found this worked really well. Our customers loved the fact that we were considering their ideas, and that we had good, valid reasons for not pursuing them; they were not being ignored.

Talking to your customers in depth is easier than ever using the internet. There are so many specialist forums and chat rooms that all you need to do is to find one which has plenty of your customers. I spent around 20 hours a week in the early years of my games business chatting to people on message boards, which pre-dated the internet, and it literally transformed my business. If you run a shop, café or similar business, it's easier for you to ask some of your customers if they wouldn't mind sparing a few minutes with you once they have bought something.

The key is to make sure you spend most time with the critical customers. They are the people who you can learn most from: they will be your most loyal customers, too, if you can turn them round by improving your business in their eyes. It's very good for your ego to talk to customers that already love you, but it won't help you progress as much as talking to the people who tried you once but don't currently plan to again.

If you can, try to get testimonials out of some customers, so you can quote them in your marketing materials. You know the sort of thing: *'I thought this was the best thing since sliced bread'* from Mrs S of Swindon. Testimonials are really powerful sales tools, giving potential customers confidence in your business.

⇁ STARTUP TIP

It's all very well to suggest talking to your customers, but what if you haven't got many, or even any? Even if you simply don't have enough, I've often found it even more useful talking to my competitors' customers than to my own. Why do they buy from your competitors? Why don't they buy from you? Ask without any pressure or emotion, and you should get excellent information. How to do this? Never miss out on an opportunity to strike up conversation with someone you don't know who you come across; this could be at a party, while you're out shopping, dropping children off at school, or wherever. Be alert, and politely ask questions. You may get the occasional strange look, but you could also transform your business.

WHEN BUSINESS IS BLEAK

I have found myself often wondering why things weren't going better. Just about every business has patches when things don't go very well. Most of the time, I have worked out, after much thinking and soul-searching, that it's because the business had managed to leave behind some of the core principles which got us into it in the first place. It is so easy to do. Once a business is up and running, all sorts of issues get in the way of us doing what we set out to do; not being able to get the right staff, marketing glitches, supplier problems, cash flow issues, all sorts. Before you know it, your focus shifts to doing what you can, rather than what you set out to achieve.

Your job, as business founder and leader, is to bring the business back on course. Go back to your business plan, and re-read it; ask yourself whether you are really delivering all the benefits you set out to offer.

Of course, sometimes business is tough for long periods of time. This might be something you can get over, or change, but it does need to be addressed.

There are two primary reasons why business might not be going well: your sales are too low, or your costs are too high. Worst of all is when you have both situations. So if business is tough, you need to look hard and honestly at whether you need to grow income or cut costs; it may be that you need to do both. You should spend some time playing with your profit and loss forecast (see Chapter Six), working out what would happen if you could push sales up by a set amount. When you have calculated what it would take to get to somewhere worthwhile, the question then is how to achieve that. Maybe you need more marketing, or more vigorous sales efforts; maybe cut out some costs which aren't really necessary. It's amazing how many costs people think they need but when their backs are against the wall they realise they can do without after all.

Business failure is often blamed on cash flow, suggesting that the underlying business was fine, but some 'unfair' cash flow situation came along and forced the business into closure. That happens extremely rarely, although there are times when it does happen.

The reality is that it often takes businesses longer to get established and profitable than their founders expect. So while they usually cease trading when their money runs out, it is inaccurate to say that cash flow caused the downfall of their business; rather, it is likely they did not develop a profitable business. Ultimately, unless a business is profitable, someone has either got to fund the losses, or the business will go bust.

Should you carry on?

The hardest part for many new businesses is to know whether to keep going or not. The danger of continuing to trade is that unless you do something differently, the results won't change, and the business will simply lose more money. At that stage, the founder is likely to be in real danger of wrongful trading, which could lead to personal bankruptcy and possibly even mean that they are disqualified from being a director of a company in future. Businesses shouldn't need to get to that stage – if you think that you are going to run out of money, go and see an accountant or lawyer, and they will help advise you on what to do next.

It might be that your business is improving steadily, but hasn't yet reached a point where you're making enough to stay open. You need to work out whether you expect to get to a worthwhile, viable business, and if so, how long it will take, and how much money you will need to get through to that point. You can then look at different ways of getting that money, to see if it is possible.

Too expensive to get to profitability

There are some businesses which could be profitable but would take so much money to get to profitability that nobody is likely to invest that much. That is really an unviable business, and the sooner everyone realises that the better. I launched a computer games magazine like that. We had fantastic customer feedback on it, but not quite enough customers. More people were buying the magazine over time, and I saw achievable, yet expensive, ways to increase this. In the end however, we worked out we couldn't have got a big enough return to justify the cost of winning the extra customers. So the magazine wasn't viable, and we shut it down.

One poor performing section holds back the rest

Sometimes businesses have some very successful elements, but these are held back by some loss-making elements. It might be possible to stop doing what is not working, which would at a stroke make the business more profitable. I bought a business out of administration once which was nicely profitable; the company running it had gone into administration because they were spending lots of money on other things which weren't working; I ended up just taking the bits which were working, and bought these for much less than they were really worth. Great for me, but try not to let that happen to you!

We're getting there… just slowly

Quite often businesses take years to build into profitability. At Crimson we know this; startups.co.uk took several years to grow into profitability, for example. We could see traffic and revenue climbing steadily, and believed that the website would reach a worthwhile place, so we carried on. But there were times when some of my management team questioned whether we should. We carried on publishing another magazine, called *PLC Director*, for about a year too long; we thought that it would reach profitability, but it didn't. That last year cost us more money; had we known it wouldn't have worked, we would have been far better stopping it sooner. Amazon didn't make profits until 2003, eight years after it opened for business. The challenge with a business which takes as long as that to break into profits is whether you can raise enough money to keep going.

The frustrating thing about business is that we just don't know what is going to happen next. Running your own business involves your judgement. I would advise you to look at as many facts as you can, and try to be as objective as you can. Then make your best decision based on those facts.

CONFIDANTS AND MENTORS

It's at times when I've been wondering what to do to try to get business out of a bad patch that I have felt most lonely and stressed out. Two things have worked really well for me: the first was talking to the people I trusted most and who knew a bit about my business; for me, that was my brother and father. In the early days of running Impressions, business wasn't going very well; I had had to lay off our office staff, and I was unhappy. My brother talked me through my concerns, and suggested I write down what I needed the business to look like for me to want to carry on with it. Then I worked backwards from there to see what kind of sales the business would need to make to fund that. I decided that I could get to that point, and set about it with renewed energy and passion. If you possibly can, find someone to talk through these issues with.

The other thing I did which worked well for me was to read business biographies. It is so easy to look at the successful businesses we see every day, and presume that they aren't facing the hardships that we are. Reading the stories behind the founding and growth of businesses shows that they've almost all been through their own hardships. Discovering how other people dealt with their challenges helped me work out how to deal with mine. Not every solution was the same, of course, but seeing people overcoming challenges often bigger than those I have faced inspired me to take another look at my issues and find a way through.

—☐ STARTUP TIP

If you don't know any entrepreneurs as friends, then seek a mentor for advice and as a sounding board. You could try posting a request for one on startups. co.uk, for example. James Hibbert, founder of bespoke tailor Dress2Kill, wrote to Sir Richard Branson, who actually replied in person and went on to offer advice and some practical help. You can't expect Sir Richard to reply to everyone, but plenty of experienced entrepreneurs are more than happy to pass on their knowledge if they get a polite request which interests them at a time when they aren't too busy. Most remember well how they felt setting out, and want to give something back to society now that they've made it. Good old networking is often the best way to find someone to help: attend trade dinners, even business angel network events. If you're young enough to meet their criteria, both the Prince's Trust and Shell Livewire offer excellent mentoring schemes.

ACTIONPOINTS

1. Track progress with monthly accounts
2. Measure results against your expectations
3. Learn from customer feedback, and adjust as necessary
4. Think what is likely to happen if business carries on as is
5. Consult an accountant if you think the business might not make it
6. Take action to cut costs or kick-start sales if needed
7. Make sure you have enough money to keep going
8. Consider finding a mentor

CHAPTER 22
Tips for success

Listen to your customers

This is by far the most important thing to do, whatever business you start. And I mean listen hard; you need to get to the crux of what your customers really want, checking you really understand what they tell you rather than just presuming you know what they mean. One person's idea of 'good service' might be extremely different from yours, for example, and what matters is your customers' definition. For as long as you give the customers what they want, in a way that they want, you should have a thriving business.

Only the paranoid survive

This means that you can never rest on your laurels, however successful you become. In fact I know a number of entrepreneurs who don't want to become too successful because they think that if they do, it will attract more competition. As owner, you need to constantly think about what might go wrong, what you might have missed, who else might be about to compete with you, and how you can keep your business on top. If this sounds tiring, that's because it is. But it works.

Work, work, work

If this is your idea of a nightmare, check you're really ready to start your own business. I confess to having occasional bad days, but by and large I love what I do and genuinely don't mind working hard. If what you're doing still excites you, you won't mind the hard work (though your family might...). You can ease off a little once you're up and running, but for as long as you're in charge, you should expect to have to lead from the front, with hard work. I really believe that leaders should arrive first and go home last most of the time.

Test, review, revise, test...

If you get your idea 75% right first time round, you're doing very well. Most entrepreneurs need to adjust what they do in the light of customer feedback. This never goes away: business is all about improving what you're already doing, to make it better. It's crucial for a startup business, though, so that enough people buy from you to make the business viable. So expect to have to adjust your product or service, or the way that you promote. Use any negative comments as a way to make your product better – find out what wasn't liked, and see how you can improve it.

Keep control over your paperwork

Businesses rapidly generate unbelievable amounts of paper: bills, receipts, ideas, plans, forms, letters, emails, faxes. In particular make very sure that you keep all your financial records in good shape – they will be far, far harder to sort out in six or nine months time. You simply have to keep on top of what money you owe to whom, and who owes you how much. Get that wrong, and it could put you out of business.

Keep your eye on cash

At an absolute minimum you should look at your bank balance every week, and predict what is going to come in over the week, and therefore what you can afford to pay out that week. Ideally do this every day; it won't change very much, so it won't take very long. Manage this well, and you're giving your business the best possible chance to survive long enough to succeed.

Share your problems

The old saying 'a problem solved is a problem halved' applies here. I have frequently been bothered by some issue or other, talked to someone about it and had them come up with a solution that hadn't occurred to me. You are inevitably going to find it hard to see the wood for the trees, as you're so fully immersed in your new business. Talking to someone who knows a bit about business (ideally the same sector) can work wonders. If you possibly can, find a mentor or non-executive director.

Stay focused

It's amazing how addictive being an entrepreneur is – and how often people want to set up all sorts of businesses once their first one starts to succeed. I have fallen into this trap too often myself. And it is a trap. Innocent drinks have a wonderful mantra:

'keep the main thing the main thing' and it really matters. The best businesses in any sector will be those most focused on that sector. Focus really works.

Back your winners

A fabulous tip told to me by Ken Williams, founder and ex CEO of Sierra, once the world's largest PC games publisher. All too often we spend our time fighting fires, working out why elements aren't working. Instead, try spending more time working out how the things that are working could be even better, and your business could really take off.

Stop activities which are losing money

This might sound obvious, but a lot of businesses continue to do things that are not profitable. If you simply stop those parts of a business which are loss-making, it automatically makes the overall business more profitable. I see far too many entrepreneurs working really hard, but not doing very well; many of these people could work far less and make more money simply by stopping certain parts of their business. Of course, sometimes you need to be willing to let a new product or service lose money while it establishes itself; the key here is to set some hard targets for minimum acceptable achievement for it to be worth your while continuing to support it. Otherwise, you could easily simply carry on with an activity which is losing money and is unlikely ever to stop.

Collect data

It is so easy not to, but the more information you can build up about your customers, the better. Feedback cards, or whatever is appropriate for your business, can build into a very nice database over time, which you can use for all sorts of reasons. Early in my first business we threw these away as we didn't have time to enter them onto a database. It was a wasted opportunity. Hang on to them, and use the data. It could save you money on marketing, enable you to take swift advantage of sale opportunities cheaply, and keep in touch with customer opinion.

Keep the faith

There will be times when you think it's all going wrong, and life will be about as bleak as you can imagine. I still vividly remember staying awake at night wondering how I would ever pay back the £500,000 I owed in my first business, and what my life would be like if I couldn't. It's negative, and, especially at night, it's easy to get into depressing thoughts. Try to go back to basics: why did you get into the business you started? Has anything changed since which alters the fundamental principle? Probably not. Use that thought to reignite your passion, and to work through the issues to find a solution. If the business is viable, there will be a solution to be found.

Bounce back

There may well be times when you get some negative feedback from somewhere, whether a potential customer, supplier or maybe a bank manager. You may well feel some anger about that – good. Channel this energy into proving that person wrong. You can succeed if you really want to and put your heart and soul into it. Imagine how satisfying it will then be to know that you have succeeded where this person said you wouldn't.

Have fun

If you ever stop enjoying it, for more than a day, stop and ask yourself why. Your business will be a large enough chunk of your life that if you're not really enjoying it, you'll become miserable and that will really harm your chances of success. You should love doing what you're doing – just remember to stop every once in a while, and remind yourself that you're in charge, running your own business. Enjoy it.

Less is more

As a principle, I love this. It applies to so much of business. Take marketing messages: the simpler the message, the easier it is to get across to potential customers. Yet it is all too easy for us to get carried away with all the ways in which our product or service is better than the rest that we turn what might have been a strong, simple message into something weaker, which is less easy to understand and remember.

The principle also applies to overall strategy. I have always sought low volume, high margin businesses because I think they're simply more forgiving and more pleasant. The 'pile 'em high, sell 'em cheap' concept certainly works in some situations, but it can mean your business needs to work very hard to be viable. If your profit margins are low and something goes wrong, you need to sell an awful lot more to make up for the mistake.

There's an old cliché you are likely to hear quite often once you've started your own business: 'turnover is vanity, profit is sanity'. Focus on profitability rather than size, and you should thrive; businesses which are more focused on size than on profitability often run into problems.

CHAPTER 23
What not to do

Ignore trends

It's normal when starting a business to base your expectations on what happened in a market 'yesterday'. You don't have very much choice; since you can't know what is happening 'today' until it has happened, let alone what might happen tomorrow. But increasingly, industries are changing more quickly, driven by the internet, mobile technology and the very rapid pace of growth in countries like India and China.

The danger is that you will create a great business which may have succeeded really well last year, but now that the market has moved on, your business isn't going to succeed.

I feel strongly about this because that is precisely what I did at Crimson. What's even more frustrating is that when I set Crimson up, I knew about the importance of these trends, and predicted them correctly; what I got wrong was just how fast the change would happen. The result was that we lost a lot of money on some magazines.

Assume the competition will ignore you

It's very frustrating, actually. You can have a fantastic idea about how to improve a product, set up a business which does really well… and then the competitors get wind of this, adapt to offer the extra ideas that you thought of… and in a stroke, remove your unique selling points. This happens all the time. I've even heard entrepreneurs saying 'it's not fair', just as a child might. And you know what? They're right; it isn't 'fair'. But it often is legal, and could make a huge difference to your business. So before you launch, think about what those competitors might do, and how your new business would cope with their reaction.

Get defensive about customer complaints

I've done this, and I've seen so many other people do it. Try not to! It's so easy to feel defensive about the business you have created. Of course you're proud of your 'baby'; you're probably also pretty reliant on customers liking it, so you don't want there to be anything wrong with it. Never get angry with a customer; always be polite, thank them for their comments and apologise if they're unhappy. Not necessarily because you agree, but because it is good for business. The best way to deal with an angry customer is to apologise and smile, which deflates their anger; it's almost impossible to stay angry with someone who's being kind and agreeing with you. You can decide whether or not to take on board the customer comment in your own time.

Rely on achieving your sales forecast

Lots of new magazines never publish a fourth edition. This is because their founders relied on the cash they would make from selling copies of their first or second edition to pay for the fourth edition to be written and printed. If sales are less than expected, there is no money to pay for the fourth edition. Founders of new businesses are almost all over-optimistic about sales. I know one founder who continues to tell me how conservative his sales forecasts are – yet he hasn't hit any of his sales targets in the last five years. As you believe your products are great, it is much harder for you to understand why people might not buy from you. Forecast as conservatively as you can, but be prepared not to hit those sales – and have a contingency plan for what to do if you don't.

Spend all your money on an initial advertising campaign

This sounds nuts, I'm sure. Surely nobody would really do this? Yet I invested in a business which did precisely this – and then went bust when the marketing campaign didn't work. Test your plans, and focus on what works.

Get distracted by other opportunities

This is certainly my single biggest flaw. I know it, and it's still there. Crimson would have been far more successful far sooner had I focused properly on our core business early on. The problem with many entrepreneurs, including me, is that when we have an idea that we like, we want to pursue it immediately, in case someone else does so first. If we pursue some of those new opportunities before our first business is properly set up and succeeding, the danger is that the first business might never achieve its potential. Focus on your core business, and you will reap the rewards.

Take on lavish premises

It's very easy to convince yourself that your business needs fancy or large premises from the start, to cope with the growth you're going to achieve. Yes, it will be more expensive in the long run to move several times; but keep your premises to an absolute minimum in the early days. Premises costs are usually a high chunk of a business's overall costs, and it's often hard and expensive to get out of any long-term commitments. Think small at first, then grow gradually. I know one ambitious business which grew its sales very well for 10 years running, but the founder said they were always one year away from profitability. Why? Because he managed to keep growing his costs, including premises, before the revenues had grown, so he would be able to cope when the business grew. The business lost money every one of those years.

Buy a flash company car

I'm sure we've all seen it; someone starts up a new business, starts feeling very proud of themselves, and goes out and spends money on a flashy new car. It's bad use of money until the business is profitable, and if you need to sell it in a hurry, or try to get out of a lease, it'll cost lots. Get your pride from building the business, then buy the car, if you want to, when you've made the money from profits.

Over to you

Y ou're probably reading this either while thinking about starting or having recently started your own business for the first time. Over the last 23 chapters I've talked about all the major elements of starting a business. But now, you're on your own.

It's up to you to decide what will work best for your business. Only you know the potential of your business, and the extent of your ambition. It is only you who can therefore take what I have said in this book and interpret it appropriately for your new venture. You should feel free to decide that some of what I have suggested won't work for you, or to add things that will matter to your business. And you are sure to need more information on some of the issues – you can literally choose from hundreds (or more) books which cover every one of the chapters in this book.

The successful entrepreneur will be comfortable taking decisions. You know your business and resources well enough to be able to weigh up when you need more help, and when you'll be able to get by.

If you haven't seen it already, I strongly recommend reading another book I publish and edited: *How They Started*. It's a book telling the story of 30 people who had ideas for new businesses, how they started those businesses and went on to build highly successful companies. You will learn as much from their experiences as you will from this book.

Jack Welch was the chief executive of one of the world's largest companies, General Electric (GE). He turned a large, strong company into a truly great one. His policy was only to be in business sectors where GE could be number one or two in market share, on the basis that the top two companies in a market will make the lion's share of the profits – and that the cost of being in businesses which were never likely to get there were substantial, in terms of loss of focus from the main opportunities.

Most of the mistakes I have made in all my significant businesses were to do with my losing focus on the business. Some of the things I tried which didn't work might well have worked had we focused more on them – but we were trying to do too much, and couldn't focus on all of it.

Seth Godin is an American business guru with a large and passionate following. On the subject of focus, he is clear: get out of things fast if you aren't going to get to somewhere worthwhile, which probably means being first or second in your market (having clearly defined the size of your market). He is equally clear about the need to keep going when it gets tough, to reach the point where things do become worthwhile. I can't tell you how tough it feels when you've been losing money for several years; when you're passionate about what you're doing, and convinced that you're doing most things well, and better than your competitors, but still aren't breaking through. It is awful, and any sane person will start to question whether they will ever get there. Very often, though, that's when you're closest to breaking through – yet many people will give up around then. Seth Godin says in his recent book *The Dip* that the vast majority of people enter a market but don't see it through; he's right. Get out early, or (if you're sure the business is viable) stay in to the end and make sure you win.

Be clear to define your market. When I say you need to be the first or second in a sector, that doesn't necessarily mean in the whole world. If you're setting up a fish and chip shop, you don't need to be the first or second best fish and chip shop in the country – but you do need to be the first or second best in the local area. You might even take the view that you need to be the first or second best fast food outlet in the area. You need to define the market you want to be best in.

It would be unwise of me to set out to be the best publisher of business books in the world, starting from our modest base in London. So I have defined our objectives clearly as to become the best publisher of small business books in the UK (I hope to add other countries to that in due course). When you achieve your goal of being the best or second best in your defined market, you and your team will feel enormous pride, and you will start to be able to make more profits as a result of being in that strong position.

Setting up and running a business is a journey. A long journey. Enjoy the ride!

Reference

Glossary

Administration

Courts can appoint an administrator to run a business which is having cash flow difficulties; these businesses are then 'in administration'. You can't sue a business in administration for any money it owed which was incurred before the administration began, in order to give the ailing business a chance to get back on its feet and trade through its difficulties.

AIM

'AIM' is the Alternative Investment Market, which is a part of the London Stock Exchange. It is a stock market for younger businesses, helping them raise money to grow, and has been a tremendous success. Lots of ambitious young businesses set a goal of floating on AIM.

Business angel

A 'business angel' is a private individual who invests his or her own money, and usually also his or her time, in private companies.

Capital cost

This is the cost of an item which will last for more than one year. The cost will be spread over several years in a business's accounts, but the business will usually need to pay the full cost to start with.

Company seal

This is a tool which indents a company's unique name and number onto paper. Every company needs one to be able to complete certain corporate documents.

Credit

When someone buys 'on credit' it means that they buy today but pay in the future. The business selling the goods or service issue the customer with an invoice stating how long the customer is being given to pay (the credit terms).

Credit control

'Credit control' is the process of collecting money owed to a business by its customers. This process involves sending statements to customers detailing what invoices are due for payment when, and usually entails phoning to remind customers that money is due and applying gentle, polite encouragement to pay.

Debenture

A 'debenture' is a formal legal acknowledgement of a debt or loan, in writing. This is normally set up in relation to an asset, usually a property, or over all assets within a business. Debentures over property are filed at the Land Registry where anyone interested can search them, and property cannot normally be sold while the debenture is still in place. Banks almost always want this security when they lend businesses money.

Dividends

A 'dividend' is a payment a company makes to its shareholders. Companies are only allowed to pay dividends out of profits they have made. Shareholders need to approve the payment of a dividend in advance at a shareholders' meeting. Shareholders need to pay income tax on dividend income they receive and companies need to deduct basic rate income tax from the dividends they pay to shareholders.

Equity

'Equity' represents the value to owners in a business (which is calculated as the value of all assets less all debts). 'Equity investors' will either own shares in a company or be a partner in a partnership. The equity owner will be entitled to a share of any profits. The same word is used in describing ways a business can raise money. Businesses can raise debt, which they need to pay back, or equity, which doesn't need to be paid back.

Factoring

'Factoring' is a way for businesses that are owed money by customers to borrow money. A specialist company called a 'factor' lends the business that sells on credit, a proportion of the value of each invoice as soon as the invoice is issued; the buyer then pays the factor the entire value of the invoice directly, after which the factor pays the balance to the seller (minus a factoring fee and an interest charge). Legally the factor buys the debt from the seller.

Franchise

A franchise is a right to operate a particular type and brand of business in a defined area.

Goodwill

This is the value of a business's reputation; it is usually calculated as the value of a business over and above any net assets in that business. It is effectively the amount someone is willing to pay at any given time over and above the net assets, owned by the company in return for all the future profits the business is expected to make.

Gross profit

The 'gross profit' is what is left after deducting the cost of producing something a business has sold from the income it has earned. So a restaurant would deduct the cost of buying food and drink and staff wages from its income from customers to work out its the gross profit.

Invoice

An 'invoice' is a document setting out the terms of a sale. This document will contain the date, quantity and value sold, the name and address of both customer and supplier, and details of any credit terms. It is often useful to have details of the bank account that the money is to be paid into on the invoice. If a business is VAT registered, its VAT number and any VAT due should be included on the invoice.

Profit margin

This is the proportion of sales revenue which is profit. Both gross profit margins and net profit margins are used a lot in business. Profit margins are usually expressed as a percentage.

Net profit

'Net profit' is a common term which usually means 'profit after tax'. Occasionally people use it to mean 'profit before tax', so be careful and clarify their meaning.

New share capital

This is money which comes into a company in return for shares in that company. Unlike debt, the company never needs to pay the money back, but instead gives the shareholder ownership of a proportion of the company.

Overheads

These are costs that are usually fixed, regardless of the level of sales a business makes. For example, a rent on a property is likely to be a substantial overhead.

Over-trading

When a business is 'over-trading', it is trading at a larger size than it can sensibly afford. This is because businesses need money to trade (called 'working capital'), and when a business is growing it will probably need more working capital. The danger of not having more money is that the business runs out of cash, even if it is otherwise successful.

USP

'USP' stands for Unique Selling Point. A business's USP is the reason why a customer might buy from this business as opposed to a competitor.

Venture capital

'Venture capital' is money that is invested by specialised funds in risky companies to help them grow. The funds are managed by venture capitalists.

Virtual business

A 'virtual business' is one that operates without dedicated premises or staff.

Wrongful trading

'Wrongful trading' occurs when a business continues to operate once it knows that it will be unlikely to pay all its bills.

Sources of startup funding

Regional venture capital funds

NAME	WEBSITE
The Capital Fund	www.thecapitalfund.co.uk
South East Growth Fund	www.segrowthfund.co.uk
East of England Fund	www.createpartners.com
South West Regional Venture Capital Fund	www.southwestventuresfund.co.uk
Advantage Growth Fund	www.midven.com
East Midlands Regional Venture Capital Fund	www.catapult-vm.co.uk
Yorkshire and Humber Fund	www.yfmventurefinance.co.uk
Capital North East	www.nel-capital.co.uk
North West Fund	www.nwef.co.uk

Sources of business angel funding

NAME	WEBSITE
Advantage Business Angels	www.advantagebusinessangels.com
Beer & Partners	www.beerandpartners.com
British Business Angel Association	www.bbaa.org.uk
Envestors	www.envestors.co.uk
Equus Capital	www.equuscapital.co.uk
Great Eastern Investment Forum	www.geif.co.uk
Hotbed	www.hotbed.uk.com

NAME	WEBSITE
London Business Angels	www.lbangels.co.uk
North West Business Angels	www.nwbusinessangels.co.uk
Oxfordshire Investment Opportunity (technology companies only)	www.oion.co.uk
Pi Capital	www.picapital.co.uk
SWAIN	www.swain.org.uk
Yorkshire Association of Business Angels	www.yaba.org.uk
Xenos	www.xenos.co.uk

NB Note that some only cover certain areas of the UK.

Other sources of help

I launched startups.co.uk in January 2000 with the aim of making good answers to every question anyone starting or running a business might have available 24/7.

It was an ambitious goal, and while we don't answer every question you might have at the site yet, we should answer most common questions. The site is full of information about how to get your business up and running, and has links to other useful sites, too. But more than that, it has loads of stories of how other people started their businesses—both famous, successful entrepreneurs, and ordinary people setting up ordinary businesses. It's free to use and you don't need to register—we make our money from advertising.

The site also has a really lively community of entrepreneurs; you can ask questions of them and you'll get all sorts of answers back, which could really help. It is also a good place to "talk" to other entrepreneurs, which can be really useful when you're facing tough times in your own business.

I know it's a bold thing to say, but I really do think it is by far the best independent site for anyone setting up a business in the UK. It has more information, and I believe more accurate and better-written information than any other site I know. Try it for yourself, and please let me know how you think we can improve it—we have lots of ideas, but I'm sure some of you will have some suggestions we haven't thought of, and I'd love to hear them.

There are two other websites I respect which you might find useful:

www.businesslink.gov.uk
This is a government-funded website, and has some really clear, helpful information and guides on it.

www.chamberonline.co.uk
This is the British Chambers of Commerce website; it is particularly helpful if you are going to trade internationally, or if you want to learn more about the Chambers of Commerce in your area.

For years, startups has also run an annual Awards competition, to celebrate and get public recognition for the best new businesses of various types. To enter your business needs to be less than three years old, and you could win a prize; best of all, though, you would get tremendous publicity for your business which could help drive it further forward. You can see details about it on its own website: www.startupsawards.co.uk.

This year we have started a series of free seminars called Startups Live. We get two successful entrepreneurs to talk about how they got started, and we have a specialist talking about a subject like how to raise money, or how to market your business. The best bit, though, is that it's a really interactive session where you can ask the speakers loads of questions to make sure you get the answers you want. We run these all round the country, and I'd love to see you at one. More details are on its website: www.startupslive.co.uk.

Other Crimson Sites

In addition to startups.co.uk, my company Crimson also publishes two other small business sites, with slightly different goals.

www.mybusiness.co.uk
Mybusiness.co.uk is designed to help all those people who are running their own business already; it has much of the same information as is on startups, but a bit more about how to run something which is already established, and obviously less about the process of getting started. We set it up because we found that many once a business was set up, its founders didn't think of themselves as being startups any more, and so didn't think the startups website was for them.

www.growingbusiness.co.uk
Growing business.co.uk is designed specially for businesses which want to grow to a reasonable size fast. It assumes businesses are already started, and focuses on how to grow rapidly—talking about how to raise growth capital, deal with the different employment issues which often crop up, what sort of IT needs growing businesses tend to have, and of course, how to make the growth happen. Again, it has lots of articles explaining growth topics, and plenty of stories of how other people have grown their businesses.

Growing Business also publishes a monthly magazine, which you can buy in larger branches of WH Smith, or you can subscribe to online.

We put on a number of different events for Growing Business, too—from awards to seminars and conferences aimed to help you learn how to grow your business, to small lunches focussed on topics like floating on AIM or buying other companies.

My Story

When I started my first business I was training to be an accountant, and, along with several friends, decided to set up a computer games publishing business. It was 1988 and the computer games industry was in its infancy, but growing rapidly – a really good time to start a business. When we started, it was just a hobby, none of us had to take the risk of giving up our jobs, or had any idea that we would go on to achieve what we did.

I had reviewed some computer games for consumer magazines before university and during summer vacations. Through this, I had got to know a few people who developed games and had formed plenty of ideas for great games. I could see that some people developing games were making good money, and I wondered whether I could sell some of my idea. I was not a programmer and I couldn't have developed a game on my own. So I sent a number of game ideas, developed into documents, to several game publishers. I got a few straight rejections, but also a reasonable amount of interest. A number of companies thought my ideas were worth pursuing, but wanted me to find people to develop these ideas into a prototype, after which they would consider whether or not to publish the game. At the same time, some of my friends in the industry were unhappy with the publishers they were developing for, so we started to wonder whether we could develop games together, and even publish them ourselves.

It was the summer of 1988, at the then peak of the property market, and I had saved up a deposit to buy a flat. I finally found a two-bedroom flat I could just about afford, but I needed to rent out one of the rooms in order to be able to pay back the mortgage I would need, but the survey showed the building owner had applied for planning permission to add on another floor to the building. I couldn't imagine I would be able to get a lodger to pay rent while there was scaffolding all round the building, so I pulled out of buying the flat, a little fed up.

A week later, I met up with my game developer friends again, and we got to talking once more about whether we should set our own business up. Spurred on by having an unused flat deposit, I went off to investigate how to get the games manufactured, marketed and sold, while some of the others explored what game to produce first. When we came back with the results of our basic research, it looked as though we ought to be able to break even fairly easily, and there was a good chance that we'd make a small profit, so we set up. In the end, I was brave (or rash) enough to put up most of the money, with my flat deposit burning a hole in my pocket; in all, we thought we could set up with about £12,500.

We decided to produce a football management game; several of the developers had built one of these types of game before, and we felt that we could improve on what was out there in several ways.

We then considered how to market it, and decided that the best way to promote the game would be to licence the rights to a famous football manager and use this to brand our game. The most successful manager at the time by far was Kenny Dalglish, at Liverpool FC. I volunteered to try to obtain the rights to use his name, having never done anything of the kind before. I phoned Liverpool football club, and amazingly, they put me straight through to Kenny. I still wonder about this – knowing rather more about football now than I did then (I was on the board at Watford FC between 2000 and 2006) it seems staggering that I got through – football managers spend relatively little time at the clubs, since they're mainly at training grounds!

I had a very pleasant conversation with Kenny, who suggested I speak to his agent and gave me the details. I put a proposal to the agent, which they accepted: we paid him a modest royalty on sales, but no advance at all. I later learned that this was extremely unusual. Furthermore, I met someone several years later who told me his company had been trying to sign the rights to Kenny's name for computer games for more than a year when we signed him up. That company was established and much better funded than we were (though they did later go bust…).

I spoke to one of the publishing companies I had interviewed for a magazine about manufacturing the games, and we agreed to publish the football game as a joint venture. The game was launched in 1989 and was an instant hit, staying at number one in the games charts for weeks. As a result of this, our company made a profit of £30,000 in its first year, which was amazing. But we also felt that the joint venture hadn't worked as well for us as we had hoped, so we decided to publish any future games under our own label, Impressions.

Our next game was offered to us by another developer known to one of the other shareholders. He had developed a game called *Raider*, and was looking for a publisher. We liked it, thought it would sell, and paid the programmer a small advance against future royalties. We then set about establishing a publishing infrastructure. In those days that meant marketing, manufacturing, sales and accounts. At this stage one of the other founders, Ed Grabowski, took on more responsibilities. We asked around, looked at trade magazine advertisers, and eventually found a sales agency, a disk duplicator, a warehousing business, a printer, and a box manufacturer. Whenever we found a potential supplier, we asked all sorts of questions, learning as we went along, and they were all very helpful. Before long, we knew what to do, and got on with doing it.

The programmer finished off the game, we sourced an illustrator for the front cover, sent all the materials to the suppliers, and the game was manufactured. Our sales agent, Robert Stallibrass of Active Sales & Marketing, had generated some orders by presenting the game's cover and an information sheet on it to the customers he knew, and our warehouse dispatched the goods. We had made our first sales as publishers!

I thought *Raider* was a really good game, but it got more modest reviews and sales than I'd hoped. We then published some more games from our Kenny Dalglish series, as well as some others, and soon started to get approached by other people wanting us to publish their games, once they'd seen our adverts in the magazines.

Eventually, Ed Grabowski went full-time, and we took on a small serviced office, a full-time PR person and an office manager. I still carried on with my accountancy exams, working on Impressions in the evenings. This is obviously an unusual arrangement, and our PR person sadly decided to take advantage by showing up late for work, taking long lunches, and not doing anything like enough work. I gave him a formal warning that unless he improved we would need to let him go. Nothing changed, and at the end of the month, I explained to him that we were terminating his employment. He was remorseful, but our cash flow was tight and we couldn't afford to keep him on doing so little. I had dismissed someone for the first time, and felt awful, despite being convinced that it was the right thing to have done.

I started to do quite a bit of business planning, talking to some of the developers, and forecasting our sales and profits. Our profits rapidly turned into losses, though, as some of the games we had sold started to be sent back. It is normal in computer games publishing, as with magazines and books, that if a game doesn't sell, the retailer or distributor can send it back to the publisher. We knew this, but hadn't taken it into account. The first thing to happen was that it reduced our cash receipts, as customers who owed us money deducted the returns amounts from what they owed us. We started to delay paying a few of our suppliers.

We took a stand at the industry's trade show, at London's Business Design Centre, and found some new distributors in places such as Spain, Italy and Australia. These distributors would fax their orders over, and I still remember the excitement every time the fax machine started, wondering how many games each customer would order. I also remember the sinking feeling when the title of the fax was 'returns request', dreading the amount a customer wanted to send back.

Then we had our first major incident. We had agreed to publish a game we were calling *Chariots of Wrath*, produced by some freelance developers. This was a 'science fiction shoot-'em-up' game with some similarities to a very major game, *Xenon 2,* published by Mirrorsoft, one of the most powerful UK game publishers at the time. We promoted our game in the press, and shortly afterwards received a legal letter from Mirrorsoft alleging that our game infringed their rights in *Xenon 2*, and suggesting that our developers had somehow obtained a pirate early version of their game, and had copied a level.

This was a massive concern for us; we were already tight for cash, and really needed to publish *Chariots of Wrath* fast, to increase our income. Our developers were up in arms, adamant that they were innocent, and we defended them. I appointed Bird & Bird, one of the best firms of solicitors for intellectual property law, to advise us, and we set up a meeting with Mirrorsoft. I found the Mirrorsoft manager's attitude very demeaning, and have rarely felt angrier; he clearly presumed we were a tiny, annoying company, and that our law firm was also. However I had to acknowledge that the two levels were remarkably similar, and in the end, to avoid further prolonging any dispute, I agreed that we would change our controversial level. I'll never know whether our developers were genuinely innocent or not, but had to accept that the similarity was substantial.

We changed the offending level, which had to be done in a huge rush. For days on end, I used to go to Euston station just to collect a disk from the Red Star transport service after midnight with the latest version on it; sometimes the package went missing, sometimes the disk didn't work. But we got there in the end. Ironically, what we changed it to ended up far better than the original, and we published the game in time.

Meanwhile I had failed my tax exam at the last stage of my accountancy qualification, and decided that I could no longer work full-time, study to retake the tax exam, and run the games publishing business. So I resigned from the accountancy firm, leaving them in early December 1990, to study full-time for a week before my last exam, and then work full-time to try to make a go of Impressions. Had I not passed, I would have had to sit four exams again in order to qualify as an accountant. Luckily, I passed, which gave me the confidence to concentrate on the games business for a while, thinking that I could always get a job as an accountant if it didn't work out.

Early in 1991, though, business started to get tougher. Our second Kenny Dalglish game hadn't done as well as the first, and we were getting more returns than we had expected, giving us real financial problems. We already had a bank overdraft, which I was personally guaranteeing, and decided to use factoring to help get us through the tight period. We also stripped our overheads right back; at this stage, I was running the business from the house I shared with friends, renting an extra room to use for the business, and Ed Grabowski was working full-time from his home.

I took over sales from the agency, and started calling our customers myself, which I loved as it got me close to the market. I would deal with the suppliers, too, and the accounts. There was too much to do, and I ended up in a horrible administrative mess, often leaving it far too late to send out invoices to our customers, which meant that they paid us even later than they should have.

Our cash flow remained very tight throughout 1990 and 1991; I would spend hours at night going over our income for the next few weeks, and therefore which bills we could pay. It was enormously stressful, and many nights I wondered whether we would ever be able to pay all our bills off. By early 1991, we owed considerably more to suppliers than people owed us, and I was personally guaranteeing something well over half a million pounds of debt. It was scary. I was also getting less and less good at coping with my workload, and with working from home. At this stage, the business was far more stressful than enjoyable.

I started talking to friends and family about this, and it was my brother who helped me most, by suggesting I drew up a list of what I would need in order to enjoy what I did. My list included an office, a marketing person, someone to manage the accounts, and someone to run the developers. I calculated how this would be feasible, with some profit left – by making fewer games selling more copies, or selling fewer copies of more games.

The games industry was expanding rapidly and there were lots of games on the market, many of them poor. The better games started to sell substantially better than the poorer games. At this stage Impressions was producing quite a few games, not spending all that much time or money on each. We felt this had to change, to produce better quality games and invest time and money into them. As we had had some success with strategy games (things like *Risk* or chess) we decided to specialise in these types of games.

This was a big decision – most games sold in Europe were action, not strategy games, so we were leaving a big part of the market behind. In reality our action games just weren't good enough to compete, while we were better at producing strategy games.

To fund even the minimalist organisation I envisaged, we would need to sell copies of our strategy games in either Japan or North America, both of which had huge markets for these sorts of games. We could have just sold our European products to customers in America, but nobody wanted European games – Americans needed American addresses on American boxes.

Most UK software publishers licensed their games to companies in the USA, taking a small cash advance, and leaving the rest up to the Americans. We wanted a bigger share of the cake than that, since these US sales would be very important in making our games viable at all. So I spent a lot of time in the States, going to trade shows, meeting other small publishers and distributors who we might be able to do a deal with.

We did a test deal with a small software company in Dallas; but we found that they didn't have a great reputation for product quality. They launched a Roman military game of ours called *Cohort*, but took ages to do so and ended up making a mess of it. In fact, we learned a great deal from this. We had been proud of this game because it was just about the first game where figures started to move in real time on the screen to players' commands, which later became enormous. But in fact it was a bit clunky, and didn't go down well in the USA at all – until they dropped the price, at which point it started to sell in pretty good quantities.

I was still living in London, working most evenings, and speaking on the phone with Americans late at night, due to the time difference. The good news was just how well my English accent went down – it seemed to be beneficial in a way which I suspect an American accent in the UK would not. My tactic was to play dumb (this was pretty easy, since I didn't know much about how things worked over there) and people seemed very willing to talk. I learned a lot and in the end decided we should open our own office over there, and sell to retailers and wholesalers directly, rather than using some sort of partner. Although it would cost some money to set up a small office, we only needed two members of staff, one to 'Americanise' the products and the other to provide customer service.

The American market was also very attractive for us. We were able to sell at a higher price per game, and by manufacturing over there, the cost of each game was smaller – so our gross profit was considerably higher. There were also no translation costs, as in Europe, and just three real magazines to promote our products in, compared to five in the UK. We were able to spend less money on advertising, and still end up with a far more prominent campaign than we had in the UK. And best of all, the strategy game market was bigger than in Europe.

So in spring 1992 I decided to move over to North America to set up a US company, intending to return to the UK once it had been set up. We decided to launch with five games in the autumn, or fall, of 1992. I decided to move over in July to set things up ready for the launch. I appointed a group of freelance sales reps to sell our games and found a company which would manufacture, store, assemble and dispatch our games for us.

First, though, we needed to raise some money. We just needed a bit more cash to get things set up, and to convert more of our games onto the IBM compatible PCs which were dominant the USA but not yet very important in Europe.

Raising money was tough. I wrote a brief business plan, and talked to lots of venture capitalists – none were interested in investing. I was livid and disheartened: here was a British company trying to expand in an important and growing field, and the people whose business it was to invest in growing companies were turning us down. Ridiculous! In fact, we fell between lots of stools: some investors considered us too small for them; technology investors felt we were a consumer products business; consumer products investors felt we were too much of a technology company. Very frustrating!

Time was running out, though; we needed to get US distribution for our products or we would go out of business. We set out to raise £50,000; my father and brother both put a bit of money in, as did one or two friends, and we got most of what we needed, but still not enough. Then someone had the idea of asking our suppliers – people who knew us, and might have more faith as a result. One of them took us up, and we scraped together £48,500. At the time, £1 was worth about $2 so we had just about $100,000 to fund our US venture.

I bought a one-way ticket to Boston and initially rented a small office in Connecticut, near an American games developer I had got to know and like, called Tom Carbone. I had met Tom just by picking up the phone and trying to speak to other American companies making strategy games; he had been very helpful, and we ended up publishing his next game.

Luckily for us, in 1992 America, Connecticut in particular, was in the depth of recession. This enabled us to get a really good deal on an office; it also made it easy to hire staff.

We launched our first game in September 1992, called *Air Force Commander*. Although this was before the internet, there were several 'online services' active in America – AOL, Compuserve and Genie. Using a dial-up modem, we could visit message boards where players were discussing different games. The day *Air Force Commander* hit the shops, we got onto these services to see how it was reviewed – and it was fine. Not great, not terrible.

We got on with the next game, which was supposed to be our big one for that autumn. *Air Bucks*, where players could build an airline from scratch, had done well in Europe, and magazines had already written glowing previews. We had orders for about 17,000 copies, which was our biggest order to date.

It was released, and, more excited than before, we got onto the message boards to see what people thought of the game. In short, they hated it. Americans were able to return any product to the store if they didn't like it, which most European consumers couldn't do back then. The bad news was that almost none of the people writing about our game wanted to keep it. This was terrible – it meant that we would not get paid for the big orders we had just sent out, and we had already used most of that money to pay wages and rent. That was a long night.

I spent ages discussing the game with these customers online, asking them in detail what they didn't like. They hated the graphics, but the good news was that they really liked the concept of the game.

I decided to offer to fix the problems with this game and told people online that we would give them a copy for free, if they would just bear with us. There was much scepticism as to whether we would really deliver, but luckily the word got out that here was a different company, where the President (as most American managing directors are known) was actually talking to customers directly. Luckily, enough of these gamers gave us a chance, and didn't return their games.

Fixing it took months and I think it was February or March the following year that we recalled the old game from the shops, and put the new one out instead. When we finally reissued the game, we launched it in a new box, as *Air Bucks 1.2*, and mailed it for free to several thousand customers. And it worked. The customers loved the game they ended up with, and while the overall sales had been tarnished, our reputation was established as a company that listened to its customers.

By then, we had launched our other games. These were largely mediocre. One game which had done reasonably well in Europe was converted to PC by a programmer we had found in Hungary. Sadly, there was a bug which meant that the game crashed from time to time. We had to fix it, but were unable to contact the programmer. After numerous attempts, we were eventually told in stilted English that the programmer was not available, because he had died suddenly! We have no idea to this day whether that was genuine, or whether it was a cunning ruse to get us off his backs. Either way, we were unable to fix the bug, which hindered sales of the game.

So by January 1993, we had launched five games; three were mediocre, with *Air Bucks* both spectacular and potentially disastrous, and the other bugged with no hope of fixing it. My reputation for delivering on my many promises to customers online was wearing thin. Our next game just had to be successful, or it would threaten our ability to sell any more to customers.

The previous Christmas, I had taken a look at this game called *Sim City* which lots of people were talking about. It had been out quite some time by then, but hadn't appealed to me at all. Until I played it. I had allowed myself two hours, and ended up spending two days pretty much solidly on it. It was truly a brilliant, innovative product which was totally absorbing. I was impressed.

But it wasn't a game. Not really. It was much more of a 'simulation'. Our speciality was history games, and it struck me that the Romans were legendary city builders; they also had plenty of interesting features in their cities, such as amphitheatres, baths, temples, and so on. They also had many enemies, and a strong army. By taking some of the elements of *Sim City* and putting them into a game form, we could create a series of levels, introducing new elements at each level, and moving players on before they began to get stuck. I called the game *Caesar* and a highly talented developer called Simon Bradbury turned this into a game throughout 1992, while I was setting up the American operation.

We reviewed *Caesar* extensively in the aftermath of the *Air Bucks* fiasco and delayed its American launch, even though we had already launched it in Europe in the autumn of 1992. In the end, we released the American version in February 1993, just before *Air Bucks 1.2* was sent out. *Caesar* was a hit. The press loved it, and the customer loved it. And sales took off – we sold tens of thousands of copies within a few months.

We had made a tiny profit in our first year of business as a company, on the back of the success of the first Kenny Dalglish game. We then lost money in each of the following three years, despite growing turnover substantially year on year. At the end of our first year of operating in America, we made a profit of several hundred thousand pounds.

We continued growing after that, launching more products, and with America as our new focus, we could make considerably more money than we could in Europe. What had begun as a way of making Europe viable, took over and became our new core. We moved to Boston and hired more and more people – within three years this office had 40 staff.

One day I remember getting a call from our UK office asking whether I had heard anything from our factoring company. I suddenly learned that they had gone bust. This was a massive shock. Legally, your factoring company owns the debts owed to you by your customers. Sure, it also owes you the balance it hasn't advanced you; but when our factoring company went bust, it cost us roughly £60,000, which was an enormous debt for a company our size. Luckily, we managed to find an American factoring company to take things over, and we survived it.

Although in our terms we were doing really well, making profits and making games our customers loved, we were still a very small part of the enormous and fast-growing American software industry. Some of our retail customers started to take advantage of that – charging us lots of money to promote their stores, and taking ages to pay their bills. And while we were profitable, the cost of making games was going up all the time, as customers expected bigger and better games every year. So I decided to try to raise some venture capital.

In contrast to my earlier experience, we had already been approached by a number of American venture capital companies. I remember one who rang up out of the blue one day, and asked me 'how much faster could you grow if I invested $2m in your company?' The downside to taking venture capital on is that you give up some of your shares and potentially get someone else telling you what to do, and by this stage, I was loving running a successful and growing company, and didn't want to give up more than I really had to.

I was attending all sorts of conferences and industry networking events, and came across a company called Davidson. They were one of the largest educational software companies in the States, with an impressive head office in LA. We eventually agreed to let them sell our games for us; in theory they had more sales muscle than we did. I was really pleased with myself for negotiating very hard with them on the commission we paid them (lower than our previous deal) and also for getting them to pay us far earlier than our customers were paying us; so we didn't need to raise venture capital after all, which I really liked.

Unfortunately we never got on all that well with Davidson. We didn't feel that their sales people did as good a job as we wanted them to, and they resented how little we were paying them. Towards the end of the distribution period, we were working on *Caesar 2*, the sequel to our hit game of 1993. By now a research company was selling reports detailing precisely how many copies different games were selling every month, so we knew how we were doing compared to other games; this information was expensive, but made a huge difference to our product development strategy. Our best game at this point had sold around 100,000 copies; we felt that *Caesar 2* really should hit 200,000 copies, but we weren't confident that it would do so with Davidson selling it.

We decided to look at other options. Sierra Online was then the largest company making PC games, and they were quoted on Nasdaq, the American stock market for technology and other fast growing companies. They ran various studios developing games, most of which were very prestigious; the head of one of these rang me one day to ask what plans we had for the future, and I went to see him, in Oregon, and decided to talk to him about distribution. We got on well, and he liked what we were up to; the big advantage was that Sierra didn't make strategy games at all at this point, which was all we did, so there was a good fit.

I knew that Sierra was interested in buying companies, and had started to think about whether I would be willing to sell Impressions. It felt that unless whoever was selling our games made as much money from them as they did from their own products, we would lose out. And running the company was increasingly stressful; I think I was probably burned out from seven years of 70–100-hour weeks, with almost no holiday. And the amount software companies were worth was life-changing money. So I was open to considering it.

He suggested a meeting between Sierra's CEO, Ken Williams, at the E3 Trade Show in LA in the spring of 1995. I went to meet him at the Beverley Hills Wilshire, a very grand hotel, and had a very quick chat to the Sierra senior management team. They asked straight out if I wanted a distribution deal, or whether I would consider selling my company. Their chief financial officer then took me for coffee to find out a bit more about my company; within five minutes he made me an offer to buy the business for a substantial amount of money. I said that I would consider it and then spent the rest of the day feeling a little weird; I was just 29 years old, and had been offered many millions of pounds.

Ken Williams later came to our stand at E3 to see our products, and I took him through what we had to show of *Caesar 2*, which he loved. Within a few days I decided to accept their offer, after discussing it with my senior managers and our larger shareholders. In the end, this deal took the pressure off me, got us the distribution arrangement I felt we needed, and paid our shareholders a fantastic return. For me, it was simply too much money not to take – to reject it felt like leaving all my wealth, now a very tangible and vast sum for me, on the table at a casino. At the end of June 1995, I sold my company to Sierra.

Caesar 2 came out in the autumn of 1995, and went on to sell not the 200,000 copies that we had hoped, but two million. Sierra made significant profit from that, as well as from our other games which they also did a good job of selling. As a result of these profits, and some other acquisitions they made shortly after us, their share price more than doubled. I had sold for shares, expecting this, and did very nicely from it.

In 1996 I decided to return to the UK, and moved back to London in the spring of 1997. I carried on working for Sierra in London, though on a part-time basis. I wanted a break from the intensity of the computer games world, and ideally to find a more balanced life. I designed *Caesar 3*, which came out in 1998 and also went on to sell millions of copies, and then stopped working with computer games altogether.

Next I invested in a few small private companies, as a business angel. I couldn't find very many companies I wanted to invest in, and became frustrated with some of the investments I did make when the business managers made bad mistakes, and in 1998 decided to set up a new company.

This was the beginning of the internet 'revolution', and I thought that I could use my knowledge of what was happening in America, together with my technical experience of creating computer games, to make a successful internet business. I researched a number of ideas, and in the end decided on publishing. I loved small, fast-growing businesses, and had seen magazines and books in America which were substantially better than anything that existed then in the UK: my plan was to bring the American quality of information to the UK small businesses, using the internet. I liked the idea of growing a business rapidly this time, having grown Impressions initially very slowly, constrained by lack of cash.

So in February 1999, I launched Crimson, a magazine and website publishing business. We launched *What Laptop* magazine in August 1999, which was a huge success, and *eBusiness* magazine in the November, which was successful for a while, but died in the dotcom crash. In January 2000, we launched www.startups.co.uk, now the UK's biggest and most popular website for small business by quite a large margin. Crimson has launched over a dozen publications in total; some have been tremendously successful, but we've also made a number of mistakes, the biggest being an absolutely disastrous acquisition of a wedding magazine. Crimson is now a successful publisher of books, magazines, websites and organiser of events for small businesses, and has acquired two other book publishing businesses specialising in travel and education/careers.

I've also invested heavily in two other businesses – a children's shoe retailer, and a book distributor, as well as smaller sums in another half a dozen private businesses ranging from a restaurant to a telecoms company. I also invested in Watford FC, the football club I support, and spent six eventful years on the board there.

Now I work for enjoyment; I love what I do, and am determined to create products I'm proud of. I continue to make many mistakes, and continue to learn. I'm enormously lucky now to meet many other successful entrepreneurs as part of what I do. Running a small business is far from easy; starting one is significantly tougher still; but if you're the right sort of person for it, then it is an absolutely fantastic way to work.

Some of my own Good, Bad and Unexpected experiences

✓ THE GOOD

- The first time I saw one of my business's computer games in a shop
- Seeing the first sales orders for our games coming over our fax machine
- Making our first profit – first for a month, then for a full year
- Hearing from customers who absolutely loved games we made
- Seeing *Kenny Dalglish Soccer Manager* take the number one position in the best-selling games chart
- Hearing from people who say their business has been transformed by information we've provided at Crimson

✓ THE BAD

- Not having enough money to pay all the bills we owed
- Hearing from customers who didn't like one of our games they'd just bought

- Reading a magazine review slagging off one of our games, written by someone who hadn't actually played the game
- Seeing requests to send loads of our games back coming out of our fax machine

✓ THE UNEXPECTED

- Kenny Dalglish agreeing to license his name for our first computer game
- Our factoring company going bust, which cost us £60,000
- Going to live in the USA
- Paying money to a company which owed us money in order to avoid the hassle and cost of fighting a court case in Italy
- Selling out for millions before I was 30
- Becoming a director of Watford Football Club

A book to make your business stand out:

BRIGHT MARKETING

WHY SHOULD PEOPLE BOTHER TO BUY FROM YOU?

Why should people bother to buy from you when they can buy from the competition?

Bright Marketing reveals that in a world of mediocrity it only takes 5% difference to stand out from the crowd. This revolutionary book shows you how you can apply simple, practical changes to your business to ensure its success.

Written by industry expert Robert Craven, MD of the Directors' Centre, this book is based on the results of his work helping thousands of companies find their edge and improve their profitability.

Author: Robert Craven
Published: May 2007
ISBN: 978-1-85458-404-5